REVIEWING THE LATEST TRENDS IN MANAGEMENT LITERATURE

REVIEW OF MANAGEMENT LITERATURE

Series Editor: Sudhir Rana

Review of Management Literature is a multidisciplinary series presenting unique and groundbreaking literature reviews and examinations of new and emerging trends in research across the management discipline and beyond.

Examining broad disciplinary areas including new research developments in fields including Marketing, Operations Management, Finance, International Business, and HRM, as well as well as more focused studies on the big data and gamification in management literature, the series also explores practical research guidance with titles examining methodologies for conducting literature reviews in management domain.

Supported by a highly reputable editorial board from across the globe, the series will be an essential research resource to access and interpret cutting-edge global developments from across the management discipline.

VOLUMES IN THIS SERIES

Exploring the Latest Trends in Management Literature, Volume 1 – Edited by Sudhir Rana, with Sakshi and Jagroop Singh

Advancing Methodologies of Conducting Literature Review in Management Domain, Volume 2 – Edited by Sudhir Rana with Jagroop Singh and Sakshi Kathuria

Review of Technologies and Disruptive Business Strategies, Volume 3 – Edited by Rahul Pratap Singh Kaurav and Vinaytosh Mishra

Reviewing the Latest Trends in Management Literature, Volume 4, Part A – Edited by Sudhir Rana with Jagroop Singh, Shubham Singhania and Sakshi Kathuria

EDITORIAL BOARD

REVIEW OF MANAGEMENT LITERATURE VOLUME 4, PART B

REVIEWING THE LATEST TRENDS IN MANAGEMENT LITERATURE

EDITED BY

SUDHIR RANA

Gulf Medical University, UAE

emerald PUBLISHING

United Kingdom – North America – Japan
India – Malaysia – China

Emerald Publishing Limited
Emerald Publishing, Floor 5, Northspring, 21-23 Wellington Street, Leeds LS1 4DL

First edition 2025

British Library Cataloguing in Publication Data
A catalogue record for this book is available from the British Library

ISBN: 978-1-83708-753-2 (Print)
ISBN: 978-1-83708-752-5 (Online)
ISBN: 978-1-83708-754-9 (Epub)

ISSN: 2754-5865 (Series)

Printed and bound by CPI Group (UK) Ltd, Croydon, CR0 4YY

CONTENTS

ABOUT THE CONTRIBUTORS

Mohammad Khaled Al-Nawayseh is an Associate Professor of Information Systems at the Management Information Systems, School of Business, University of Jordan. His areas of expertise encompass health information systems, data analytics and technology diffusion. His research interests are diverse and include recent topics such as the implementation of health information technologies, the analysis of large-scale healthcare datasets and the study of factors influencing the adoption and diffusion of new technologies in organizational settings.

Mohammad A.K. Alsmairat is an Associate Professor of Supply Chain Management at American University in the Emirates. He is a distinguished graduate of Girne American University in Cyprus, where he earned his PhD in Supply Chain Management. He also has a Master's in Business Administration from Mutah University and a double Bachelor's major in Computer Information Systems (CIS) and Business Administration. Dr Alsmairat's research interests include supply chain management, logistics, big data analysis in the supply chain, blockchain, supply chain sustainability and business model management. He has also written numerous papers and articles for high-indexed journals.

Biswajit Behera is working as a doctoral researcher in the School of Management, National Institute of Technology (NIT) Rourkela, India. He has completed his post-graduation in commerce from the School of Commerce, G.M. University, Sambalpur, Odisha. His research interest is in the areas of workplace deviance, generational differences at the workplace, innovative work behaviour, employee engagement, employee creativity and workforce diversity and inclusion.

Elvira Anna Graziano, PhD, is an Associate Professor of Financial Markets and Institutions at the Department of Social Sciences, Link Campus University. Her research interests include behavioural finance, neurofinance and FinTech. She serves as an Associate Editor for several prominent scientific journals and is the Delegate of the Rector for University Rankings. She is also a member of a Nudge Unit at the Lazio Region, composed of leading national and international behavioural economists. Graziano has received the AIDEA award for young business scholars (2012), the EuroMed Conference Best Abstract Award (2016) and the EuroMed Conference Best Paper Award (2024).

Aleena Ilyaz is a Junior Research Fellow at the Department of Management Studies, Jamia Millia Islamia, New Delhi. Her research interests include new ways of working (NWW), creativity, leadership, emotional and mental well-being. As a young scholar and a lifelong learner, she is focused on improving the robustness and impact of her research by creating and collaborating. She further strengthens her academic pursuits by actively participating in workshops on new research methodologies and national and international conferences. She values the interplay between intellectual rigour and creative expression, ensuring that both nourish her mind and soul.

Anshul Jain is working as a research scholar in the Department of Commerce and Management, Banasthali Vidyapith, Rajasthan, India. She has completed her graduation from Delhi University and post-graduation from Indra Gandhi University, Haryana. Her research interest is in the areas of banking, sustainable development in banking sector and studying the behaviour of banking employees and customers.

Luay Jum'a is an Associate Professor of Logistics and Supply Chain Management (SCM) at the German Jordanian University (GJU). He holds a PhD in SCM from Brunel University and an MSc in Marketing Management from the University of Surrey in the United Kingdom, both renowned for their management programs. Ranked among the top 10 scientists in Business and Management, Decision Science and Operations Management in Jordan by the 2024 World Scientists Rankings, Dr Jum'a has published extensively and served as an academic reviewer for leading journals. His research focuses on supply chain management, logistics operations, disruptive technologies and sustainability.

Khyati Kochhar is working as an Assistant Professor in the Department of Commerce and Management, Banasthali Vidyapith, Rajasthan, India. She has completed her PhD in Management from Banasthali Vidyapith. She has more than 13 years of experience as an Assistant Professor and attended many national and international conferences and guided many research scholars in completing their PhD.

Devyani Negi is currently perusing PhD from the Department of Commerce, Delhi School of Economics, University of Delhi. She is also an Assistant Professor (guest basis) at the Department of Commerce, Hindu College, University of Delhi. She has completed her MPhil from Department of Commerce, Delhi School of Economics, University of Delhi. Her area of interest includes finance and investment mainly capital markets. She has published three research papers in ABDC, Scopus and UGC Care-listed journals.

Gerardo Petroccione, PhD in Management, is an Adjunct Professor of Banking at Link Campus University and Rome City Institute. His expertise includes consumer payment behaviour and behavioural finance. He was a Visiting Scholar at NYU Stern, Universitat Oberta de Catalunya, Pan-European University and UCD Michael Smurfit Graduate Business School. Formerly Coordinator of the Italian PhD Society (SIDRI) at the University of Rome 'Tor Vergata', he now leads its Report Area. He received the EuroMed Conference Best Paper Award in September 2024. Petroccione oversees peer review for 'Bancaria' (ABI) and collaborates with Assonebb on 'Bankpedia'. He is also a chartered accountant and a freelance journalist.

Yasmeen Shamsi Rizvi, a distinguished academician in the field of Human Resource Management and Organizational Behaviour, is renowned for her prolific research contributions. Holding a PhD along with an MBA and M.Sc. from AMU, India, she possesses a strong academic foundation complemented by certifications from esteemed institutions worldwide. As a Professor at the Department for Management Studies, Jamia Millia Islamia, New Delhi, Dr Yasmeen imparts knowledge across various management domains. With over 23 years of teaching experience, including at prestigious management institutions like Indian Institute of Management Lucknow, she has shaped the minds of countless future leaders. Yasmeen's research prowess is evident through her extensive publications in reputable international and national journals. Her contributions extend beyond academia, as evidenced by her involvement in Management Development Programmes for senior professionals across various sectors. She has also headed the training and engagement function at Max Super Speciality Hospital, Saket, New Delhi.

Somesh Kumar Sharma earned his M.Tech in Industrial Engineering and PhD with Gold Medal from the Indian Institute of Science, Bangalore, India. He is currently working as an Associate Professor at the National Institute of Technology Hamirpur, India. His research interests are agent technology, maintenance management, high-tech manufacturing, aviation studies, international business, optimization, re-engineering, strategic management and international marketing. He has published 50+ research papers in Scopus/SCI/SCIE/SSCI-indexed reputed international journals under publishers T & F, IEEE, Emerald Publishing, Science Direct and InderScience.

Dario Siggia, qualified as a University Associate Professor with a PhD in Agricultural Economics and Policy, works for the Italian Ministry of Foreign Affairs and teaches in Istanbul. Formerly a Cabinet Member for the Italian Minister of Education, he is also a Visiting Professor at Warsaw University of Life Sciences. He was Policy Advisor at the European Parliament and visiting researcher at London South Bank University and Universitat Politècnica de Catalunya. Awarded the Best Reviewer Award by *Euromed Journal of Business* (2022) and EuroMed Academy (2013), he has authored numerous papers in international journals and presented at global conferences.

Amit Kumar Singh is a Professor in the Department of Commerce, Delhi School of Economics, University of Delhi. His areas of expertise include Finance and Investment Management, with a particular focus on the Initial Public Offerings market, and has a teaching experience of more than 20 years. He has authored/co-authored five books and published over 90 research papers in reputed journals. He serves as an editorial board member and reviewer for several reputed journals, such as *Indian Journal of Finance*, *Orissa Journal of Commerce*, *Indian Journal of Research in Capital Market*, *FIIB Business Review*, *Indian Economic Journal*,

MUDRA and more. He was honoured with the IIF Laureate 2021 Award and the IIF Research Professor Award 2021 for his outstanding contributions to commerce.

Vikram Singh is pursuing his PhD from the National Institute of Technology, Hamirpur. He earned his M.Tech. Degree from Himachal Pradesh Technical University Hamirpur and B.Tech. with Honours from Himachal Pradesh University Shimla. He worked as an Assistant Professor in the Mechanical Engineering Department at SIRDA Institute of Engineering Technology, Mandi, Himachal Pradesh, India. He supervised more than 10 M.Tech. thesis at SIRDA Institute of Engineering Technology. His contribution is also acknowledged in the thesis of M.Tech. Scholars of NIT Hamirpur. His research interests are agent technology, maintenance management, high-tech manufacturing, Industry 4.0 and aviation studies.

Ekta Singhal works at Lal Bahadur Shashtri Institute of Management, New Delhi, India. She has an excellent academic record and a great aptitude for teaching and research. She obtained her PhD in Marketing Management from the Department of Commerce and Business Administration (MONIRBA), University of Allahabad, India, and her Master's in Business Administration and her Bachelor's in Commerce from Delhi University, India. She has been awarded various academic scholarships. She has presented her research papers at various conferences held all over India and has published many papers in internationally known journals.

Sankalp Srivastava is the founder of i8CLOUD, a tech consulting firm specialising in cloud technologies and AI-driven solutions. He holds a PGDM from the International Management Institute (IMI), New Delhi, and a B.Tech from Government Engineering College (BIET), Jhansi. With over 15 years of experience in cloud technologies, Sankalp's work spans entrepreneurship, generative AI and large language models (LLMs). He is particularly focused on exploring the applications of AI to optimise business operations, create innovative solutions and drive digital transformation across industries.

Parijat Upadhyay has rich experience of teaching and research in the domain of Information Systems and Supply Chain Management and is currently associated with Indian Institute of Management, Shillong. An alumnus of Symbiosis and XLRI Jamshedpur, he was associated with reputed academic institutes like IMT Ghaziabad and IMT Nagpur. He has been taking courses like Management Information Systems, Supply Chain Management, Digital Transformation of Business and IT Project Management. Dr Parijat has published extensively reputed international journals like *International Journal of Information and Management*, *Technology Forecasting and Social Change*, *Internet Research*, *Journal of Enterprise Information Management*, *Management Decision*, *Benchmarking: An International Journal*, *International Journal of Educational Management*, *VINE Journal of Information and Knowledge Management* and others.

PREFACE

Literature reviews play a crucial role in advancing scholarly understanding by organising, synthesising and critiquing the vast body of existing knowledge. They provide researchers and practitioners with comprehensive insights into current developments, highlight gaps in the research and suggest pathways for future exploration. As the landscape of business and management continues to evolve rapidly, literature reviews become invaluable in helping to navigate these changes by offering a clear view of where the field stands and where it is heading.

We are pleased to introduce the fourth volume, Part B of the Review of Management Literature series, continuing our mission to consolidate and present the latest trends and research in management. This volume offers an in-depth exploration of contemporary topics shaping management thought and practice, particularly in three core areas: human resource management, sustainability and technology.

In the realm of human resources, this volume covers topics like performance orientation, employee engagement and workplace behaviour, providing a comprehensive analysis on how organizations can foster a productive and positive work environment. It also delves into issues like workplace deviance and the factors influencing employee happiness, exploring both positive and negative behaviours within organizations.

In context of sustainability, this volume explores critical areas such as sustainable human resource management, the adoption of green banking and finance and the integration of Artificial Intelligence (AI) in driving sustainable financial practices. These reviews provide insights into how businesses can align their operations with sustainable goals and adapt to the increasing emphasis on eco-friendly practices.

In the domain of technology, the volume addresses the impact of emerging technologies on business processes and strategic decision-making. Topics such as digital leadership, multi-agent technology in manufacturing and the intersection of AI with supply chain resilience offer a comprehensive look at how technological advancements are reshaping industries. Furthermore, the role of technology in driving social and economic emancipation in developing regions is discussed, offering insights into the broader implications of tech adoption in underrepresented areas.

As we continue to face rapid digitalisation and shifting organizational environments, this collection of reviews will be an invaluable resource for scholars, practitioners and policymakers. It synthesises knowledge across a wide array of disciplines, offering both conceptual frameworks and practical recommendations for adapting to the ongoing changes in the global business landscape.

We extend our gratitude to the authors, reviewers and our editorial team, whose dedication has been instrumental in producing this volume. We are confident that this work will serve as a valuable reference, advancing both theory and practice in management. As always, we welcome feedback and look forward to future contributions in this ever-evolving field.

Warm regards,
The Editorial Team
Review of Management Literature

Role of Emerging Technologies in Indigenous Emancipation: A Systematic Literature Review

Sankalp Srivastava and Parijat Upadhyay

Indian Institute of Management Shillong, India

ABSTRACT

Indigenous communities worldwide face significant challenges, including cultural endangerment, health disparities and economic inequities. This systematic literature review examines the intersection of emerging technologies, particularly artificial intelligence (AI) and generative AI, with the well-being of indigenous communities. Contributions are compiled from both policy and academic databases to review systematically in order to identify the impact of digitalization and AI on indigenous populations. The review analyzes both the positive outcomes and potential biases associated with these applications in the domains of culture, language, health and economic development. This review reveals that while emerging technologies offer significant potential to empower indigenous communities, their development and implementation must be approached with cultural sensitivity to mitigate potential biases. Findings highlight key opportunities and challenges, emphasizing the need for inclusive design and community engagement to ensure that emerging applications are both effective and respectful of indigenous cultures worldwide.

Keywords: Indigenous communities; artificial intelligence; generative artificial intelligence; large language models; indigenous data sovereignty; decolonizing AI

1. INTRODUCTION

Indigenous communities globally face persistent challenges, often rooted in historical and ongoing social exclusion (Matthews, 2024). This marginalization is evident in their disproportionate representation (Williamson, 2001) in negative

Reviewing the Latest Trends in Management Literature
Review of Management Literature, Volume 4B, 1–26

ISSN: 2754-5865/doi:10.1108/S2754-58652025000004B001

socioeconomic statistics. Furthermore, past technological advancements, while promising, have often fallen short in adequately addressing these communities' unique needs. For instance, early machine translation systems frequently exhibited higher error rates when translating indigenous languages (Ishida, 2006), hindering effective communication and knowledge sharing. While modern knowledge-based systems excel at providing tailored solutions to complex problems, they currently lack effective methods for representing traditional knowledge (TK) (Thomson, 2000) in a way that meets the unique needs of diverse communities. For instance, the lack of collaborative partnerships between researchers and tribes in the United States (Credo & Ingram, 2021) has resulted in frequent under or the misrepresentation of American Indian and Alaska Native people in research and health statistics, hindering efforts to address health disparities effectively.

Emerging digital technologies offer opportunities for indigenous peoples to develop new ways of representing their knowledge, reclaiming cultural heritage and connecting with their communities (Botes & Rossi, 2021). A great example is how New Zealand has focused on the preservation of Maori indigenous communities (Stillman & Craig, 2006) via integrating them with the mainstream. Within indigenous communities, new digital versions of historic artefacts are being utilized for a variety of purposes (Newell, 2012). For instance, GIS mapping can be used to support Maori land management (Lischer-Katz, 2022) in New Zealand, and 3D scanning enables the digital repatriation of indigenous cultural heritage held by overseas institutions.

A number of studies vividly illustrate the transformative potential of artificial intelligence (AI) in the field of indigenous emancipation (Robinson et al., 2022). The infusion of AI has potentially augmented the benefits conferred by digitalization (Ratten, 2024). Existing AI technologies are being used in an amazing range of problem areas. These include facial recognition (Kleider-Offutt et al., 2024), natural language processing, robotics and autonomous vehicles (Kaufman et al., 2024) and virtual agents of many kinds. For example, Gumbo's investigation into the digitization of research and higher education suggests that AI can play a key role in accelerating sustainable development (Gumbo, 2023), which will enable indigenous communities to advance into contemporary educational paradigms. Indigenous communities can be empowered, and historical injustices rectified through the use of AI (Eglash et al., 2024), as demonstrated by computational reparations through generative justice in science, technology, engineering and mathematics (STEM) students.

AI also has shed light on the intricate relationship between technological advancement and colonial biases (Irwin & White, 2019) in the preservation of indigenous knowledge (Asuquo et al., 2023). Given the challenges posed by digitalization for indigenous people, emancipatory online learning must carefully balance the need to preserve indigenous legacies (Williamson, 2001) with the avoidance of imposing colonial structures. Although the debate on AI ethics predates many current discussions, it is still important because it emphasizes how software design must take ethics into account to prevent prejudices against indigenous communities (Thomson, 2000).

Generative artificial intelligence (GAI) distinguishes itself from predictive AI through its capacity for continuous learning and human guided development. By integrating human feedback into its decision-making processes, GAI moves beyond static predictions engaging in a more collaborative and iterative approach to problem-solving. While traditional AI systems analyze and learn from input data, generative AI goes a step further by creating new data that is similar, yet distinct (Marr, 2023) With its reputation for producing new content, insights, and solutions on its own (Ishida, 2006), generative AI holds great potential to reduce prejudice, promote inclusivity and elevate the voices of indigenous people in the digital sphere. It has the potential to empower indigenous communities by giving them back control over their narratives (Thomson & Schmoldt, 2001) and allowing them to cocreate culturally relevant content. This highlights how technology can help transmit culture.

Indigenous communities can be given previously unheard-of opportunities to take control of their stories, collaborate on content that reflects their cultural values and navigate the digital world with greater respect and autonomy with the strategic application of generative AI technologies. Through this review, the authors aim to explore how the adoption of generative AI serves to empower indigenous communities, both economically and socially.

The dominant reality is that non-native entities often control the collection, sharing and narration of data concerning indigenous peoples. This external control perpetuates the marginalization of indigenous voices (Starblanket et al., 2019) and perspectives in mainstream narratives. Digital empowerment within indigenous communities go beyond simply having access to technology (Kandiuk, 2016). It's about leveraging technology to support self-determination (Leditschke et al., 2024), cultural revitalization and social justice (Fomunyam, 2020). It recognizes the historical context of colonization and the digital divide (Dirks, 2021), aiming to bridge those gaps in a way that empowers indigenous people.

Equitable and affordable access to infrastructure, including broadband internet (Chiu et al., 2009), computers and mobile devices, is crucial for indigenous community involvement and equalizing educational opportunity (Berry, 2020). However, access must also encompass culturally relevant content and platforms that reflect indigenous languages, values and knowledge systems (Tsai & Wang, 2019). Furthermore, digital empowerment necessitates moving beyond basic digital literacy to cultivate the ability to critically evaluate online information (Arawjo & Mogos, 2021), create digital content and utilize technology for advocacy, storytelling and cultural preservation (Santano et al., 2021).

Examining technology adoption within indigenous communities requires a nuanced understanding of the factors influencing their choices and experiences. The Unified Theory of Acceptance and Use of Technology (UTAUT) (Venkatesh et al., 2003) offers a comprehensive framework, emphasizing the impact of performance expectancy, effort expectancy, social influence and facilitating conditions on technology acceptance. Additionally, the Ability–Motivation–Opportunity (AMO) theory (Appelbaum et al., 2001) highlights the crucial role of individual capabilities, motivation and access to resources in shaping technology adoption. However, it's essential to recognize that these models, while valuable, may not fully encapsulate the unique cultural, historical and socio-economic contexts of indigenous communities. Further research is needed to adapt and refine these models, ensuring they are grounded in indigenous perspectives (Ruster & Brown, 2020) and reflect the values, knowledge systems (Raut et al., 2024) and aspirations of these communities.

This systematic literature review seeks to bridge a critical gap in our understanding of how emerging technologies with a focus on generative AI can be leveraged ethically and effectively to empower indigenous communities. While the potential benefits are significant, there is a pressing need for rigorous research that examines both the opportunities and challenges presented by this rapidly evolving technology. This review aims to provide a comprehensive overview of existing research exploring the intersection of generative AI and indigenous communities, synthesizing key findings and identifying emerging trends and analyze the specific ways in which generative AI can empower indigenous communities, both economically and socially, while also examining potential risks and unintended consequences.

It also aims to identify best practices and guidelines for developing and implementing generative AI applications in collaboration with indigenous communities, ensuring cultural sensitivity, data sovereignty and equitable outcomes. Ultimately, this review seeks to inform the responsible development and deployment of generative AI, ensuring that this transformative technology contributes to the well-being and self-determination of indigenous communities worldwide.

2. THEORETICAL BACKGROUND

Indigenous communities face significant challenges in exercising control over their data (Tapu & Fa'agau, 2022). This study delves into the landscape of indigenous digital empowerment, grounding its exploration within the established frameworks of the UTAUT(Venkatesh et al., 2003) and the AMO theory (Appelbaum et al., 2001).

The UTAUT, as articulated by Venkatesh et al., provides a comprehensive lens through which to understand technology adoption. It posits that four key constructs, performance expectancy, effort expectancy, social influence and facilitating conditions, are central to the decision to adopt and utilize a technology.

Technology should be utilized in a way that aligns with indigenous values and priorities, ensuring that digital tools and platforms are culturally appropriate, respectful of indigenous knowledge systems (Chan, 2018) and contribute to the well-being of indigenous communities. Ultimately, digital empowerment supports indigenous self-determination (Stichel et al., 2019) by enabling communities to make their own decisions about how technology is used and governed. This includes advocating for data sovereignty – the right of indigenous peoples to own, control and access their own data – and promoting indigenous-led technology initiatives and ensuring that technology benefits, rather than exploits, indigenous communities (Vasileva & Okhlopkov, 2021).

Performance expectancy, a pivotal factor within UTAUT (Schomakers et al., 2022), centres on the belief that using a specific technology will enhance job or task performance. In the context of indigenous communities, this translates to understanding how AI tools are perceived in terms of their potential to address community-identified needs and aspirations. Effort expectancy, on the other hand, considers the perceived ease of use associated with a technology. For AI to be successfully integrated into indigenous contexts, it is crucial that the tools and platforms are designed with user-friendliness in mind, acknowledging varying levels of digital literacy within communities.

Beyond individual perceptions of usefulness and ease of use, the UTAUT recognizes the significant role of social influence (Schomakers et al., 2022). This construct highlights how the subjective norms within a community, shaped by influential individuals and groups, can either encourage or hinder technology adoption. Examining the role of elders, knowledge holders and community leaders in shaping perceptions of AI is essential. Finally, facilitating conditions, the fourth construct of UTAUT, emphasizes the importance of a supportive environment for technology adoption. This encompasses access to reliable internet connectivity, appropriate hardware and software and ongoing technical support, all of which are crucial considerations for ensuring equitable access to AI within indigenous communities.

Complementing the UTAUT, the AMO theory, rooted in organizational behaviour research, provides a complementary lens through which to understand the factors that enable or hinder individual and collective action. This theory posits that for any behaviour to occur, individuals or groups must possess the necessary abilities (knowledge, skills, resources), be motivated to engage in the behaviour (driven by needs, values, goals) and operate within an environment that provides opportunities for action. Applying this framework to indigenous digital empowerment requires a multifaceted approach.

First, assessing the digital literacy levels within indigenous communities and identifying any skills gaps is paramount. This includes not only technical proficiency but also critical thinking skills related to data privacy, algorithmic bias and the ethical implications of AI. Second, understanding the motivations driving indigenous communities to engage with AI is crucial. This requires recognizing the inherent right to self-determination and the desire to leverage technology for cultural revitalization, language preservation and economic development (Alghatrifi & Khalid, 2019). Finally, creating opportunities for meaningful engagement with AI is essential. This encompasses fostering partnerships between indigenous communities, technology developers and policymakers to ensure that AI applications are developed and deployed in a culturally sensitive and beneficial manner.

By integrating the comprehensive framework of UTAUT with the action-oriented lens of AMO theory, this study aims to provide a nuanced and holistic understanding of the factors that contribute to successful and empowering AI adoption within indigenous communities. This integrated approach recognizes the complex interplay of individual perceptions, social influences, environmental factors and the fundamental right of indigenous peoples to self-determination in the digital age.

3. METHODS

3.1 Review Scope, Boundaries and Phases

For this review, we have considered indigenous reports and publications, academic databases which includes Scopus and Web of Science, online databases and government websites published between 1990 and 2024. A tabular list of the sources is provided in Table 1.

To ensure our systematic review was both methodical and replicable, we reviewed not only academic journals but also indigenous databases, government websites and other online sources. This comprehensive approach allowed us to cover local reports on indigenous communities, providing a well-rounded perspective. We conducted our search using structured keywords as mentioned

Table 1. Secondary Data Sources for Data Collection.

Secondary Sources	Type	Original Source/Website
Reports and Publications	ILO, UNESCO, WWF, Niti Ayog, Corporate Reports, GSMA, etc.	ILO (www.ilo.org) UNESCO (www.unesco.org) WWF (www.worldwildlife.org) Niti Ayog (www.niti.gov.in) GSMA (www.gsma.com)
Academic Journals	Scopus and Web of Science (Clarivate)	Scopus (www.scopus.com) Web of Science (www.webofscience.com)
Online Databases	World Bank's World Development Indicators	World Bank (data.worldbank.org)
Government Websites	Government websites dedicated to indigenous affairs	Ministry of Tribal Affairs: India (tribal.nic.in) National Commission for Scheduled Tribes: India (ncst.nic.in) National Indigenous Australians Agency (indigenous.gov.au) Te Puni Kōkiri (Ministry of Māori Development): New Zealand (tpk.govt.nz) Ministry of Cultures, Decolonization, and Depatriarchalizing: Bolivia (minculturas.gob.bo)

Source: Compiled by authors.

in the abstract, employing both backward and forward source searches. This involved examining references cited in relevant studies and exploring more recent publications that have cited these key studies. By incorporating these approaches, we ensured a thorough examination of the existing literature.

Given that Generative AI is a relatively novel concept, our research was conducted in two phases. Initially, we focused on literature concerning indigenous people and digitalisation/AI, which is a well-researched area. Subsequently, we extended our study to include generative AI, identifying gaps that could be addressed by its application. This included reviewing industry reports and publication from institutions like UNESCO, ILO, etc. and also which highlight the need for informed consent and cultural sensitivity to avoid misuse and misappropriation of indigenous data. These reports provide a robust framework to support the ethical use of AI.

Our research was structured around clearly formulated questions, developed at the outset of the review process. This protocol ensured that our examination of digital empowerment for indigenous people using generative AI was comprehensive and focused.

Our review on the digital empowerment of indigenous people utilizing generative AI has been developed around our research questions. The review process has been shown in Fig. 1.

We conducted our literature review in three phases (Rana et al., 2023).

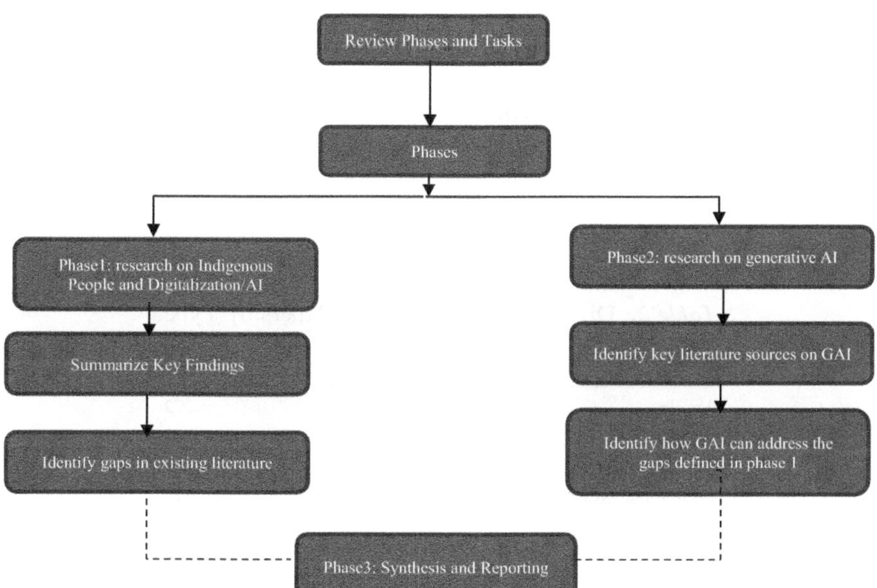

Fig. 1. Review Phases and Tasks. *Source:* Created by the authors based on review phases.

(1) *Phase 1*: Initial Search
   - Search Strategy: A comprehensive search was conducted across multiple databases and sources (Table 2), including academic journals (SCOPUS, Web of Science), reports and publications (ILO, UNESCO, WWF, Niti Ayog, Corporate Reports, GSMA), online databases (World Bank's World Development Indicators) and government websites dedicated to indigenous affairs.
   - Article Selection: Articles were screened based on predefined inclusion/ exclusion criteria, including relevance to the research question, focus on indigenous communities and discussion of digitalization or AI.
   - Data Extraction: Relevant data were extracted from selected articles, including key findings, methodologies and gaps identified in the literature.

(2) *Phase 2*: Identification of Generative AI Literature
   - Separate Search for Generative AI: A focused search was conducted specifically targeting literature on generative AI. Integration of Findings: The generative AI literature was analyzed to identify potential gaps and opportunities for application in the context of indigenous digital empowerment.
   - Integration with Phase 1 Findings: The findings from Phase 2 were integrated with the existing literature on indigenous digitalization and AI to identify synergies and potential areas for further exploration.

(3) *Phase 3*: Synthesis and Reporting
   - Data Synthesis: Findings from both phases of the literature review were synthesized to draw broad theoretical conclusions and identify overarching themes related to digital empowerment and Generative AI for indigenous communities.
   - Reporting: A structured report was prepared following the PRISMA guide lines (Fig. 2), including a flow diagram illustrating the search process, details of included/excluded studies and a narrative synthesis of key findings.

Table 2. Distribution of Analyzed Papers by Type.

Paper Type	Count
Article	272
Book	44
Conference Paper	120
Conference Review	15
Editorial	8
Letter	1
Note	5
Review	23
Short Survey	3

Source: Compiled by authors.

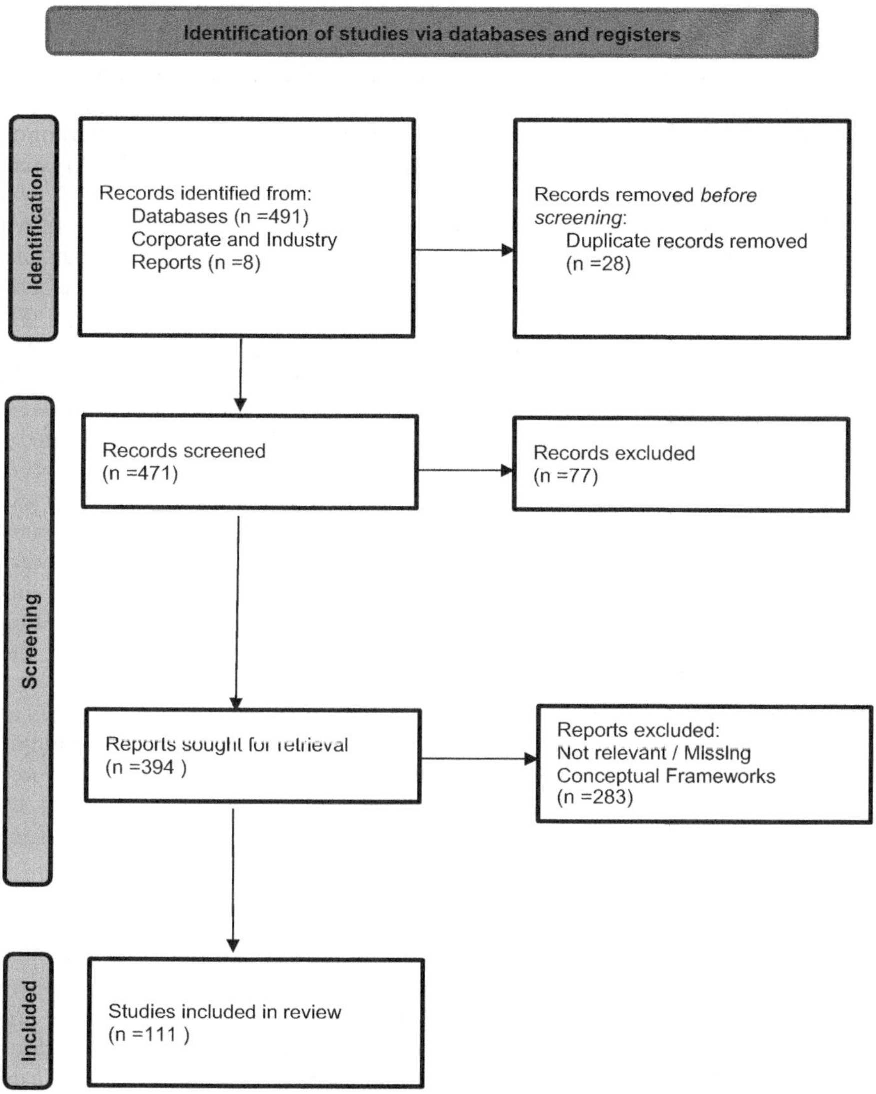

Fig. 2. PRISMA Flow Diagram. *Source:* Adapted from M.J. Page et al. (2021).

3.2 Selection Criteria

A characteristic of a systematic review is that it should be methodical and replicable. To ensure a process which is replicable and specific to our study, we not only reviewed academic journals but also indigenous databases, government websites and other online databases. This also ensured that we covered local reports on indigenous communities. Only publications in English language were considered for this study.

We started our review with Scopus and Web of Science databases. Keywords mentioned at the start of paper were used and only published articles were considered. In addition of the databases, different government and corporate reports were also considered. Only articles with indigenous AND AI were considered.

We searched on these various sources using structured keywords. Our search string used was TITLEABSKEY ("indigenous communities" OR "indigenous people" OR "indigenous") AND (TITLEABSKEY ("artificial intelligence" OR "generative AI" OR "generative artificial intelligence" OR "deep learning" OR "large language models" OR "LLM") OR TITLEABSKEY ("decolonial AI" OR "decolonizing AI" OR "ethical AI" OR "ethical artificial intelligence")). In the initial search, 476 documents were found in Phase 1, and 15 documents were shortlisted in Phase 2. In the first stage of screening, 28 duplicates and articles having exactly similar themes were excluded. Post that, 77 documents were excluded based on publication stage, publication type and language. In the second stage, articles not directly talking about the impact of AI or digitalization on indigenous populations or which were missing any conceptual frameworks were excluded which accounted to total of 283. Articles which did not provide any conceptual frameworks or were non empirical were also excluded. Finally, after doing a full analysis of the documents, we also included eight government and corporate reports, which increased our final count to 111.

Additionally, we conducted both backward and forward source searches as part of our comprehensive literature review process. This involved examining references cited in relevant studies (backward search) as well as exploring more recent publications that have cited the key studies identified (forward search). By incorporating these approaches, we ensured a thorough examination of the existing body of literature.

3.3 Research Boundaries

Since Generative AI is a relatively novel concept, we conduct our search in two separate phases also. First, we discovered the literature on indigenous people and digitalization/AI as this is a well reached topic. We then did separate research on Generative AI and then tried to extend current study, identifying what all gaps can be answered using Generative AI.

3.4 Search Protocol

High-quality reviews combine research to derive broad theoretical conclusions about the implications of a body of literature, forming relationships between theory and evidence as well as between evidence and theory (Siddaway et al., 2019).

Our inclusion criteria mandated that articles directly address digital empowerment for indigenous communities and explicitly identify gaps or limitations in current research on this topic. Furthermore, included studies needed to demonstrate a clear need for innovative approaches, such as GAI, to address these gaps. We prioritized articles presenting empirical research findings or proposing conceptual frameworks (Singh, 2024).

Conversely, we excluded studies focusing on unrelated topics or populations outside the scope of indigenous communities. Articles lacking robust methodologies or failing to provide sufficient evidence were also excluded.

3.5 Data Synthesis

Given the nature of the research questions and the anticipated heterogeneity of the included studies, a meta-analysis was not conducted. Instead, we employed a narrative synthesis approach to synthesize the findings from the selected studies. This approach allowed for a comprehensive and nuanced understanding of the complex relationships between generative AI and indigenous communities, even when the studies are diverse in design and outcome measures.

The narrative synthesis involved grouping the studies based on key themes and concepts related to generative AI and indigenous communities, such as cultural preservation, language revitalization, economic empowerment, education, etc. Within each theme, we summarized the findings of individual studies, highlighting key results, strengths and limitations and analyzed the summarized findings to identify patterns, trends and relationships across the studies. This involved comparing findings, exploring potential explanations for differences and identifying areas of agreement and disagreement.

Based on the identified patterns and relationships, we developed a synthesized narrative that provides a comprehensive and coherent overview of the evidence on generative AI and indigenous communities. This narrative will address the research questions, highlight key findings and discuss the implications for policy, practice, and future research.

4. FINDINGS

The findings of our systematic review have been categorized into seven broad categories as shown in Fig. 3. These include indigenous knowledge, digital transformation in education, health data decolonization, data and governance, societal impact, cultural preservation and the role of Generative AI.

All papers that were shortlisted from various academic databases were thoroughly studied and analyzed in depth. An additional column was then created in the exported and collated spreadsheet from these databases. This new column was titled ‘Theme’ and was carefully populated with the relevant thematic category for each paper after a detailed review and assessment.

The thematic grouping process played a critical role in synthesizing the vast amount of information collected from the shortlisted papers. By categorizing the papers into these seven broad themes (Fig. 3), it became easier to identify patterns, commonalities and gaps in the literature. This structured approach not only

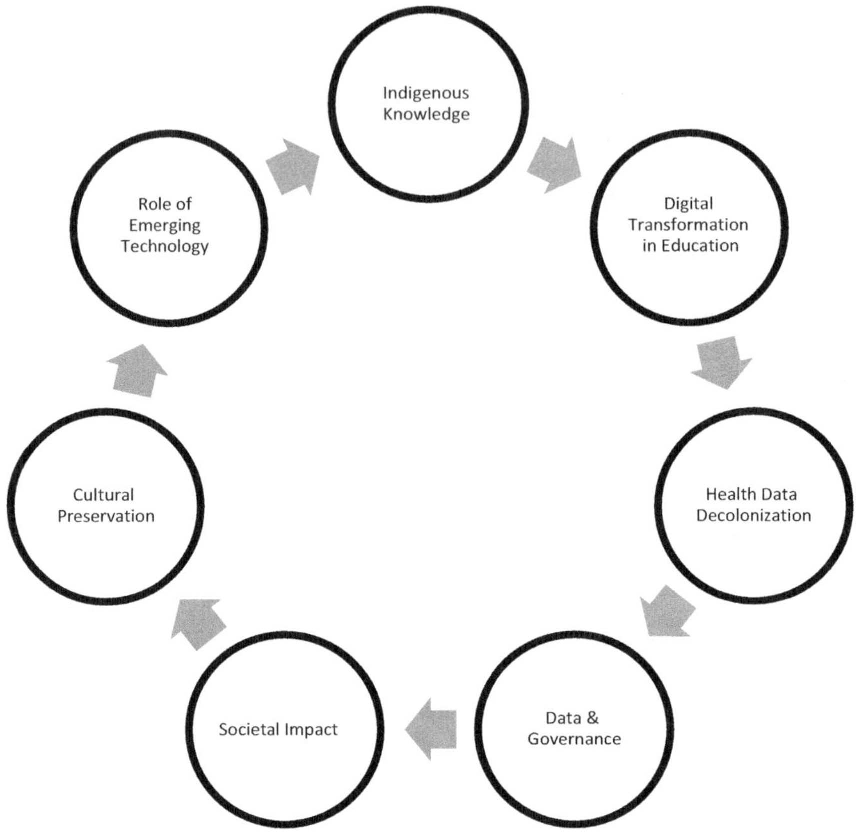

Fig. 3. Key Themes From Our Literature Review. *Source:* Developed by the authors.

facilitated a more focused and coherent analysis but also allowed for a deeper exploration of each theme. Additionally, it enabled the identification of emerging trends and areas that warrant further research, thereby contributing to a more nuanced understanding of the subject matter under investigation.

4.1 Indigenous Knowledge and Access

The recognition and inclusion of indigenous knowledge systems are increasingly emphasized as crucial for the survival of indigenous languages and cultural resources, which face significant challenges to their long-term preservation. Digitalization plays a vital role in this effort, as evidenced by initiatives that digitize folk tales, music and cultural heritage onto compact discs featuring narration, dialogue and music (Chan, 2018). It is essential for local communities to develop integrated, user friendly and nonintrusive preservation processes to continue local appropriation and codesign of tools (Stichel et al., 2019). TK is valuable to modern industry, particularly biotechnology, pharmaceutical and agribusiness corporations, as well as to those who historically relied on it. Despite its significance in the global economy, indigenous communities rarely receive credit or payment for TK exploitation due to the current global intellectual property regime's western conception of knowledge and individual ownership, facilitating misappropriation (Amechi, 2015). Such misappropriations must be identified and rectified.

4.2 Digital Transformation in Education

The digital transformation in education, especially within higher education, has been critically examined by multiple authors who argue that digitization efforts often perpetuate colonial legacies and inequities (Gumbo, 2023). This theme underscores the importance of reevaluating digital practices to ensure they positively contribute to educational equity and access. Preserving and teaching indigenous languages is also crucial. Machine learning algorithms can analyze vast amounts of data from digital archives to recognize patterns in indigenous languages, aiding in their preservation and revitalization (Fiorucci et al., 2020). AI can predict which languages are most at risk of extinction and help develop strategies for their preservation (Arista, 2023).

4.3 Health Data Decolonization

Decolonizing health data is vital to address disparities and achieve health equity. Modern digital health practices must be redesigned to dismantle colonial structures embedded within healthcare systems. This requires moving beyond simply incorporating technology into existing frameworks and instead, centring indigenous voices and priorities in the development and implementation of health technologies. Multiple initiatives have addressed this issue, such as the adoption of wearable AI-powered electrocardiogram sensors for early ailment detection (Zobair et al., 2023) and the feasibility of AI-assisted diabetic retinopathy for indigenous populations (Scheetz et al., 2021). Studies have also explored whether AI and machine learning have been utilized to detect disease onset in primary healthcare settings among indigenous populations (Jeong et al., 2023). Many studies focus on decolonizing health data and identifying health-related issues within historically marginalized indigenous populations.

4.4 Data and Governance

Data governance is increasingly crucial, especially in the research and health sectors. Emphasis on data ethics covers topics such as consent, privacy and the fair use of data, highlighting the necessity of strong governance frameworks to ensure responsible and ethical data use. Strategic priorities concerning digitization and resource allocation must be adjusted following setbacks from previous ineffective digital strategies (Kandiuk, 2016). These adjustments are vital for enhancing the capacity to adhere to legal obligations regarding the acquisition, preservation and provision of access.

The imperative for robust data governance is intensifying, particularly in sectors like research and healthcare where sensitive information is paramount. This emphasis on data ethics, encompassing crucial aspects like informed consent, privacy and equitable data use, underscores the need for comprehensive governance frameworks to ensure responsible and ethical data.

4.5 Technological Impact on Society

Digitalization has significantly impacted the lives of indigenous populations. The traditional knowledge digital library (TKDL) addresses concerns regarding TK and the prevailing traditions of intellectual property (Thomas, 2010). Since 2011, hubs established by Dell, Intel, Microsoft and Computer Aid International have accelerated the digitization and inclusion of remote and low-income communities in the global digital economy (Balan et al., 2018). Understanding how technologies like social media platforms communicate, share information and participate in social change is also crucial although they can have both positive and negative influences on indigenous youth (Rice et al., 2016).

The imperative for robust data governance is intensifying, particularly in sectors like research and healthcare where sensitive information is paramount. This emphasis on data ethics, encompassing crucial aspects like informed consent, privacy and equitable data use, underscores the need for comprehensive governance frameworks to ensure responsible and ethical data practices.

4.6 Cultural Preservation and Technology

The role of technology in preserving cultural heritage and supporting access to cultural and historical resources is growing in importance (Brown, 2008). Studies provide information to support policies that respect ethnic identity by classifying people and identifying the aspects of cultural identity most susceptible to change (Espinosa Zárate et al., 2023). Creating digital systems to preserve intangible cultural heritage is a growing conversation.

Participatory design approaches ensure that digital artefacts respect the diversity of cultural perspectives (Rehm & Rodil, 2017). Participatory design, as Rodil suggests, is essential for ensuring that digital artefacts are developed with input from indigenous communities, respecting the diversity of cultural perspectives and avoiding the pitfalls of technological imposition. This approach ensures that technology serves as a tool for empowerment and self-representation rather than a means of further control or misrepresentation.

4.7 Role of Generative AI

Generative AI presents both promising opportunities and complex challenges for digital empowerment within indigenous communities. On the one hand, it has the potential to identify and mitigate historical biases embedded in existing datasets, paving the way for more inclusive and equitable AI applications. By carefully curating training data and incorporating indigenous knowledge systems, generative AI could help create datasets that ethically represent indigenous perspectives and avoid perpetuating harmful stereotypes (Mohamed et al., 2020; Prabhakaran et al., 2022). This is particularly crucial for combating algorithmic bias, which can exacerbate existing inequalities and marginalize already vulnerable communities.

Moreover, generative AI offers powerful tools for cultural revitalization and preservation. It can be used to regenerate and digitize indigenous data, including languages, stories, songs and TK, helping to prevent the extinction of endangered cultures (An indigenous Perspective on Generative AI, 2023). For instance, AI-powered language models can assist in language learning, translation and the creation of culturally relevant educational materials.

However, it's crucial to acknowledge the potential risks associated with generative AI. Without careful consideration and community oversight, these technologies could be misused in ways that further exploit indigenous data and knowledge (Generative AI in the classroom risks further threatening indigenous inclusion in schools, 2024). Issues of data ownership, intellectual property rights and the potential for misrepresentation or cultural appropriation must be carefully addressed (Patnaik et al., 2024; Srinivasan & Uchino, 2020). Therefore, a collaborative and ethical approach, guided by indigenous data sovereignty principles and community protocols, is essential to ensure that generative AI is developed and deployed in a way that empowers, rather than harms, indigenous communities.

Prioritizing the involvement and participation of indigenous communities in the creation and execution of digital technologies and AI projects is essential for decolonizing these fields. This entails forming partnerships with indigenous communities that are based on respect and consultation in order to guarantee that their opinions and voices are heard throughout the decision-making process. Digital technologies can be used as tools for empowerment and cultural revitalization by placing a priority on indigenous sovereignty and self-determination (Mohamed et al., 2020).

Our review concentrated on areas where generative AI can support indigenous emancipation because it was centred on digital empowerment through the use of AI while adhering to the above guidelines, which have been identified by numerous studies.

The literature reviewed encompasses various aspects of indigenous communities (Table 3), including the integration of indigenous perspectives into mainstream business, digitalization, and the preservation of indigenous knowledge. This systematic and rigorous approach to narrative synthesis allowed us to draw meaningful conclusions from the body of literature, even in the absence of a quantitative meta-analysis.

5. DISCUSSION

This systematic literature review examined the intersection of emerging technologies and indigenous communities, revealing key insights and highlighting

Table 3. Key Challenges and Opportunities for Indigenous Knowledge Access and Preservation.

Challenge	Opportunity	Example/Solution's Proposed in Reviewed Articles
Loss of Indigenous Languages and Cultural Resources	Digitalization for Preservation	Develop digital archives for storing and sharing folk tales, music, and cultural heritage in collaboration with indigenous communities.
Lack of Control Over Preservation Processes	Community-Driven Preservation	Establish community-based digital repositories with indigenous leadership and control over access.
Misappropriation of Traditional Knowledge	Protecting Intellectual Property Rights	Develop benefit-sharing mechanisms that ensure fair compensation for indigenous communities when their knowledge is used commercially.
Endangerment of Indigenous Languages	AI-Powered Language Preservation	Use machine learning to analyze language data, identify patterns and aid in revitalization efforts.
Health Data Colonization	Adoption of AI technologies in health sector	AI-powered wearable tech/identifying diseases prior to onset through patterns.
Technological Impact/Bias Removal	Identifying colonial biases and handling them	More indigenous participation to include their perspectives and avoid data colonization.

Source: Compiled by the authors based on literature reviewed.

areas for further exploration. In our review of the literature, we identified several limitations in existing research studies. Primarily, these studies tend to focus either on the positive or negative aspects of digitalization and AI, rarely providing a balanced perspective. Our research aims to fill this gap by examining how generative AI, as an extension of AI, can impact the lives of indigenous people in a balanced manner.

5.1 Theoretical Contribution

This review underscores the limitations of traditional technology adoption models in fully capturing the multifaceted realities of indigenous contexts (Jokhu & Kutay, 2020). While these frameworks offer valuable insights, they fall short of addressing the culturally specific factors (LaFrance & Nichols, 2008) that significantly influence technology adoption within indigenous communities. Therefore, this study proposes an expansion of these theoretical models by incorporating three critical variables: culture, biases and indigenous involvement.

First, the integration of culture as a variable necessitates moving beyond a superficial understanding of cultural influence to consider the profound impact of indigenous worldviews (Fox et al., 2020), values and protocols on technology perception and use. This requires recognizing the diversity of indigenous cultures and understanding how technology intersects with TK systems (Lewis, 2023), language preservation efforts (Zulfadrim et al., 2021) and self-governance aspirations. Second, acknowledging and mitigating the biases inherent in technology design and development is paramount.

Secondly, acknowledging the pervasive presence of biases within technology design and implementation (Sandoval et al., 2023) is crucial. This includes recognizing how algorithmic bias (Pan et al., 2019), data sovereignty concerns (Leslie et al., 2022) and the digital divide can perpetuate existing inequalities and marginalize indigenous voices. Incorporating this variable necessitates a critical examination of power dynamics embedded within technology development and a commitment to decolonizing digital spaces.

Finally, centring indigenous involvement (Paul et al., 2020) throughout all stages of technology design, implementation and evaluation is paramount. This participatory approach recognizes the agency and expertise of indigenous communities, ensuring that technology serves as a tool for self-determination rather than a means of further control or assimilation.

While some of these frameworks, like the UTAUT or AMO, offer valuable insights into factors influencing technology acceptance, they often fall short of addressing the unique cultural, historical and socioeconomic realities of indigenous communities. However, the emergence of generative AI presents a unique opportunity to move beyond these limitations and develop more inclusive and culturally grounded frameworks.

Generative AI, particularly in the form of LLM, can be trained on massive text and code datasets. In this context, we can envision training an LLM on existing research, which would include academic papers, conference proceedings and potentially even code implementations of these models. Datasets related to indigenous cultures could encompass texts in indigenous languages, ethnographic studies, accounts of TK systems and documentation of historical interactions with technology. With this training, the LLM could then be used to

- Identify Discrepancies and Gaps: The LLM could analyze the language and assumptions embedded within existing research, comparing it to the cultural contexts present in the indigenous datasets.
- Terminological Bias: Where terms used in existing research have different meanings or connotations in indigenous cultures.
- Missing Variables: Identifying factors highly relevant to indigenous technology adoption that are absent or underemphasized in the models.
- Assumptions of Universality: Highlighting where these research works assume universal human behaviour that may not hold true in specific cultural contexts.

Training a large language model on datasets representing indigenous cultures could provide valuable insights for constructing culturally relevant technology adoption frameworks. Imagine feeding the LLM a corpus comprising texts in I\indigenous languages, traditional stories and documentation of ecological knowledge. As the LLM processes these data, it would begin to identify recurring themes, values and practices central to these cultures.

For instance, the LLM might recognize the significance of community consensus or the interconnectedness of humans and nature within these cultures. These identified elements, often absent or underrepresented in models like the UTAUT and AMO, could then be translated into novel variables or constructs within the technology adoption framework. This process could involve either adapting existing variables to better reflect indigenous values or proposing entirely new factors derived from the unique insights gleaned from the indigenous datasets.

Generative AI possesses the capability to construct highly detailed and contextually nuanced simulations, offering a powerful tool for understanding technology adoption within specific indigenous communities. By leveraging this technology, researchers and policymakers can move beyond abstract models and delve into the intricate interplay of cultural values, community dynamics and historical contexts that shape technology acceptance.

By providing a safe space for experimentation and foresight, these simulations can pave the way for more equitable, ethical and ultimately beneficial technology implementation. By harnessing the power of generative AI in a responsible and culturally sensitive manner, we can move beyond generic models and develop technology adoption frame works that are truly inclusive, equitable and responsive to the needs and aspirations of indigenous communities.

5.2 Societal and Policy Implications

The inclusion of indigenous perspectives in research is not merely an act of inclusivity, it is a societal imperative with profound implications. Indigenous communities, with their unique histories, cultures and knowledge systems, hold a wealth of understanding that can reshape our approach to societal issues. By embracing these perspectives, we embark on a journey towards a more just, equitable and sustainable future.

The integration of indigenous methodologies into technical and professional communication (Al-hassan, 2023) and UX research carries significant societal and policy implications (Fig. 4). By moving beyond decolonial approaches that lack actionable strategies, and instead embracing indigenous-centred methods like the integrative approach, third space, Afrikology and predominantly indigenous methodologies, TPC and UX practitioners can contribute to more equitable and just technological development.

Policy frameworks should encourage and incentivize the adoption of these approaches, particularly in areas like localization and translation where indigenous epistemologies are often overlooked. Furthermore, recognizing the potential of indigenous methodologies, such as the focused life story interview method, for ethically designing AI systems, necessitates policy support for research and development in this domain. By centring indigenous voices and knowledge systems, we can foster technological innovation that respects cultural diversity and promotes digital empowerments for all.

By incorporating indigenous worldviews, research becomes culturally grounded, reflecting the specific contexts and needs of indigenous communities. This leads to

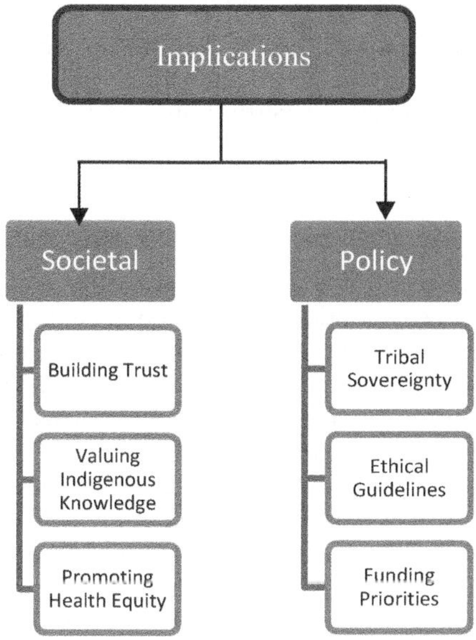

Fig. 4. Factors in Societal and Policy Implications. *Source:* Developed by the authors.

more effective and relevant solutions, whether addressing health disparities, environmental degradation, or social injustices. Moreover, this inclusion empowers indigenous communities by validating their knowledge systems and recognizing their agency in shaping research agendas. It fosters a sense of ownership and self-determination, enabling indigenous peoples to actively participate in research processes and influence outcomes that directly affect their lives.

The societal implications are far reaching. Without accurate data and representation, communities remain invisible in research (Credo & Ingram, 2021), leading to policies and interventions that fail to address their unique needs. This perpetuates cycles of health disparities, limiting access to quality healthcare and exacerbating existing inequalities. Moreover, the lack of collaboration stifles scientific progress. Indigenous knowledge systems, developed over millennia, hold invaluable insights into health, environmental sustainability and social well-being. By excluding these perspectives, we limit understanding of these critical issues and miss opportunities for innovative solutions.

Addressing this issue requires a paradigm shift in both societal attitudes and policy approaches. This paradigm shift also necessitates a significant change in policy. Policies must be developed in consultation and collaboration with indigenous communities, ensuring their voices are heard and their priorities are reflected in research agendas. This includes respecting indigenous data sovereignty, ensuring ownership and control over their knowledge and information. Funding agencies should prioritize research projects that are led by or conducted in genuine partnership with indigenous communities, supporting self-determination and capacity building. Furthermore, ethical guidelines for research involving indigenous communities must be strengthened and strictly enforced, ensuring respect for cultural protocols, intellectual property rights and free, prior and informed consent.

5.3 Limitations and Scope for Future Research

While emerging technologies like generative AI offer a powerful new lens for understanding technology adoption in indigenous communities, several limitations and avenues for future research warrant consideration.

In terms of data availability and representation, the effectiveness of AI-driven approaches hinges on the availability of comprehensive and representative datasets. However, existing datasets often lack representation from indigenous communities or misrepresent their knowledge and experiences (Santano et al., 2021; Tsai & Wang, 2019). This raises critical questions: How can we ensure data sovereignty (Thomson, 2000) and ethical data governance in AI research involving indigenous communities? What strategies can be employed to develop and curate culturally appropriate and representative datasets (Credo & Ingram, 2021)? Future research should prioritize collaborative efforts with indigenous communities to collect, curate and annotate data in culturally sensitive and ethical ways. This includes ensuring data sovereignty and community ownership of data.

Algorithmic Bias: While generative AI can help identify existing biases, it's crucial to acknowledge that algorithms themselves can perpetuate or even amplify biases present in the training data (Williamson, 2001). This is particularly concerning in the context of indigenous communities, who have historically faced systemic bias and discrimination. Key questions emerged are as follows: How can we develop AI models that are sensitive to the cultural contexts (Fomunyam, 2020; Tsai & Wang, 2019) and values of indigenous communities? What methods can be used to detect and mitigate bias in AI algorithms used in indigenous contexts? Future work must critically examine and mitigate potential biases within AI models to ensure equitable and just outcomes.

Indigenous Involvement: The use of AI in indigenous contexts raises important questions regarding consent, data privacy and the potential for misuse. How can we ensure that AI technologies are developed and deployed in a way that respects indigenous knowledge systems (Lewis, 2023) and protocols? What mechanisms are needed to ensure meaningful participation (Mohamed et al., 2020) and consent from indigenous communities in AI research and development? Ongoing dialogue and collaboration with indigenous communities are essential to establish ethical guidelines and best practices for AI development and deployment.

Beyond Prediction to Empowerment: Future research should move beyond simply predicting technology adoption to exploring how generative AI can empower indigenous communities (Eglash et al., 2024). How can generative AI be used to revitalize indigenous languages, preserve cultural heritage (Santano et al., 2021) or support economic development in indigenous communities? What design principles should guide the development of AI technologies that align with indigenous values and aspirations? This includes co-designing technologies that align with indigenous values, support self-determination and promote cultural revitalization.

By acknowledging these limitations and pursuing these research directions, we can harness the potential of generative AI to contribute to more equitable and just technology adoption processes that benefit indigenous communities.

6. CONCLUSION

Generative AI holds immense potential to positively impact the lives of indigenous people across diverse domains, from healthcare and language preservation to environmental monitoring and economic empowerment. As our technical exploration of advanced AI technologies, such as natural language generation, federated learning, 3D reconstruction, and predictive analytics, has revealed, there are creative and powerful ways to adapt these innovations to address the specific needs and challenges faced by indigenous communities. However, the true measure of success lies not just in technical prowess, but equally in the ethical considerations that must be woven into the fabric of these advancements. Upholding principles of data sovereignty, cultural integrity and collaborative development processes are not merely boxes to be ticked but rather foundational pillars upon which impactful and sustainable solutions must be built to ensure the benefits of these technologies are equitably distributed and aligned with the values and aspirations of indigenous peoples.

To this end, we propose a collaborative approach that empowers indigenous stake holders as equal partners in the research, development, and deployment of generative AI systems. This means not only soliciting input and feedback from indigenous communities but also centring their knowledge, values and decision-making processes throughout the entire lifecycle of these technologies. By forging deep and lasting partnerships, we can ensure that the benefits of generative AI are equitably distributed, the risks and harms are mitigated and the unique cultural identities and aspirations of indigenous peoples are respected and amplified.

Furthermore, by engaging in meaningful dialogues with indigenous communities, developing trust-based relationships and fostering a spirit of mutual learning, we can ensure that the potential benefits of generative AI are equitably distributed and that any risks or challenges associated with these technologies are proactively addressed. This collaborative approach is essential to unlocking the true transformative potential of generative AI in supporting the needs and aspirations of indigenous peoples around the world. This collaborative approach also necessitates a fundamental shift in the research and development paradigm, moving away from extractive models that have historically exploited indigenous knowledge and resources and towards models that prioritize capacity building, reciprocal knowledge exchange and the establishment of sustainable, long-term partnerships built on trust and mutual respect.

The future of generative AI in supporting indigenous communities is bright, promising a tapestry of benefits. To realize this potential, a collaborative approach is essential. Researchers, technologists and indigenous stakeholders must work together, ensuring that these powerful tools are developed and deployed in a manner that is respectful, beneficial, and empowering. By prioritizing ethical frameworks and community engagement in future research and applications, we can foster the creation of sustainable, culturally sensitive solutions. This will not only improve lives and preserve the rich heritage of indigenous communities worldwide, but also establish a blueprint for ethical AI innovation that respects and uplifts the diversity of human cultures and societies.

REFERENCES

Al-hassan, M. (2023). Revolutionizing methods and methodologies: Advancing Indigenous-centered research methodologies in user experience research (UXR), technical and professional communication practice. In *Proceedings of the 41st ACM international conference on design of communication* (pp. 103–109). https://doi.org/10.1145/3615335.3623018

Alghatrifi, I., & Khalid, H. (2019). A systematic review of UTAUT and UTAUT2 as a baseline framework of information system research in adopting new technology: A case study of IPV6 adoption. In *2019 6th International conference on research and innovation in information systems (ICRIIS)* (pp. 1–6). https://doi.org/10.1109/ICRIIS48246.2019.9073292

Amechi, E. P. (2015). Leveraging traditional knowledge on the medicinal uses of plants within the patent system: The digitisation and disclosure of knowledge in South Africa. *Potchefstroom Electronic Law Journal, 18*(1), 3072–3101. https://doi.org/10.4314/pelj.v18i1.04

Appelbaum, E., Bailey, T., Berg, P., & Kalleberg, A. L. (2001). Do high performance work systems pay off? In *Research in the sociology of work* (Vol. 10, pp. 85–107). Emerald Publishing Limited (MCB UP). https://doi.org/10.1016/S0277-2833(01)80022-4

Arawjo, I., & Mogos, A. (2021). Intercultural computing education: Toward justice across difference. *ACM Transactions on Computing Education, 21*(4), 1–33. https://doi.org/10.1145/3458037

Arista, N. (2023). Maoli intelligence: Indigenous data sovereignty and futurity. In S. Cave & K. Dihal (Eds.), *Imagining AI* (1st ed., pp. 218–234). Oxford University Press. https://doi.org/10.1093/oso/9780192865366.003.0014

Asuquo, M. E., Okenjom, G. P., Okpa, O. E., & Eyiene, A. E. (2023). Opportunities and challenges in digitization of Indigenous knowledge and implication for educational management in the Nigerian context. In T. M. Masenya (Ed.), *Advances in information quality and management* (pp. 87–104). IGI Global. https://doi.org/10.4018/978-1-6684-7024-4.ch005

Balan, S., Lajitha, C. S., Mathew, J., Sreedhanya, L. R., & Bhaskara Rao, V. (2018). Design of a Novel IEC 61850 based merging unit for substation automation. In *2018 International CET conference on control, communication, and computing (IC4)* (pp. 101–105). https://doi.org/10.1109/CETIC4.2018.8530933

Berry, J. E. (2020). The internet: An educational system for equalizing educational opportunity. In R. Papa (Ed.), *Handbook on promoting social justice in education* (pp. 1587–1607). Springer International Publishing. https://doi.org/10.1007/978-3-030-14625-2_74

Botes, M. W., & Rossi, A. (2021). Visualisation techniques for consent: Finding common ground in comic art with Indigenous populations. In *2021 IEEE European symposium on security and privacy workshops (EuroS&PW)* (pp. 292–297). https://doi.org/10.1109/EuroSPW54576.2021.00037

Brown, D. (2008). "Ko to ringa ki nga rakau a te Pakeha"—Virtual *Taonga* Maori and museums. *Visual Resources*, *24*(1), 59–75. https://doi.org/10.1080/01973760801892266

Chan, C. S. C. (2018). Sustainability of Indigenous folk tales, music and cultural heritage through innovation. *Journal of Cultural Heritage Management and Sustainable Development*, *8*(3), 342–361. https://doi.org/10.1108/JCHMSD-06-2017-0044

Chiu, R.-F., Yeh, Y.-S., Chi, S., Lee, R., Wu, A., Chang, H.-J., & Chang, L. (2009). Kaohsiung county broadband mobile network. In *2009 10th ACIS international conference on software engineering, artificial intelligences, networking and parallel/distributed computing* (pp. 36–41). https://doi.org/10.1109/SNPD.2009.42

Credo, J., & Ingram, J. C. (2021). Perspective developing successful collaborative research partnerships with AI/AN communities. *International Journal of Environmental Research and Public Health*, *18*(17), 9089. https://doi.org/10.3390/ijerph18179089

Dirks, L. G. (2021). Collaborative research results dissemination: Applying postcolonial theory to Indigenous community contexts. In K. Toeppe, H. Yan, & S. K. W. Chu (Eds.), *Diversity, divergence, dialogue* (Vol. 12646, pp. 394–403). Springer International Publishing. https://doi.org/10.1007/978-3-030-71305-8_33

Eglash, R., Robinson, K. P., Bennett, A., Robert, L., & Garvin, M. (2024). Computational reparations as generative justice: Decolonial transitions to unalienated circular value flow. *Big Data & Society*, *11*(1). https://doi.org/10.1177/20539517231221732

Espinosa Zárate, Z., Camilli Trujillo, C., & Plaza-de-la-Hoz, J. (2023). Digitalization in vulnerable populations: A systematic review in Latin America. *Social Indicators Research*, *170*(3), 1183–1207. https://doi.org/10.1007/s11205-023-03239-x

Fiorucci, M., Khoroshiltseva, M., Pontil, M., Traviglia, A., Del Bue, A., & James, S. (2020). Machine learning for cultural heritage: A survey. *Pattern Recognition Letters*, *133*, 102–108. https://doi.org/10.1016/j.patrec.2020.02.017

Fomunyam, K. G. (2020). Theorising the itinerant curriculum as the pathway to relevance in African higher education in the era of the fourth industrual revolution. *International Journal of Education and Practice*, *8*(2), 248–256. https://doi.org/10.18488/journal.61.2020.82.248.256

Fox, J., McKnight, J., Sun, Y., Maung, D., & Crawfis, R. (2020). Using a serious game to communicate risk and minimize psychological distance regarding environmental pollution. *Telematics and Informatics*, *46*, 101320. https://doi.org/10.1016/j.tele.2019.101320

Gumbo, M. (2023). Digitisation of higher education and research: Raising inclusivity and equity issues for Indigenous students. *South African Computer Journal*, *35*(1). https://doi.org/10.18489/sacj.v35i1.1107

Irwin, R., & White, T. H. (2019). Decolonising technological futures: A dialogical tryptich between Te Haumoana White, Ruth Irwin, and Tegmark's artificial intelligence. *Futures*, *112*, 102431. https://doi.org/10.1016/j.futures.2019.06.003

Ishida, T. (2006). Communicating culture. *IEEE Intelligent Systems*, *21*(3), 62–63. https://doi.org/10.1109/MIS.2006.44

Jeong, K., Mallard, A. R., Coombe, L., & Ward, J. (2023). Artificial intelligence and prediction of cardiometabolic disease: Systematic review of model performance and potential benefits in Indigenous populations. *Artificial Intelligence in Medicine*, *139*, 102534. https://doi.org/10.1016/j.artmed.2023.102534

Jokhu, P. D., & Kutay, C. (2020). Observations on appropriate technology application in Indigenous community using system dynamics modelling. *Sustainability*, *12*(6), 2245. https://doi.org/10.3390/su12062245

Kandiuk, M. (2016). The rhetoric of digitization and the politicization of Canadian heritage. *Library Trends*, *65*(2), 165–179. https://doi.org/10.1353/lib.2016.0029

Kaufman, R., Costa, J., & Kimani, E. (2024). Effects of multimodal explanations for autonomous driving on driving performance, cognitive load, expertise, confidence, and trust. *Scientific Reports*, *14*(1), 13061. https://doi.org/10.1038/s41598-024-62052-9

Kleider-Offutt, H., Stevens, B., Mickes, L., & Boogert, S. (2024). Application of artificial intelligence to eyewitness identification. *Cognitive Research: Principles and Implications*, *9*(1), 19. https://doi.org/10.1186/s41235-024-00542-0

LaFrance, J., & Nichols, R. (2008). Reframing evaluation: Defining an Indigenous evaluation framework. *Canadian Journal of Program Evaluation*, *23*(2), 13–31. https://doi.org/10.3138/cjpe.23.003

Leditschke, A., Nichols, J., Farrow, K., & Agius, Q. (2024). The ethics and cultural sensitivities of data management: Some considerations. In J. Nichols & B. Mehra (Eds.), *Data curation and information systems design from Australasia: Implications for cataloguing of vernacular knowledge in galleries, libraries, archives, and museums (Advances in librarianship)* (Vol. 54, pp. 23–39). Emerald Publishing Limited. https://doi.org/10.1108/S0065-283020240000054003

Leslie, H. A., Van Velzen, M. J. M., Brandsma, S. H., Vethaak, A. D., Garcia-Vallejo, J. J., & Lamoree, M. H. (2022). Discovery and quantification of plastic particle pollution in human blood. *Environment International*, *163*, 107199. https://doi.org/10.1016/j.envint.2022.107199

Lewis, J. E. (2023). Imagining Indigenous AI. In S. Cave & K. Dihal (Eds.), *Imagining AI* (1st ed., pp. 210–217). Oxford University Press. https://doi.org/10.1093/oso/9780192865366.003.0013

Lischer-Katz, Z. (2022). The emergence of digital reformatting in the history of preservation knowledge: 1823–2015. *Journal of Documentation*, *78*(6), 1249–1277. https://doi.org/10.1108/JD-04-2021-0080

Marr, B. (2023). A short history of ChatGPT: How we got where we are today. https://www.forbes.com/sites/bernardmarr/2023/05/19/a-short-history-of-chatgpt-how-we-got-to-where-we-are-today/

Matthews, A. (2024). Sculpting the social algorithm for radical futurity. *AI & Society*, *39*(1), 75–86. https://doi.org/10.1007/s00146-023-01760-8

Mohamed, S., Png, M.-T., & Isaac, W. (2020). Decolonial AI: Decolonial theory as sociotechnical foresight in artificial intelligence. *Philosophy & Technology*, *33*(4), 659–684. https://doi.org/10.1007/s13347-020-00405-8

Newell, J. (2012). Old objects, new media: Historical collections, digitization and affect. *Journal of Material Culture*, *17*(3), 287–306. https://doi.org/10.1177/1359183512453534

Page, M. J., McKenzie, J. E., Bossuyt, P. M., Boutron, I., Hoffmann, T. C., Mulrow, C. D., Shamseer, L., Tetzlaff, J. M., Akl, E. A., Brennan, S. E., Chou, R., Glanville, J., Grimshaw, J. M., Hróbjartsson, A., Lalu, M. M., Li, T., Loder, E. W., Mayo-Wilson, E., McDonald, S., … Moher, D. (2021). The PRISMA 2020 statement: An updated guideline for reporting systematic reviews. *Journal of Clinical Epidemiology*, *134*, 178–189. https://doi.org/10.1016/j.jclinepi.2021.03.001

Pan, X., Song, M. L., Zhang, J., & Zhou, G. (2019). Innovation network, technological learning and innovation performance of high-tech cluster enterprises. *Journal of Knowledge Management*, *23*(9), 1729–1746. https://doi.org/10.1108/JKM-06-2018-0371

Patnaik, R., Patra, S. K., Mahapatra, D. M., & Baral, S. K. (2024). Adoption and challenges underlying OTT platform in India during pandemic: A critical study of socio-economic and technological issues. *FIIB Business Review*, *13*(3), 356–363.

Paul, M., Upadhyay, P., & Dwivedi, Y. K. (2020). Roadmap to digitalisation of an emerging economy: A viewpoint. *Transforming Government: People, Process and Policy*, *14*(3), 401–415. https://doi.org/10.1108/TG-03-2020-0054

Prabhakaran, V., Qadri, R., & Hutchinson, B. (2022). Cultural incongruencies in artificial intelligence. (Version 1). *arXiv*. https://doi.org/10.48550/ARXIV.2211.13069

Rana, S., Singh, J., & Kathuria, S. (2023). Parameters and decision elements of writing effective literature review papers: Empirical evidence from multiple stakeholders on POWER framework. In S. Rana, J. Singh, & S. Kathuria (Eds.), *Review of management literature* (Vol. 2, pp. 1–25). Emerald Publishing Limited. https://doi.org/10.1108/S2754-586520230000002001

Ratten, V. (2024). Artificial intelligence, digital trends and globalization: Future research trends. *FIIB Business Review*, *13*(3), 286–293. https://doi.org/10.1177/23197145231222774

Raut, S. K., Alon, I., Rana, S., & Kathuria, S. (2024). Knowledge management and career readiness: A review and synthesis. *Journal of Knowledge Management*, *28*(7), 1821–1866. https://doi.org/10.1108/JKM-02-2023-0140

Rehm, M., & Rodil, K. (2017). Introducing the tripartite digitization model for engaging with the intangible cultural heritage of the city. In A. L. Brooks & E. Brooks (Eds.), *Interactivity, game creation, design, learning, and innovation* (Vol. 196, pp. 297–304). Springer International Publishing. https://doi.org/10.1007/978-3-319-55834-9_35

Rice, E. S., Haynes, E., Royce, P., & Thompson, S. C. (2016). Social media and digital technology use among Indigenous young people in Australia: A literature review. *International Journal for Equity in Health*, *15*(1), 81. https://doi.org/10.1186/s12939-016-0366-0

Robinson, C., Macdonald, J., Perry, J., Nadji, J., Nadji, S., McCartney, S., Taylor, A., Hunter, F., Cooper, D., Moyle, F., Drummond, A., Borovac, C., Van Bodegraven, S., Gilfedder, M., Setterfield, S., & Douglas, M. (2022). Coproduction mechanisms to weave Indigenous knowledge, artificial intelligence, and technical data to enable Indigenous-led adaptive decision making: Lessons from Australia's joint managed Kakadu National Park. *Ecology and Society*, *27*(4), art36. https://doi.org/10.5751/ES-13747-270436

Ruster, L. P., & Brown, G. (2020). Termination for cultural misalignment: Setting up contract terms to ensure community well-being in the development of AI. *International Journal of Community Well-Being*, *3*(4), 523–537. https://doi.org/10.1007/s42413-020-00081-8

Sandoval, M. H., Alvear Portaccio, M. E., & Albala, C. (2023). Life expectancy by ethnic origin in Chile. *Frontiers in Public Health*, *11*, 1147542. https://doi.org/10.3389/fpubh.2023.1147542

Santano, D., Esmaeili, H., Thwaites, H., & Amar, S. (2021). Unmasking the Mah Meri mask: A digitization journey for AR and VR. *Virtual Creativity*, *11*(1), 33–51. https://doi.org/10.1386/vcr_00041_1

Scheetz, J., Koca, D., McGuinness, M., Holloway, E., Tan, Z., Zhu, Z., O'Day, R., Sandhu, S., MacIsaac, R. J., Gilfillan, C., Turner, A., Keel, S., & He, M. (2021). Real-world artificial intelligence-based opportunistic screening for diabetic retinopathy in endocrinology and Indigenous healthcare settings in Australia. *Scientific Reports*, *11*(1), 15808. https://doi.org/10.1038/s41598-021-94178-5

Schomakers, E.-M., Lidynia, C., Vervier, L. S., Calero Valdez, A., & Ziefle, M. (2022). Applying an extended UTAUT2 model to explain user acceptance of lifestyle and therapy mobile health apps: Survey study. *JMIR mHealth and uHealth*, *10*(1), e27095. https://doi.org/10.2196/27095

Siddaway, A. P., Wood, A. M., & Hedges, L. V. (2019). How to do a systematic review: A best practice guide for conducting and reporting narrative reviews, meta-analyses, and meta-syntheses. *Annual Review of Psychology*, *70*(1), 747–770. https://doi.org/10.1146/annurev-psych-010418-102803

Singh, P. (2024). Navigating the digital dimensions of the metaverse: A systematic review and research agenda exploring implications across industries and customers. *FIIB Business Review*. https://doi.org/10.1177/23197145241247704

Srinivasan, R., & Uchino, K. (2020). Biases in generative art – A causal look from the lens of art history. (Version 2). *arXiv*. https://doi.org/10.48550/ARXIV.2010.13266

Starblanket, D., Lefebvre, S., Legare, M., Billan, J., Akan, N., Goodpipe, E., & Bourassa, C. (2019). Nanâtawihowin Âcimowina Kika-Môsahkinikêhk Papiskîci-Itascikêwin Astâcikowina [Medicine/healing stories picked, sorted, stored]: Adapting the collective consensual data analytic procedure (CCDAP) as an Indigenous research method. *International Journal of Qualitative Methods*, *18*. https://doi.org/10.1177/1609406919896140

Stichel, B., Blake, E., Maasz, D., Stanley, C., Winschiers-Theophilus, H., & Afrikaner, H. (2019). Namibian Indigenous communities reflecting on their own digital representations. In *Proceedings of the 9th international conference on communities & technologies - Transforming communities* (pp. 51–59). https://doi.org/10.1145/3328320.3328378

Stillman, L., & Craig, B. (2006). Incorporating Indigenous world views in community informatics. In E. M. Trauth (Ed.), *Social inclusion: Societal and organizational implications for information systems* (pp. 237–246). Springer. https://doi.org/10.1007/11915034_47

Tapu, I. F., & Fa'agau, T. K. (2022). A new age Indigenous instrument: Artificial intelligence and its potential for (de)colonialized data. *Harvard Civil Rights - Civil Liberties Law Review*, *57*(2), 715–753. https://search.informit.org/doi/10.3316/agispt.20230215083222

Thomas, P. N. (2010). Traditional knowledge and the traditional knowledge digital library: Digital quandaries and other concerns. *International Communication Gazette*, *72*(8), 659–673. https://doi.org/10.1177/1748048510380799

Thomson, A. J. (2000). Elicitation and representation of traditional ecological knowledge for use in forest management. *Computers and Electronics in Agriculture*, *27*(1–3), 267–281. https://doi.org/10.1016/S0168-1699(00)00103-4

Thomson, A. J., & Schmoldt, D. L. (2001). Ethics in computer software design and development. *Computers and Electronics in Agriculture*, *30*(1–3), 85–102. https://doi.org/10.1016/S0168-1699(00)00158-7

Tsai, C.-H., & Wang, C.-P. (2019). *Study on the digitalization of festival culture in Taiwan's aboriginal literature* (pp. 383–386). https://doi.org/10.35745/ecei2019v2.098

Vasileva, O., & Okhlopkov, V. (2021). School education for the Indigenous small-numbered peoples of the North: Between cultural preservation and educational quality. *Voprosy Obrazovaniyal Educational Studies Moscow*, *4*, 285–310. https://doi.org/10.17323/1814-9545-2021-4-285-310

Venkatesh, V., Morris, M. G., Davis, G. B., & Davis, F. D. (2003). user acceptance of information technology: Toward a unified view. *MIS Quarterly*, *27*(3), 425. https://doi.org/10.2307/30036540

Williamson, A. (2001). Emancipatory learning via the internet: A model for reducing Maori socio-economic exclusion in Aotearoa/New Zealand. In W. Kim, T.-W. Ling, Y.-J. Lee, & S.-S. Park (Eds.), *The human society and the internet internet-related socio-economic issues* (Vol. 2105, pp. 100–113). Springer. https://doi.org/10.1007/3-540-47749-7_8

Zobair, K. M., Houghton, L., Tjondronegoro, D., Sanzogni, L., Islam, M. Z., Sarker, T., & Islam, M. J. (2023). Systematic review of Internet of medical things for cardiovascular disease prevention among Australian first nations. *Heliyon*, *9*(11), e22420. https://doi.org/10.1016/j.heliyon.2023.e22420

Zulfadrim, T. Y., & Kanegae, H. (2021). *Analysis of the impact of technology on culture in indigenous communities: Mentawai Islands, Indonesia: 2nd Southeast Asian Academic Forum on sustainable development (SEA-AFSID 2018)*, Jogjakarta, Indonesia. https://doi.org/10.2991/aebmr.k.210305.049

Artificial Intelligence in Sustainable Finance: A Comprehensive Literature Review and an Integrative Framework

Elvira Anna Graziano[a], Gerardo Petroccione[a] and Dario Siggia[b]

[a]*Link Campus University, Italy*
[b]*University of Palermo, Italy*

ABSTRACT

The rapid emergence of Artificial Intelligence (AI) as a pivotal technology in the financial sector has generated increasing interest in its potential to advance economic and environmental sustainability. This research utilizes a systematic literature review (SLR) approach to analyze 40 articles from reputable scientific journals in the fields of economics and finance, using the Elton Bryson Stephens Company (EBSCO) database, which is known for its reliability in these areas. The primary aim is to assess emerging trends, pinpoint gaps and delve into the challenges associated with the implementation and utilization of AI within the realm of sustainable finance (SF). By delivering a methodical overview of the current literature, this study presents the first comprehensive review dedicated to the intersection of AI and SF. The findings indicate that, despite the potential for AI to revolutionize SF, there are significant hurdles to overcome, particularly concerning regulatory compliance, ethical considerations and the integration of AI-driven decision-making systems.

Keywords: Artificial Intelligence; sustainable finance; ESG; fintech; sustainability; systematic literature review

1. INTRODUCTION

In recent years, the developments in technological innovation within organizations have captured heightened scholarly interest (Mariani et al., 2023). This surge in attention is due to companies increasingly leveraging diverse

Reviewing the Latest Trends in Management Literature
Review of Management Literature, Volume 4B, 27–51

ISSN: 2754-5865/doi:10.1108/S2754-58652025000004B002

technologies to enhance their innovation capabilities and achieve better innovation outcomes (Wamba-Taguimdje et al., 2020; Akter et al., 2021). This trend mirrors the transformative impact of Artificial Intelligence (AI), which, integrated into the financial sector since the 1950s (Ng, 2020), is now emerging as a dominant technology in the 2020s (Hilpisch, 2020). AI's rapid advancement across sectors underscores its potential to reshape corporate competitiveness, job markets and economic development globally (Bughin et al., 2018; Lin, 2024).

According to the European Union (EU), AI is defined as 'the ability of a system to correctly interpret external data, learn from that data, and use that knowledge to achieve specific goals and tasks through flexible adaptation' (Haenlein & Kaplan, 2019). AI, with rapid pervasiveness, has taken a central role in the digital transformation of society and, perhaps, ushered in a new era (Blanco-Ruiz et al., 2024). The size of the AI market is expanding, with an estimated annual growth rate between 19% and 36%, leading to total revenues of around USD 2 trillion by 2030 (Fortune Business Insights, 2023). The process is aided by the computing power of new processors, the continued increase in the volume of data produced worldwide, which is expected to reach 175 zettabytes (1 billion gigabytes) in 2025, and the number of jobs that can be automated, which in the Organization for Economic Cooperation and Development (OECD) countries is 14%, and another 32% will face substantial changes. In 2021, 8% of enterprises and 28% of large companies in the EU were already using AI technologies (Eurostat, 2021). The acceleration has been brought about by the pandemic crisis that has shifted many work processes to advanced technologies and the cloud, spread the Internet of Things (IoT) and machines and broadened consumer familiarity with Information Technology, triggering the consequent demand for AI-based solutions. By 2035, AI by ensuring improved forecasting, optimized operations, efficient resource allocation and personalized available digital solutions can increase labour productivity by between 11% and 37% (Eager et al., 2020). For these reasons, it has been placed among the priorities of the European Union. The European Parliament's resolution of 12 February 2019 on a comprehensive industrial policy on robotics and AI, together with the Council's General Guideline of 6 December 2022, encourages the development of AI, but emphasizes, at the same time, that malicious or negligent use could threaten digital security, physical and public safety, people's fundamental rights, to the point of being a threat to democracy. The resolution emphasizes the need to work with ethical standards to ensure a human-centred (anthropocentric) development of AI, accountability and transparency in algorithmic decision-making systems; while AI brings great advantages in automation and decision-making, it carries an inherent risk when the algorithms used are static and opaque. Hence the need to develop AI systems by the principles of transparency and accountability, enabling human understanding of automated actions, extending clarity to the entire automated decision-making process and preventing developer-generated bias.

Finance, on the other hand, according to the OECD (2024), is 'the management of financial resources, including activities such as lending, investment, fundraising, and financial risk management'. It plays a crucial role not only in personal lives but also in the operations of businesses, communities and governments. The integration of AI in the financial sector has led to significant advancements, improving operational efficiency, risk management and personalization of financial services.

In addition to traditional finance, the importance of sustainable finance (SF) is emerging. The United Nations defines SF as 'the process of considering environmental, social and governance (ESG) factors in investment decisions, resulting in increased long-term investment in sustainable economic activities and projects'. In recent years, there has been an increasing interest in the relationship between ESG practices and firm value (Chouaibi et al., 2022). This growing focus aligns with the principles of SF, which aims to promote investments that not only generate financial returns but also have a positive impact on the environment and society. Additionally, incorporating AI in financial decision-making can enhance the effectiveness and precision of sustainable investments, ensuring that they contribute meaningfully to environmental and social goals (Alkurdi et al., 2023).

In the global financial sector, there is an expansion of AI solutions for algorithmic trading, fraud detection, credit risk assessment and customer experiences, due to the ability to quickly and more accurately analyze large amounts of data. In the domestic banking sector, the Cipa-ABI 2021 survey on AI, carried out also to verify the state of the art and banks' strategies in the algorithmic age, already highlighted the first benefits obtained in the improvement of internal and customer-facing efficiency, cyber security and the trend to extend the scope of applications, including anti-money laundering (AML). Orientations were confirmed and extended by a subsequent ABI Lab report, according to which 68% of credit institutions are investing in AI and 22% have defined a centralized supervision or a specific competence centre. The use of this family of technologies, like all innovations, involves reflections on all its aspects, starting with the methodologies to be adopted and the skills required (ABI Lab Report, 2024).

The convergence of AI and SF presents a unique opportunity to promote a greener and more inclusive economy. AI can analyze vast volumes of data to identify sustainable practices and predict the environmental impact of economic activities, thereby facilitating informed decisions that are aligned with ESG criteria.

The integration of AI into finance, as defined by the EU and the OECD, and the emergence of SF, as defined by the United Nations, are key pillars in building a more efficient and responsible financial future. These developments highlight the crucial role of AI in driving progress and innovation in the financial sector, paving the way for a sustainable and prosperous economy.

Given this scientific framework (Alaimo et al., 2022), the purpose of this paper is to provide an in-depth and organized perspective on the convergence of AI and SF, as it plays a significant role in shaping future practices and promoting an ethical approach in the use of such technologies in the financial sector. This analysis is intended to contribute to the understanding of the potential and challenges of this convergence, highlighting the need for preventive regulation and a responsible approach in the development of AI to ensure a positive and sustainable impact on society and the global economy (Taddeo & Floridi, 2018).

Hence, this paper aims to provide a systematic review of existing literature and present an integrative framework to better understand how AI can be used to promote SF. This framework will help identify future research areas and strategies needed to address the ethical and operational challenges associated with implementing AI in the financial sector.

The remainder of the paper is structured as follows: Section 2 presents a conceptual framework that clarifies the main ideas of the study. Sections 3, 4 and 5 outline the applied methodology, the research questions and the review protocols. Section 6 provides a descriptive analysis, while Section 7 focuses on the thematic analysis of the literature. Section 8 introduces the integrative framework, followed by conclusions in Section 9, and a discussion of future research directions in Section 10.

2. CONCEPTUAL FRAMEWORK FOR ANALYZING AI AND SF

This section highlights the effects of developing technologies on the financial sector and their contributions to environmental and economic sustainability, and it offers a conceptual framework intended to clarify the connections between AI and SF.

One important technological advancement that enables computers to learn from data and make fully or partially autonomous judgements is AI. In particular, AI uses sophisticated methods and algorithms to evaluate enormous volumes of data, find intricate patterns, predict market trends, control risk and improve financial choices (Goodell et al., 2021). Financial applications benefit from AI in several ways.

The conceptual framework, which focuses on three main areas, examines the function of AI in SF, as seen in Fig. 1.

The first section, financial applications, outlines the different domains in which AI might be applied to advance sustainable financial practices. Among these uses, risk management is essential since AI enables organizations to more precisely and successfully identify and reduce financial threats. AI is also used in market forecasting, where it is used to improve investment strategies and predict trends, especially concerning sustainable financial models. AI also makes portfolio optimization easier by bringing portfolios into compliance with sustainability standards like ESG factors. Lastly, it helps to enhance the distribution of resources, increasing process efficiency and directing it towards sustainability.

The second area, emerging technologies, focuses on leveraging sophisticated tools to facilitate data management and analysis from a SF perspective. To gather and process vast amounts of data for improved forecasting and strategic decision-making in SF, the utilization of big data is essential. In addition to big data, AI-driven advanced analytics offer more precise forecasting models and facilitate instantaneous assessment of investment performance and market trends,

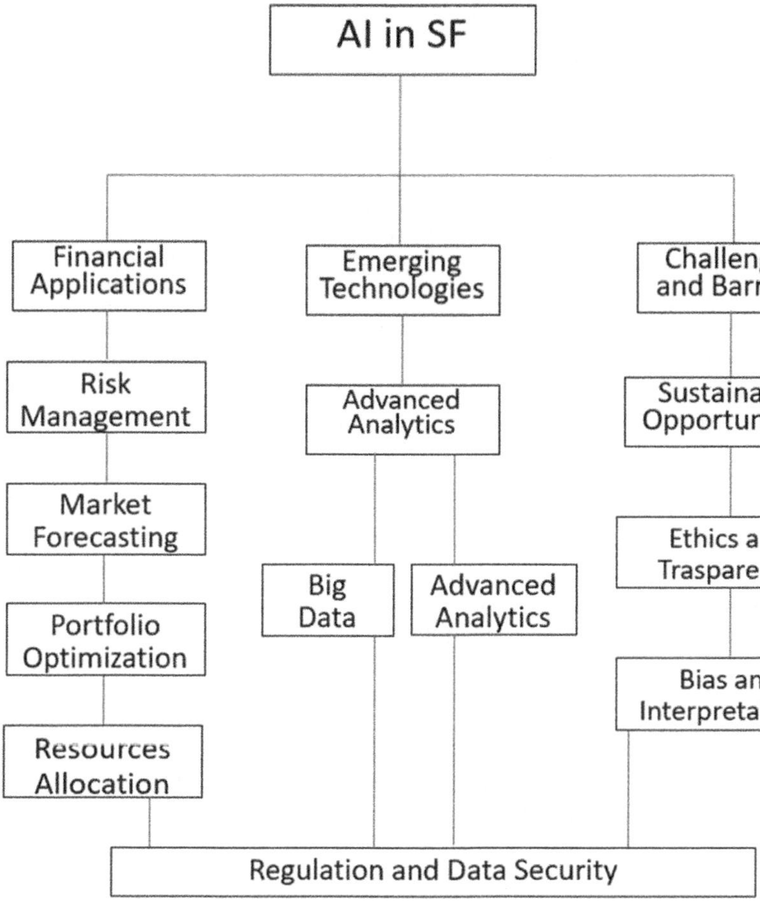

Fig. 1. Conceptual Framework. *Source:* The author.

hence augmenting the effectiveness of sustainable decision-making. The third section, challenges and barriers, lists the principal problems and prospects of the application of AI in SF. Among the opportunities, AI's ability to provide sustainable opportunities is particularly noteworthy as it may improve financial processes' efficiency, transparency and alignment with sustainability objectives.

To guarantee that decision-making processes are just and responsible, several significant obstacles must be overcome, such as the requirement to uphold a high standard of ethics and openness in the application of AI. A further concern is the interpretability of AI models, which is closely related to the management of potential biases in AI systems that may result in biased or poor outcomes. Data security and regulations form the cornerstone of this conceptual framework, ensuring that AI is used following current security and data protection laws. This is a fundamental element for the implementation of AI in SF, ensuring trust and compliance with global standards.

3. METHODOLOGY

To investigate all aspects of the existing literature thoroughly and pragmatically, a systematic literature review (SLR) methodology has been applied in this study (Vrontis et al., 2020). SLRs originated in the healthcare field (Mulrow & Cook, 1998), but over the last 15 years, SLRs represent a relevant building block for knowledge advancement in other fields (Durach et al., 2017), such as education, management, marketing, finance, psychology and information technology (Williams Jr. et al., 2020). Specifically, SLR allows scholars to identify, evaluate, summarize and criticize the studies carried out in a particular field (Booth et al., 2021; Dezi et al., 2018; Maheshwari & Chatnani, 2023; Rosado-Pinto & Loureiro, 2020). In detail, this type of literature review enhances the quality of review procedures and results by implementing transparent protocols and replicable processes (Crossan & Apaydin, 2010), and it helps one to understand what is missing and what are the possible future lines of research in a specific area (Vrontis & Christofi, 2019). Lack of novelty and poor understanding of theory appear when researchers do not have a systematic understanding of the principal body of knowledge (Schmenner et al., 2009). As suggested by various researchers, it is possible to find many advantages in applying an SLR instead of other review methodologies (e.g. traditional narrative reviews or overview) (e.g. Dada, 2018; Vrontis & Christofi, 2019; Wang & Chugh, 2014), such as (Baima et al., 2021; Battisti et al., 2019): (i) increase the quality of the review procedure and results; (ii) reduce the probability of making errors during the analysis; (iii) increase the legitimacy of the process based on the replicability of the steps applied during the review process; (iv) allow for data synthesis and literature mapping of a specific research area and (v) frequently enable synthesis of current literature with the opportunity of developing a theoretical framework with which scholars can develop future lines of research.

Based on these considerations, the use of the SLR method was guided by the desire to increase the knowledge of the topic of AI and sustainable finance, providing a comprehensive overview of the current state of research, identifying key trends and gaps and offering insights for future studies in this evolving field.

An effective SLR plan is essential to producing a robust and unbiased foundation of knowledge that helps scholars avoid factors compromising reliability and limiting contribution (Weber et al., 2024; Williams Jr. et al., 2020). For these reasons, as suggested by Tranfield et al. (2003), we conducted a systematic review consisting of five steps: (1) formulate the research question, (2) define the review protocols, (3) analyze the results through descriptive analysis, (4) perform a thematic analysis and synthesize the data and (5) construct an integrative framework.

4. RESEARCH QUESTION

First of all, a systematic review is navigated by one (Xiao & Nicholson, 2013) or more research questions (Nguyen et al., 2018), from which search strings for the scientific database searches are defined (De Menezes & Kelliher, 2011). After an initial theoretical study and discussion among the authors, and by taking the opinions of academics and practitioners (Adams et al., 2017), we developed the following research question: 'What is the key role played by AI in promoting sustainable financial practices, and how can AI-driven insights help integrate ESG factors into financial strategies?'.

5. DEFINITION OF THE REVIEW PROTOCOLS

Once the research question is defined, the second essential step is to define a protocol that represents a system of rules chosen to manage the process and minimize bias (Brereton et al., 2007), for developing a systematic, transparent and replicable process (e.g. Dada, 2018; Leonidou et al., 2018). Following Nolan and Garavan (2016), we applied explicit inclusion and exclusion criteria in our literature review. These criteria were derived from the purposes of our study and were guided by the research question formulated in the first step of the systematic review method.

To achieve effective and appropriate results, clear rules for article selection and exclusion were adopted during the literature review. First, following previous studies, we chose EBSCO as the main database to define the limits of the search, as it is one of the main databases of economic studies offering a vast source of information. Searches were conducted to find article titles and abstracts using a combination of 'keywords' mixed with Boolean operators 'AND' and 'OR' to identify the correct search strings, and to identify relevant literature exploring the intersection of AI and SF. The research was carried out by topic (including searching by title, summary and keywords) instead of full-text search to increase the relevance of results (Sousa et al., 2022).

Several keyword combinations involving both AI and SF were considered to thoroughly analyze the interaction between these two fields. The combinations included keywords such as 'Artificial Intelligence', OR 'AI', along with key concepts in SF, such as financial decision-making, financial innovation, financial market analysis, financial risk management, financial sector regulation and SF. This comprehensive approach was adopted to ensure that all relevant aspects of the relationship between AI and SF were explored. By utilizing a broad range of keywords, we aimed to capture the multifaceted nature of how AI technologies can influence and enhance sustainable financial practices. This method provided a holistic view, enabling us to identify potential benefits, challenges and future directions for integrating AI into SF, thus highlighting its significant implications for the industry.

Furthermore, as with other SLRs, we defined some exclusion criteria (e.g. Baima et al., 2021; Christofi et al., 2017; Pereira et al., 2023; Vrontis et al., 2021). Following other systematic reviews (Leonidou et al., 2018), we considered academic journals (scholarly peer-reviewed journals) as the type of publication because they are commonly considered to contain validated knowledge that is likely to have the greatest impact on the field (e.g. Keupp et al., 2012; Vrontis et al., 2020). In particular, we excluded editorials, commentary essays, book chapters, conference proceedings, working papers and other non-reference publications (López-Duarte et al., 2016), as such research is usually subject to a less rigorous peer-review process (Laufs & Schwens, 2014). To provide an accurate and representative context of relevant academic research, we excluded contributions that were not in English (Follmer & Jones, 2018), due to language limitations of the researchers, or without full text available (Vrontis & Christofi, 2019).

As can be seen from Fig. 2, initially 283 potentially relevant articles were identified. Following the exclusion criteria described above, the number of articles was reduced to 130 for further evaluation. Subsequently, 94 articles not strictly related to AI in economic sustainability or financial decision-making were excluded. Furthermore, as suggested by Endres and Weibler (2017), to increase the number of relevant articles, we cross-referenced the studies selected so far to recognize additional articles that had been overlooked by search engines and also searched Google Scholar and SSRN. These peer-reviewed academic studies were also screened according to the inclusion and exclusion criteria of this systematic review. This additional search contributed to the inclusion of a further four articles (three from Google Scholar and one from SSRN).

The data were collected in August 2024, resulting in a set of 40 articles published from 2009 to 2024. The overall strategy of the review methodology is illustrated in Fig. 2.

Next, a data extraction form was devised to extract and summarize significant data from the final sample and the content analysis was carried out manually (e.g. Vrontis & Christofi, 2019). In detail, we decided to use a data extraction form to report technical features of the selected articles, summarize key findings and describe methodological characteristics (Nguyen et al., 2018). Following Danese et al. (2018) and Nolan and Garavan (2016), we recorded data into Microsoft Excel files and performed a careful process with the main aim of guaranteeing the accuracy and reliability of the data collected. The findings are reported in the next section.

Finally, based on the information recovered through the data extraction form, the rest of this research focuses on examining and reporting the results of the systematic review, using descriptive and thematic analysis, as well as mapping the field and synthesizing the findings into an integrative framework.

6. DESCRIPTIVE ANALYSIS

The analysis of the existing literature has revealed various trends regarding research at the intersection of AI and SF. To facilitate future study, specific observations were made on the chosen articles to give an initial map of the existing literature and highlight potential gaps. In particular, the collected data

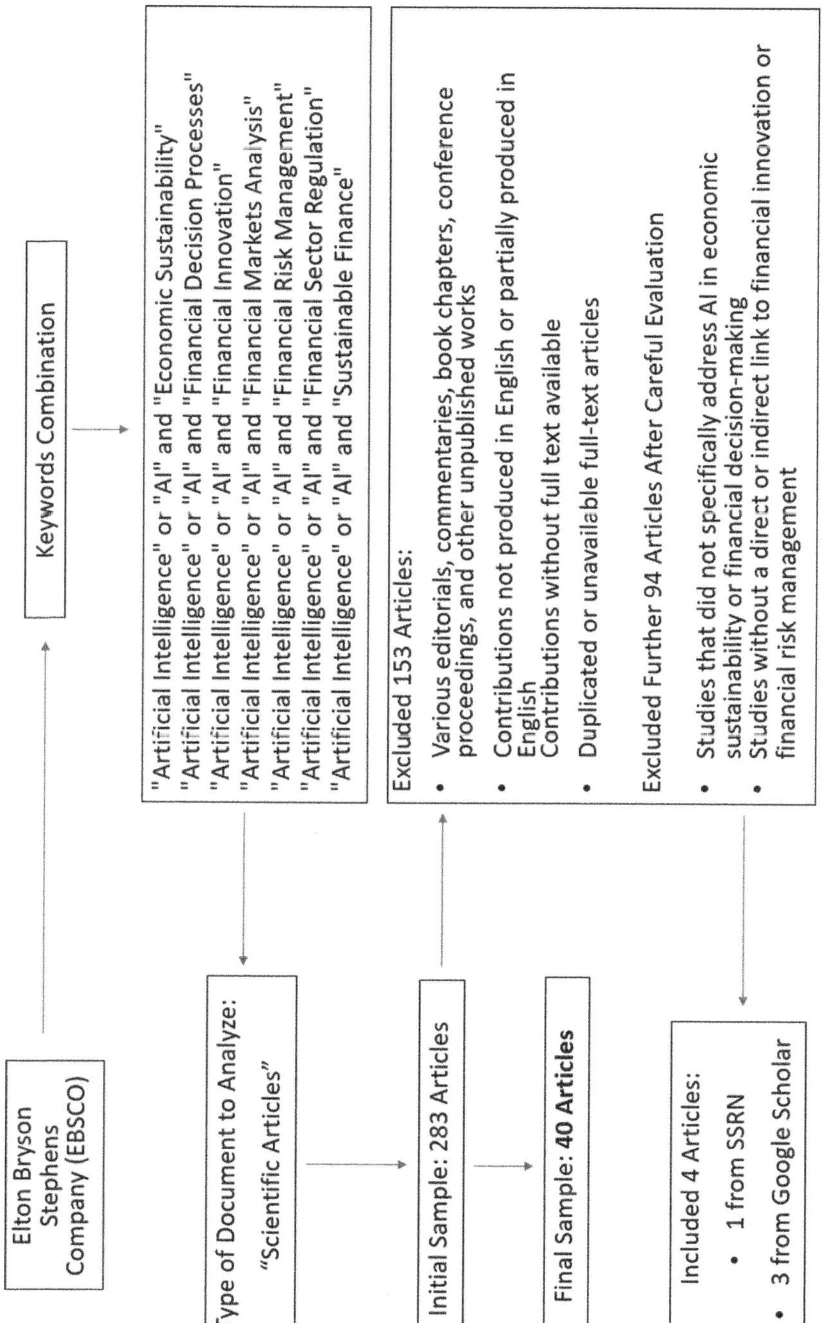

Fig. 2. Search Strategy. *Source:* Data Items collected from Literature Survey.

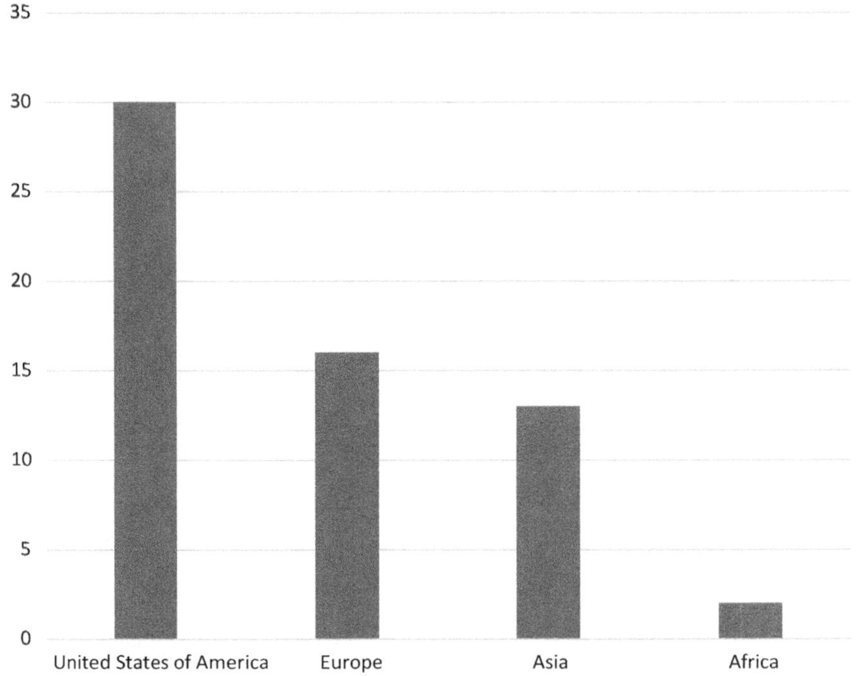

Fig. 3. Geographical Distribution of Authors. *Source:* Data Items collected from Literature Survey.

were examined considering the geographic distribution of the authors, the distribution of journals by area of interest and the evolution of publications over time.

Firstly, as shown in Fig. 3, the geographical distribution of authors reveals a strong concentration in the United States, with 30 authors. This is followed by Europe with 16 authors, Asia with 13 and finally Africa with 2 authors.

In addition, Fig. 4 provides a comprehensive overview of the distribution of journals according to different subject areas, allowing an easy understanding of the main areas of interest in AI and SF. This visualization helps identify which areas have greater editorial representation and indicates dominant trends in academic research. For example, there is a strong concentration of journals in the area of finance and risk management and the area of economics and sustainability, while fewer publications appear in journals related to AI and intelligent systems. This comment highlights the importance of further exploring the intersections between AI and SF and suggests possible opportunities for future research and academic development.

Furthermore, Table 1 shows the temporal history of articles about the influence of AI on SF from 2009 to 2024. A large increase in the number of articles published is noticed, culminating in 2020 with 10 publications, indicating a period

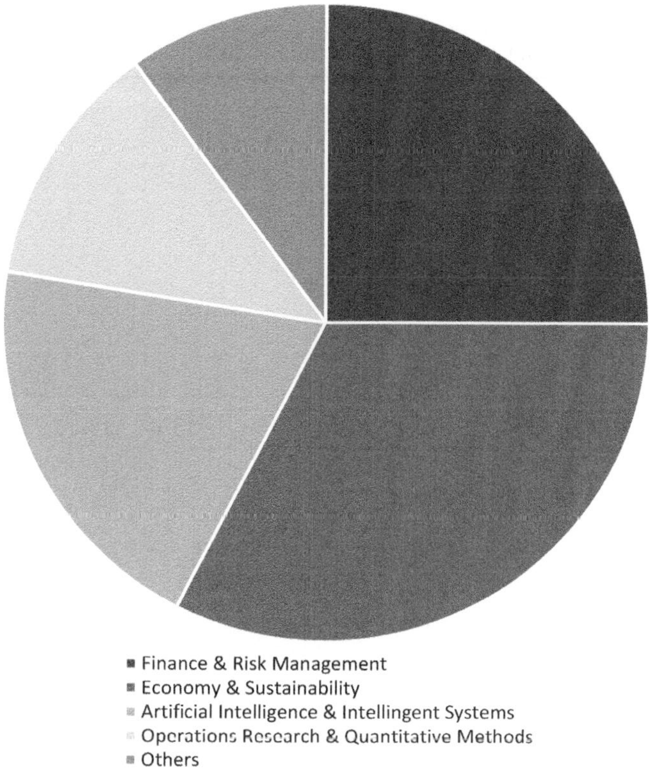

Fig. 4. Distribution of Journals by Area of Interest. *Source:* Data Items collected from Literature Survey.

of high interest within the scientific community. Although there is a little fall in the following years, beginning in 2021, interest rebounds in 2022 and continues strong in subsequent years, demonstrating that AI research in SF is still active

Table 1. Evolution of Research.

Journal	2009	2012	2018	2019	2020	2021	2022	2023	2024	Total
JRMFI			1	2	3			2		8
FM				1						1
JFQA						1				1
EE			1							1
JRR							1			1
ISAFM	1									1

(Continued)

Table 1. *(Continued)*

Journal	2009	2012	2018	2019	2020	2021	2022	2023	2024	Total
QF							1			1
SAJBM							1			1
JORS		1								1
JSBMSEE							1			1
JFRM								1		1
AAI						1				1
EIS					1					1
JIFS						1				1
PLOS ONE					1					1
SSRN							1			1
USVAEPA							1			1
JBR							1			1
JFP								1		1
WJARR									2	2
H									1	1
RQFA							1			1
AOR							1			1
TCE								1		1
EE								1		1
LFMR					1					1
SD					1					1
RP								2		2
IJME					1					1
IJIM					1					1
NC					1					1
Total	1	1	2	3	10	3	9	8	3	*40*

Source: Data Items collected from Literature Survey.

Note: *JRMFI*, Journal of Risk Management in Financial Institutions; *FM*, Financial Management; *JFQA*, Journal of Financial and Quantitative Analysis; *EE*, Engineering Economics; *JRR*, Journal of Risk Research; *ISAFM*, Intelligent Systems in Accounting, Finance & Management: International Journal; *QF*, Quantitative Finance; *SAJBM*, South African Journal of Business Management; *JORS*, Journal of the Operational Research Society; *JSBMSEE*, Journal of Sustainable Business and Management Solutions in Emerging Economies; *JFRM*, Journal of Financial Risk Management; *AAI*, Applied Artificial Intelligence; *EIS*, Enterprise Information Systems; *JIFS*, Journal of Intelligent & Fuzzy Systems; *PLOS ONE*, Public Library of Science ONE; *SSRN*, Social Science Research Network; *USVAEPA*, The USV Annals of Economics and Public Administration; *JBR*, Journal of Business Research; *JFP*, Journal of Financial Planning; *WJARR*, World Journal of Advanced Research and Reviews; *H*, Heliyon; *RQFA*, Review of Quantitative Finance and Accounting; *AOR*, Annals of Operations Research; *TCE*, The Chinese Economy; *EE*, Energy Economics; *LFMR*, Law and Financial Markets Review; *SD*, Sustainable Development; *RP*, Resources Policy; *IJME*, The International Journal of Management Education; *IJIM*, International Journal of Information Management; *NC*, Nature Communications.

and increasing. Another crucial consideration is the concentration of articles in certain scientific journals. In particular, *the Journal of Risk Management in Financial Institutions (JRMFI)* stands out for the number of articles published, as many as eight, distributed between 2020 and 2024. This implies that the publication has given special attention to topics of AI applied to finance, considerably adding to the scholarly literature on the subject. Other journals, such as *Financial Management (FM)*, *Journal of the Operational Research Society (JORS)*, *South African Journal of Business Management (SAJBM)*, and *Enterprise Information Systems (EIS)*, have a more intermittent presence, indicating a lower or less consistent interest in this particular area. However, the diversity of publications engaged suggests that interest in AI in SF extends across several academic areas, from pure finance to management and technology industries.

The highest number of publications (eight articles) appears to be in *the Journal of Risk Management in Financial Institutions (JRMFI)*, indicating its prominence in the field. Other journals show much lower numbers, typically publishing one or two articles each, which suggests that AI's role in SF is a specialized topic, receiving focused but not widespread attention across a broader range of journals.

The concentration in JRMFI suggests that certain journals may have a niche focus on SF and AI, while many others contribute sporadically. Additionally, journals such as *Resources Policy (RP)* and *The USV Annals of Economics and Public Administration (USVAEPA)* show slightly higher publication activity but remain far below JRMFI. This pattern highlights the need for further research dissemination across more journals to foster diverse academic engagement on this evolving subject.

7. THEMATIC ANALYSIS OF THE LITERATURE

In this section, we briefly analyze the results of a review of the 40 selected studies, taking a multidisciplinary approach focusing on the influence of AI on SF.

In particular, the results of the review of 40 selected studies focusing on the impact of AI on SF will be briefly presented. The analyses were divided into two main categories, 'Application of Artificial Intelligence (AI) in the Financial Sector' and 'Emerging Technologies and Sustainable Finance'. This decision allowed for a separate analysis of the impact of AI in the financial sector and its consequences on economic sustainability. In the following sections, the different issues addressed in the literature will be examined, highlighting specific applications of AI in the financial sector and discussing their implications for SF.

7.1 Application of AI in the Financial Sector

AI technologies have been increasingly integrated into financial regulation to address the challenges posed by the complexity and volume of transactions (Nembe et al., 2024). The use of AI and machine learning (ML) has increased rapidly in recent years, transforming the way companies operate (Herrmann, 2023). The financial services sector is no exception, where AI and ML are being implemented to improve operational efficiency, enhance customer experience and mitigate risk (Gupta et al., 2023). Studies on the application of AI in the financial sector are numerous and diverse (Akour et al., 2024; Johora et al., 2024; Lin, 2024; Nembe et al., 2024). AI refers to the use of algorithms and other computational techniques to automate or augment decision-making processes. In finance, AI is used to analyze large data sets, identify patterns and insights and make predictions based on historical data (Lim, 2024).

Research by Leung et al. (2009) and Sanford and Moosa (2012) has shown that the use of neural network-based and Bayesian models can be more effective in managing risk in financial trading than traditional models. For example, these studies have shown greater accuracy in market forecasting and better portfolio management. Gejke (2018) and Das (2019), in turn, found that AI can improve financial risk management through data analysis and detection of patterns that are not easily identifiable. In particular, these technologies have been able to identify investment opportunities and mitigate financial risks effectively. Mayenberger (2019) and Van Thiel and Van Raaij (2019), on the other hand, highlighted how AI/ML-based modelling methods can be successfully used to detect credit card fraud and perform credit risk assessments. These studies have shown how such methods can increase accuracy in fraud prevention and identification of high-risk loans. Antoncic et al. (2020) along with Brotcke (2020) highlighted how the use of big data and AI techniques can improve business performance evaluation and risk management. For example, an improvement in accuracy in assessing the credibility of companies and a greater understanding of financial risks was noted. Yang et al. (2020) and Grennan and Michaely (2021) conducted a study on the impact of AI technologies on firm performance and stock markets. Their results showed that the adoption of these technologies can lead to improved operational efficiency, more effective portfolio management and greater market transparency. Jankova et al. (2021), on the other hand, applied type-2 fuzzy logic to equity market modelling, showing that this methodology can increase the accuracy of investment forecasts. Vesna (2021), on the other hand, evaluated the effectiveness of AI technologies in risk management in the financial sector, highlighting how they can improve risk management through more accurate and interpretable models than traditional methods used to date. Weng and Huang (2021) developed an integrated approach to assessing credit claims using various AI-based modelling techniques, showing that this approach can provide better results than traditional methods at a lower cost. Yubo (2021), on the other hand, examined the effect of innovation in financial management on firm performance, showing how innovation in this area can improve firms' operational efficiency and competitiveness, with AI playing a particular role in supporting such innovations. In addition, Larkin et al. (2022) analyzed people's reactions to risk management advice provided by AI compared to advice from a human expert, finding that people generally prefer advice from human sources rather than AI-based systems. Li et al. (2022) explore the use of case-based reasoning in the context of financial risk assessment, showing that their proposed model provides reliable and understandable predictions of financial risk. Elouidani and Outouzzalt (2022) analyze the role of new AI techniques in supporting SF through a bibliometric study. This research provides an overview of the interdisciplinary approach to the topic and highlights how AI is replacing traditional methods with promising results.

Matsepe and Van der Lingen (2022) identify factors influencing the adoption of emerging technologies in the financial sector, suggesting that industry leaders need to understand them to make informed decisions about adopting new technologies. Mihov et al. (2022) show that combining human expertise with AI leads to significant improvements in financial decisions by using AI algorithms to optimize portfolios and send orders to buy or sell securities or financial assets to their respective markets or counterparties. Butler and Brooks (2023) highlight the potential of AI-based digital technologies in effectively addressing operational risk in the financial sector. Grimwade (2023) examine the impact of the digital revolution on banks' operational risk profile, noting the importance of strengthening existing controls and developing new ones to address future challenges.

Viswanathan and Makwani (2023) focus on optimizing investment management through the use of AI, demonstrating that this technology can improve the accuracy of financial forecasts and the quality of investment decisions.

Elias et al. (2024) examine how AI contributes to promoting sustainable financial decision-making. The study focuses on how these technologies optimize resource allocation, drive financial innovation and support sustainable practices in financial institutions. The methodology includes a thorough literature review and an analysis of AI-driven clustering and optimization techniques in financial decision-making. Additionally, the authors present case studies of institutions that have integrated AI and ML to enhance sustainability. The findings reveal that AI and ML improve decision-making efficiency, particularly in risk management and resource allocation, while also contributing to more sustainable financial practices through increased transparency and compliance. These technologies help reduce operational costs and foster financial innovation, leading to more sustainable business models (SBMs). The study provides a strategic perspective on how AI and ML can reshape the financial sector towards greater sustainability.

7.2 Emerging Technologies and SF

The articles analyzed in this section focus mainly on the integration of sustainability and AI in companies and financial sectors, with a focus on social impact and financial performance.

Antoncic (2020a, 2020b) and Goralski and Tan (2020) highlight the importance of including sustainability in business decisions, suggesting using big data and AI to gain competitive advantages. Vinuesa et al. (2020) and Liengpunsakul (2021) analyze how AI affects the achievement of the Sustainable Development Goals (SDGs), while Danila and Nastase (2021) and Kumar et al. (2022) explore the use of big data and AI in the context of sustainable development and SF. In addition, several types of research have focused on optimization and efficiency, as demonstrated by Srivastava et al. (2023), concerning energy consumption, and Wang et al. (2023), concerning natural resource utilization, both using ML algorithms. Truby et al. (2020) and Truby (2020) discuss the risks and opportunities related to regulating AI in the financial sector, while Fava (2023) explores the potential of using generative AI in tax planning. Harjoto et al. (2022) explore the link between corporate social responsibility and bondholder returns. Di Vaio et al. (2020) conducted a bibliometric analysis of the literature regarding the role of AI in creating SBMs, identifying a gap in research related to AI and SBMs about the United Nations SDGs. This same gap is also addressed by Nishant et al. (2020), who examine the potential of AI in addressing challenges related to environmental sustainability. Both studies suggest a comprehensive review and future perspectives on the use of AI in SBMs and in promoting environmental governance, integrating bibliometric approaches and analysis of challenges and opportunities in the field of sustainability.

Yang (2023) analyzes the impact of the size of the green financial market on renewable energy production in China, suggesting that an increase in the size of the green financial market may foster the development of renewable energy.

Oyewole et al. (2024) provide a comprehensive review of how AI is playing a crucial role in fostering sustainability within the finance sector. The study explores how AI-driven solutions can enhance sustainable practices by improving financial decision-making, resource management and risk assessment. The methodology includes an extensive review of current literature on AI applications in SF, combined with analyses of specific AI-driven tools and models that support green finance initiatives. The authors also present examples from real-world cases where AI has been successfully integrated into financial institutions to promote sustainability. The findings show that AI contributes to more efficient resource allocation, promotes transparency and enhances compliance with sustainability standards. Furthermore, AI supports the development of innovative financial products that align with environmental and social goals, ultimately helping to drive the transition towards a more sustainable financial system.

Finally, Pattnaik et al. (2024) analyze the use of AI in the banking, financial services and insurance (BFSI) sector, aiming to provide an overview of research trends, thematic frameworks and gaps in the literature. Through bibliometric analysis, they identify numerous benefits of AI and ML adoption, including enhancements in digital finance, cybersecurity, behavioural finance and risk management.

8. INTEGRATIVE FRAMEWORK OF FUTURE CHALLENGES IN THE APPLICATION OF AI IN SF

The integration of AI into SF presents significant potential but also complex challenges that require strategic attention and innovative solutions. In this context, it is crucial to anticipate future challenges and develop an integrative framework to address them effectively.

Among the barriers, ethical concerns surrounding transparency, bias and the interpretation of AI models are paramount. Ensuring that AI-driven decisions are accountable and ethically sound is essential for maintaining trust and avoiding unintended consequences in financial markets. Furthermore, as can be seen from Fig. 5, the framework emphasizes the importance of addressing data security and financial regulation to safeguard market stability and protect investor privacy.

On the side of challenges, the framework identifies a need for knowledge sharing and collaboration among diverse stakeholders, including financial intermediaries, regulators, academics and other sectors. Encouraging cross-sector collaboration will help foster innovation, while regulatory supervisors must work closely with the industry to manage AI biases and ensure model interpretability.

Advanced analytics and shifts in AI approaches will also play a pivotal role in shaping the future of SF. Changes in how these technologies are implemented can have a lasting impact on risk management, market forecasting, portfolio optimization and resource allocation.

In conclusion, this framework provides a structured roadmap for navigating the barriers and challenges associated with the application of AI in SF. By fostering collaboration, promoting transparency and ensuring regulatory compliance, it paves the way for the responsible and effective integration of AI in advancing more sustainable and inclusive financial practices.

9. CONCLUSIONS, IMPLICATIONS AND LIMITATIONS

Climate change is one of the most significant and urgent challenges of our time, impacting not only the environment but also the global economy. Climate risks, both physical and transitional, pose substantial threats to financial operations and economic stability. Physical risks encompass extreme weather events such as hurricanes, floods and droughts, while transitional risks are associated with the shift towards a low-carbon economy, involving changes in policies, technologies and market behaviours (European Central Bank, 2020).

This research explores the impact of AI on SF through an in-depth literature review of 40 selected articles. The study is divided into two main categories: 'Use of Artificial Intelligence (AI) in the Financial Sector' and 'Emerging Technologies and Sustainable Finance'. This categorization allows for a detailed exploration of the various facets of this complex topic.

Our study is the first systematic analysis to focus on the integration of AI and SF, integrating the most recent academic findings up to 2024. The integrative framework provides useful advice for future efforts to apply AI to SF, allowing for proactive management of emerging difficulties and the deployment of successful solutions to promote more sustainable and equitable financial practices. The findings have major significance for both the academic community and financial practitioners, establishing the groundwork for future research and development in this area. Our work differs from past literature assessments in that it takes a systematic review method rather than relying just on bibliometric analyses. While previous reviews are important for investigating publishing

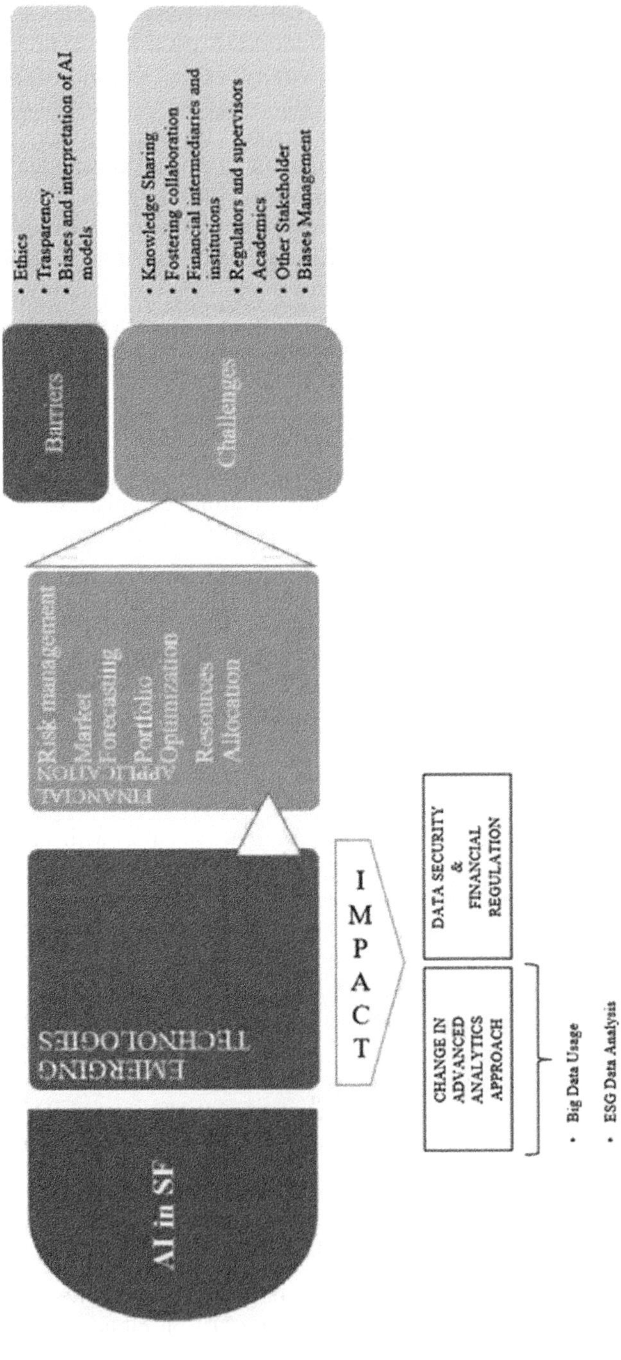

Fig. 5. The Integrative Framework. *Source:* The author.

patterns and identifying prominent authors or articles, they frequently lack in-depth analyses of thematic frameworks and particular gaps in the literature. In contrast, our research gives a comprehensive and up-to-date overview of AI applications in the banking industry by studying broad trends, thematic frameworks and current developments. This study divides existing research into two primary themes and includes a review of the most recent publications and technical breakthroughs. This thematic segmentation and in-depth study of developing research fields distinguishes our work, providing fresh insights and a solid foundation for future research.

AI has demonstrated its potential to significantly enhance the efficiency and accuracy of financial operations. Various studies indicate that techniques such as artificial neural networks and support vector machines are effective for credit scoring and credit risk assessment (Leung et al., 2009; Sanford & Moosa, 2012). These techniques not only improve forecast accuracy but also help reduce operational costs and associated risks. Additionally, the application of AI in operational risk management and financial crisis prevention is an area of growing interest (Gejke, 2018; Das, 2019), with AI integration offering the potential to identify and mitigate these risks more effectively.

However, this study has certain limitations (Graziano et al., 2024). First, the exclusive use of the EBSCO database may have constrained the search scope, possibly overlooking contributions available in other databases or less commonly used sources. Second, focusing solely on published articles might have introduced selection bias, excluding valuable research that is unpublished or found only in less accessible formats. To enhance the comprehensiveness of future research, it would be beneficial to include a broader range of databases and consider exploring the practical implications of AI in SF through specific case studies or empirical research. This would provide a better understanding of the impact of emerging technologies on financial and environmental outcomes.

10. FUTURE RESEARCH AGENDA

This analysis highlights several promising areas for future research on the intersection of AI and SF. Considering the rapid evolution of AI technologies and the growing need for sustainability in the financial sector, several opportunities emerge to deepen understanding and improve practical applications. This final section discusses some of the main directions that could guide future investigations, providing recommendations on how the field can evolve to address emerging challenges and exploit new opportunities.

One important topic for future research is the creation of more complex AI algorithms capable of better assessing ESG concerns. Current models frequently struggle with the complexity and variety of ESG data, reducing their accuracy. Future research should focus on developing algorithms that can handle unstructured data, combining various ESG measures and offering more trustworthy, actionable insights to investors. Addressing issues like data inconsistencies, poor transparency in ESG reporting and biases in datasets will be crucial.

Furthermore, using AI techniques such as ML and natural language processing (NLP) to evaluate qualitative ESG data has the potential to greatly improve decision-making in SF.

Another key issue for future research is the development of more accurate and comprehensive models for climate risk prediction and management. Existing models are frequently constrained by their reliance on previous data and inability to accurately forecast future situations in a quickly changing environment. Future research should focus on combining AI with predictive analytics and scenario modelling to deliver more forward-thinking insights. It will be critical to address issues such as data shortages, particularly in emerging nations, and the substantial uncertainty around climate change implications. Creating models that not only evaluate historical patterns but also simulate several future situations is crucial in both risk assessment and strategy planning for sustainable investments.

In addition to these areas, the development of AI-powered decision-support systems to assist investors in making informed judgements regarding sustainable investments is a promising topic for future study. These tools should not only provide financial analysis but also assess possible social and environmental implications, integrating investment decisions with larger sustainability objectives. Future research should look into how to integrate AI models into investor decision-making processes, ensuring that ethical issues and long-term sustainability are taken into account in investing plans. Furthermore, investigating how AI may be used to analyze the real-world impact of sustainable investments on social good will be critical to promoting openness and accountability.

Lastly, the significance of AI for corporate governance and regulatory compliance needs to be further investigated in future studies. Making sure AI systems abide by current rules, such as those about corporate transparency and anti-discrimination laws, is crucial as these systems grow more and more important in financial decision-making. Future research should examine how AI might improve corporate governance procedures, especially in guaranteeing moral conduct and enhancing ESG reporting transparency. Researchers should also focus on identifying potential hazards associated with the misuse of AI in financial decision-making, such as the amplification of biases and exclusionary practices.

Hence, although AI has enormous potential to revolutionize SF, it is essential to take a responsible and regulated approach to avoid potential negative consequences and ensure that the benefits are distributed fairly (Taddeo & Floridi, 2018). Only through careful and thoughtful integration of smart technologies into financial practices can we hope to promote a sustainable and ethically just future for all.

However, in any application field of AI algorithms, the continuous interaction between human resources of proven expertise and the evolution of the algorithms, regardless of the methods used, can lead to measurable improvements in results. An over-reliance on algorithmic decision-making increases the possibility of distortion, exclusion or unintentional discriminatory impacts, particularly in unsupervised settings. This emphasizes how crucial human control is to the creation and application of AI systems, especially in industries like finance where social and ethical ramifications are substantial. In actuality, AI through the use of algorithms should be viewed as a helper and adjunct to human decision-making.

The AML laws have consistently upheld this idea, emphasizing the need to strike a balance between human oversight and AI efficiency to reduce risks and guarantee adherence to ethical standards.

REFERENCES

ABI Lab Report. (2024). *Italian banks' investment and research priorities*. https://www.abilab.it/-/news/priorit%C3%A0-investimento-ricerca-2024

Adams, R. J., Smart, P., & Huff, A. S. (2017). Shades of grey: Guidelines for working with the grey literature in systematic reviews for management and organizational studies. *International Journal of Management Reviews*, *19*(4), 432–454.

Akour, I., Alzyoud, M., Alquqa, E., Tariq, E., Alzboun, N., Al-Hawary, S., & Alshurideh, M. (2024). Artificial Intelligence and financial decisions: Empirical evidence from developing economies. *International Journal of Data and Network Science*, *8*(1), 101–108.

Akter, S., Wamba, S. F., Mariani, M., & Hani, U. (2021). How to build an AI climate-driven service analytics capability for innovation and performance in industrial markets? *Industrial Marketing Management*, *97*, 258–273.

Alaimo, L. S., Fiore, M., & Galati, A. (2022). Measuring consumers' level of satisfaction for online food shopping during COVID-19 in Italy using POSETs. *Socio-Economic Planning Sciences*, *82*, 101064.

Alkurdi, A., Al Amosh, H., & Khatib, S. F. (2023). The mediating role of carbon emissions in the relationship between the board attributes and ESG performance: European evidence. *EuroMed Journal of Business*. (ahead-of-print). https://doi.org/10.1108/emjb-08-2022-0144

Antoncic, M. (2020a). A paradigm shift in the board room: Incorporating sustainability into corporate governance and strategic decision-making using big data and artificial intelligence. *Journal of Risk Management in Financial Institutions*, *13*(4), 290–294.

Antoncic, M. (2020b). Uncovering hidden signals for sustainable investing using Big Data: Artificial intelligence, machine learning and natural language processing. *Journal of Risk Management in Financial Institutions*, *13*(2), 106–113.

Antoncic, M., Bekaert, G., Rothenberg, R. V., & Noguer, M. (2020). Sustainable investment – Exploring the linkage between alpha, ESG, and SDG's. *ESG and SDG's*, *8*, 34–46.

Baima, G., Forliano, C., Santoro, G., & Vrontis, D. (2021). Intellectual capital and business model: A systematic literature review to explore their linkages. *Journal of Intellectual Capital*, *22*(3), 653–679.

Battisti, E., Miglietta, N., Salvi, A., & Creta, F. (2019). Strategic approaches to value investing: A systematic literature review of international studies. *Review of International Business and Strategy*, *29*(3), 253–266.

Blanco-Ruiz, M., Adá-Lameiras, A., & Atauri-Mezquida, D. (2024). New trends in digital marketing: Analysis of the social conversation on X.com about Metaverse and artificial intelligence. *FIIB Business Review*. (ahead of print). https://doi.org/10.1177/23197145241281033

Booth, A., James, M. S., Clowes, M., & Sutton, A. (2021). *Systematic approaches to a successful literature review*. SAGE.

Brereton, P., Kitchenham, B. A., Budgen, D., Turner, M., & Khalil, M. (2007). Lessons from applying the systematic literature review process within the software engineering domain. *Journal of Systems and Software*, *80*(4), 571–583.

Brotcke, L. (2020). Modifying model risk management practice in the era of AI/ML. *Journal of Risk Management in Financial Institutions*, *13*(3), 255–265.

Bughin, J., Seong, J., Manyika, J., Chui, M., & Joshi, R. (2018). *Notes from the AI frontier: Modeling the impact of AI on the world economy*. McKinsey Global Institute.

Butler, T., & Brooks, R. (2023). On the wicked problem of quantifying and managing non-financial risks and the role of digital technology in providing solutions. *Journal of Risk Management in Financial Institutions*, *17*(1), 53–70.

Chouaibi, S., Chouaibi, J., & Rossi, M. (2022). ESG and corporate financial performance: The mediating role of green innovation: UK common law versus Germany civil law. *EuroMed Journal of Business*, *17*(1), 46–71.

Christofi, M., Leonidou, E., & Vrontis, D. (2017). Marketing research on mergers and acquisitions: A systematic review and future directions. *International Marketing Review*, *34*(5), 629–651.

CIPA. (2021). *The digital transformation of banking*. https://www.cipa.it/rilevazioni/tecnologiche/2021/Rilevazione_tecnologica_2021.pdf

Crossan, M. M., & Apaydin, M. (2010). A multi-dimensional framework of organizational innovation: A systematic review of the literature. *Journal of Management Studies*, *47*(6), 1154–1191.

Dada, O. (2018). A model of entrepreneurial autonomy in franchised outlets: A systematic review of the empirical evidence. *International Journal of Management Reviews*, *20*(2), 206–226.

Danese, P., Manfè, V., & Romano, P. (2018). A systematic literature review on recent lean research: State-of-the-art and future directions. *International Journal of Management Reviews*, *20*(2), 579–605.

Danila, A. C., & Nastase, C. E. (2021). A bibliometric analysis of the global research on big data for sustainable development. *The USV Annals of Economics and Public Administration*, *21*, 42–49.

Das, S. R. (2019). The future of fintech. *Financial Management*, *48*(4), 981–1007.

De Menezes, L. M., & Kelliher, C. (2011). Flexible working and performance: A systematic review of the evidence for a business case. *International Journal of Management Reviews*, *13*(4), 452–474.

Dezi, L., Battisti, E., Ferraris, A., & Papa, A. (2018). The link between mergers and acquisitions and innovation: A systematic literature review. *Management Research Review*, *41*(6), 716–752.

Di Vaio, A., Palladino, R., Hassan, R., & Escobar, O. (2020). Artificial intelligence and business models in the sustainable development goals perspective: A systematic literature review. *Journal of Business Research*, *121*, 283–314.

Durach, C. F., Kembro, J., & Wieland, A. (2017). A new paradigm for systematic literature reviews in supply chain management. *Journal of Supply Chain Management*, *53*(4), 1–19.

Eager, J., Whittle, M., Smit, J., Caccia Guerra, G., & Lale-Demoz, E. (2020). *Opportunities of artificial intelligence*. European Parliament.

Elias, O., Esebre, S. D., Abijo, I., Timothy, A. M., Babayemi, T. D., Makinde, E. O., & Fatoki, I. E. (2024). Harnessing artificial intelligence to optimize financial technologies for achieving sustainable development goals. *World Journal of Advanced Research and Reviews*, *23*(2), 616–625.

Elouidani, R., & Outouzzalt, A. (2022). Artificial intelligence for a sustainable finance: A bibliometric analysis. In J. Kacprzyk, M. Ezziyyani, & V. E. Balas (Eds.), *International conference on advanced intelligent systems for sustainable development* (pp. 536–551). Springer Nature.

Endres, S., & Weibler, J. (2017). Towards a three-component model of relational social constructionist leadership: A systematic review and critical interpretive synthesis: Relational social constructionist leadership. *International Journal of Management Reviews*, *19*(2), 214–236.

European Central Bank. (2020). *Guide on climate-related and environmental risks*. https://www.bankingsupervision.europa.eu/legalframework/publiccons/pdf/climate-related_risks/ssm.202005_draft_guide_on_climate-related_and_environmental_risks.en.pdf

Eurostat. (2021). *Artificial intelligence in EU enterprises*. https://ec.europa.eu/eurostat/web/products-eurostat-news/-/ddn-20210413-1

Fava, D. (2023). The future of tax planning: Leveraging generative AI in high-net-worth contexts. *Journal of Financial Planning*, *36*(10), 54–57.

Follmer, K. B., & Jones, K. S. (2018). Mental illness in the workplace: An interdisciplinary review and organizational research agenda. *Journal of Management*, *44*(1), 325–351.

Fortune Business Insights. (2023). *Artificial intelligence market*. https://www.fortunebusinessinsights.com/industry-reports/artificIAl-intelligence-market-100114

Gejke, C. (2018). A new season in the risk landscape: Connecting the advancement in technology with changes in customer behavior to enhance the way risk is measured and managed. *Journal of Risk Management in Financial Institutions*, *11*(2), 148–155.

Goodell, J. W., Kumar, S., Lim, W. M., & Pattnaik, D. (2021). Artificial Intelligence and machine learning in finance: Identifying foundations, themes, and research clusters from bibliometric analysis. *Journal of Behavioral and Experimental Finance*, *32*, 100577. https://doi.org/10.1016/j.jbef.2021.100577

Goralski, M. A., & Tan, T. K. (2020). Artificial intelligence and sustainable development. *International Journal of Management in Education, 18*(1), 100330.

Graziano, E. A., Musella, F., & Petroccione, G. (2024). Cashless payment: Behavior changes and gender dynamics during the COVID-19 pandemic. *EuroMed Journal of Business, 0*(0).

Grennan, J., & Michaely, R. (2021). Fintechs and the market for financial analysis. *Journal of Financial and Quantitative Analysis, 56*(6), 1877–1907.

Grimwade, M. (2023). The potential impacts of the digital revolution on the operational risk profiles of banks. *Journal of Risk Management in Financial Institutions, 17*(1), 71–88.

Gupta, P., Anand, A., Singh, J., Rana, S., & Kumar, A. (2023). Study on artificial intelligence (AI) initiatives in e-service delivery systems: A service process perception model. *International Journal of Services Operations and Informatics, 12*(4), 344–366.

Haenlein, M., & Kaplan, A. (2019). A brief history of artificial intelligence: On the past, present, and future of artificial intelligence. *California Management Review, 61*(4), 5–14.

Harjoto, M. A., Hoepner, A. G., & Nilsson, M. A. (2022). Bondholders' returns and stakeholders' interests. *Review of Quantitative Finance and Accounting, 59*(4), 1271–1301.

Herrmann, H. (2023). What's next for responsible artificial intelligence: A way forward through responsible innovation. *Heliyon, 9*(3).

Hilpisch, Y. (2020). *Artificial intelligence in finance*. O'Reilly Media.

Jankova, Z., Jana, D. K., & Dostal, P. (2021). Investment decision support based on interval type-2 fuzzy expert system. *Engineering Economics, 32*(2), 118–129.

Johora, F. T., Hasan, R., Farabi, S. F., Akter, J., & Al Mahmud, M. A. (2024). AI-powered fraud detection in banking: Safeguarding financial transactions. *The American Journal of Management and Economics Innovations, 6*(06), 8–22.

Keupp, M. M., Palmié, M., & Gassmann, O. (2012). The strategic management of innovation: A systematic review and paths for future research. *International Journal of Management Reviews, 14*(4), 367–390.

Kumar, S., Sharma, D., Rao, S., Lim, W. M., & Mangla, S. K. (2022). Past, present, and future of sustainable finance: Insights from big data analytics through machine learning of scholarly research. *Annals of Operations Research*, 1–44.

Larkin, C., Drummond Otten, C., & Árvai, J. (2022). Paging Dr. JARVIS! Will people accept advice from artificial intelligence for consequential risk management decisions? *Journal of Risk Research, 25*(4), 407–422.

Laufs, K., & Schwens, C. (2014). Foreign market entry mode choice of small and medium-sized enterprises: A systematic review and future research agenda. *International Business Review, 23*(6), 1109–1126.

Leonidou, E., Christofi, M., Vrontis, D., & Thrassou, A. (2018). An integrative framework of stakeholder engagement for innovation management and entrepreneurship development. *Journal of Business Research*. Advance online publication. https://doi.org/10.1016/j.jbusres.2018.11.054

Leung, M. T., Chen, A. S., & Mancha, R. (2009). Making trading decisions for financial-engineered derivatives: A novel ensemble of neural networks using information content. *Intelligent Systems in Accounting, Finance and Management, 16*(4), 257–277.

Li, W., Paraschiv, F., & Sermpinis, G. (2022). A data-driven explainable case-based reasoning approach for financial risk detection. *Quantitative Finance, 22*(12), 2257–2274.

Liengpunsakul, S. (2021). Artificial intelligence and sustainable development in China. *The Chinese Economy, 54*(4), 235–248.

Lim, T. (2024). Environmental, social, and governance (ESG) and artificial intelligence in finance: State-of-the-art and research takeaways. *Artificial Intelligence Review, 57*, 76.

Lin, A. K. (2024). The AI revolution in financial services: Emerging methods for fraud detection and prevention. *Jurnal Galaksi, 1*(1), 43–51.

López-Duarte, C., Vidal-Suárez, M. M., & González-Díaz, B. (2016). International business and nation culture: A literature review and research agenda. *International Journal of Management Reviews, 18*(4), 397–416.

Maheshwari, S., & Chatnani, N. N. (2023). Applications of artificial intelligence and machine learning-based supervisory technology in financial markets surveillance: A review of literature. *FIIB Business Review*. (ahead of print). https://doi.org/10.1177/23197145231189990

Mariani, M. M., Machado, I., & Nambisan, S. (2023). Types of innovation and artificial intelligence: A systematic quantitative literature review and research agenda. *Journal of Business Research, 155*, 113364.

Matsepe, N. T., & Van der Lingen, E. (2022). Determinants of emerging technologies adoption in the South African financial sector. *South African Journal of Business Management, 53*(1), 2493.

Mayenberger, D. (2019). How to overcome modeling and model risk management challenges with artificial intelligence and machine learning. *Journal of Risk Management in Financial Institutions, 12*(3), 241–255.

Mihov, A.-H., Firoozye, N., & Treleaven, P. (2022). Towards augmented financial intelligence. *SSRN*. https://doi.org/10.2139/ssrn.4148057

Mulrow, C. D. & Cook, D. (Eds.). (1998). *Systematic reviews: Synthesis of best evidence for health care decisions*. American College of Physicians.

Nembe, J. K., Atadoga, J. O., Mhlongo, N. Z., Falaiye, T., Olubusola, O., Daraojimba, A. I., & Oguejiofor, B. B. (2024). The role of artificial intelligence in enhancing tax compliance and financial regulation. *Finance & Accounting Research Journal, 6*(2), 241–251.

Ng, C. W. (2020). The future of AI in finance. In I. Bartoletti, A. Leslie, & S. M. Millie (Eds.), *The AI book: The artificial intelligence handbook for investors, entrepreneurs and FinTech visionaries* (pp. 6–8). John Wiley & Sons.

Nguyen, D. H., de Leeuw, S., & Dullaert, W. E. H. (2018). Consumer behaviour and order fulfilment in online retailing: A systematic review. *International Journal of Management Reviews, 20*(2), 255–276.

Nishant, R., Kennedy, M., & Corbett, J. (2020). Artificial intelligence for sustainability: Challenges, opportunities, and a research agenda. *International Journal of Information Management, 53*, 102104.

Nolan, C. T., & Garavan, T. N. (2016). Human resource development in SMEs: A systematic review of the literature. *International Journal of Management Reviews, 18*(1), 85–107.

OECD. (2024). *Finance for sustainable development*. OECD. https://www.oecd.org/en/topics/finance-for-sustainable-development.html

Oyewole, A. T., Adeoye, O. B., Addy, W. A., Okoye, C. C., Ofodile, O. C., & Ugochukwu, C. E. (2024). Promoting sustainability in finance with AI: A review of current practices and future potential. *World Journal of Advanced Research and Reviews, 21*(3), 590–607.

Pattnaik, D., Ray, S., & Raman, R. (2024). Applications of artificial intelligence and machine learning in the financial services industry: A bibliometric review. *Heliyon, 10*(1), e23492. https://doi.org/10.1016/j.heliyon.2023.e23492

Pereira, V., Hadjielias, E., Christofi, M., & Vrontis, D. (2023). A systematic literature review on the impact of artificial intelligence on workplace outcomes: A multi-process perspective. *Human Resource Management Review, 33*(1), 100857.

Rosado-Pinto, F., & Loureiro, S. M. C. (2020). The growing complexity of customer engagement: A systematic review. *EuroMed Journal of Business, 15*(2), 167–203.

Sanford, A. D., & Moosa, I. A. (2012). A Bayesian network structure for operational risk modeling in structured finance operations. *Journal of the Operational Research Society, 63*, 431–444.

Schmenner, R. W., Van Wassenhove, L., Ketokivi, M., Heyl, J., & Lusch, R. F. (2009). Too much theory, not enough understanding. *Journal of Operations Management, 27*(5), 339–343.

Sousa, A., Calçada, E., Rodrigues, P., & Pinto Borges, A. (2022). Cryptocurrency adoption: A systematic literature review and bibliometric analysis. *EuroMed Journal of Business, 17*(3), 374–390.

Srivastava, P. R., Mangla, S. K., Eachempati, P., & Tiwari, A. K. (2023). An explainable artificial intelligence approach to understanding drivers of economic energy consumption and sustainability. *Energy Economics, 125*, 106868.

Taddeo, M., & Floridi, L. (2018). How AI can be a force for good. *Science, 361*(6404), 751–752.

Tranfield, D., Denyer, D., & Smart, P. (2003). Towards a methodology for developing evidence-informed management knowledge by means of systematic review. *British Journal of Management, 14*(3), 207–222.

Truby, J. (2020). Governing artificial intelligence to benefit the UN sustainable development goals. *Sustainable Development, 28*(4), 946–959.

Truby, J., Brown, R., & Dahdal, A. (2020). Banking on AI: Mandating a proactive approach to AI regulation in the financial sector. *Law and Financial Markets Review*, *14*(2), 110–120.

Van Thiel, D., & Van Raaij, W. F. (2019). Artificial intelligence credit risk prediction: An empirical study of analytical artificial intelligence tools for credit risk prediction in a digital era. *Journal of Risk Management in Financial Institutions*, *12*(3), 268–286.

Vesna, B. A. (2021). Challenges of financial risk management: AI applications. *Management: Journal of Sustainable Business and Management Solutions in Emerging Economies*, *26*(3), 27–34.

Vinuesa, R., Azizpour, H., Leite, I., Balaam, M., Dignum, V., Domisch, S., & Nerini, F. (2020). The role of artificial intelligence in achieving the sustainable development goals. *Nature Communications*, *11*(1), 1–10.

Viswanathan, S., & Makwani, D. (2023). How machine learning can help in investment management. *IUP Journal of Financial Risk Management*, *20*(2), 22–32.

Vrontis, D., & Christofi, M. (2019). R&D internationalization and innovation: A systematic review, integrative framework and future research directions. *Journal of Business Research*. Advanced online publication. https://doi.org/10.1016/j.jbusres.2019.03.031

Vrontis, D., Christofi, M., & Katsikeas, C. S. (2020). An assessment of the literature on cause-related marketing: Implications for international competitiveness and marketing research. *International Marketing Review*, *37*(5), 977–1012.

Vrontis, D., Makrides, A., Christofi, M., & Thrassou, A. (2021). Social media influencer marketing: A systematic review, integrative framework and future research agenda. *International Journal of Consumer Studies*, *45*(4), 617–644.

Wamba-Taguimdje, S. L., Wamba, S. F., Kamdjoug, J. R. K., & Wanko, C. E. T. (2020). Influence of artificial intelligence (AI) on firm performance: The business value of AI-based transformation projects. *Business Process Management Journal*, *26*(7), 1893–1924.

Wang, C. L., & Chugh, H. (2014). Entrepreneurial learning: Past research and future challenges. *International Journal of Management Reviews*, *16*(1), 24–61.

Wang, J., Wang, K., Dong, K., & Zhang, S. (2023). Assessing the role of financial development in natural resource utilization efficiency: Does artificial intelligence technology matter? *Resources Policy*, *85*, 103877.

Weber, P., Carl, K. V., & Hinz, O. (2024). Applications of explainable artificial intelligence in finance: A systematic review of finance, information systems, and computer science literature. *Management Review Quarterly*, *74*(2), 867–907.

Weng, C. H., & Huang, C. K. (2021). A hybrid machine learning model for credit approval. *Applied Artificial Intelligence*, *35*(15), 1439–1465.

Williams, R. I., Jr., Clark, L. A., Clark, W. R., & Raffo, D. M. (2020). Re-examining systematic literature review in management research: Additional benefits and execution protocols. *European Management Journal*. https://doi.org/10.1016/j.emj.2020.09.007

Xiao, S. H., & Nicholson, M. (2013). A multidisciplinary cognitive behavioural framework of impulse buying: A systematic review of the literature. *International Journal of Management Reviews*, *15*(3), 333–356.

Yang, X. (2023). Role of green finance and investment in sustainable resource development in China. *Resources Policy*, *86*, 104219.

Yang, J., Ying, L., & Gao, M. (2020). The influence of intelligent manufacturing on financial performance and innovation performance: The case of China. *Enterprise Information Systems*, *14*(6), 812–832.

Yubo, C. (2021). Innovation of enterprise financial management based on machine learning and artificial intelligence technology. *Journal of Intelligent and Fuzzy Systems*, *40*(4), 6767–6778.

Literature Review and Meta-analysis on Trends of Multi-agent Technology in High-Tech Product Manufacturing

Vikram Singh and Somesh Kumar Sharma

National Institute of Technology, Hamirpur, India

ABSTRACT

Multi-agent technology (MAT) has emerged as a transformative framework for high-tech manufacturing (HTM), significantly advancing automation and organizational progress. Despite its growing application, research on MAT for HTM remains unevenly distributed, with certain critical areas lacking sufficient investigation. This gap in research presents challenges for fully leveraging MAT to optimize manufacturing processes. This review addresses this gap by analyzing past, present and future trends in MAT and HTM research. It proposes two classification schemes and conducting a meta-analysis to systematically examine the data. The analysis highlights the areas such as Shopfloor Production, Inventory Control, Inspection and Quality Control, as well as Techniques of Fundamental Research (static and mathematics) and Applied Research, have received comparatively fewer publications. The review identifies 43 active MAT and 30 HTM journals, revealing fluctuating research trends over the past 14 years, with a notable increase in the last three years. The problem statement behind this research is to address the gaps in MAT and HTM literature, particularly in underrepresented areas, to drive future innovation. Based on these findings, the study suggests focusing future research on the identified gaps to enhance understanding and application of MAT in HTM. The study aims to provide valuable references and insights for readers, researchers and scholars, thereby advancing the field and fostering innovation in HTM.

Keywords: Multi-agent technology; high-tech product; manufacturing sectors; classification schemes; simple meta-analysis

Reviewing the Latest Trends in Management Literature, Volume 4B
Review of Management Literature, Volume 4B, 53–89

Published under exclusive licence by Emerald Publishing Limited
ISSN: 2754-5865/doi:10.1108/S2754-58652025000004B003

1. INTRODUCTION

The Industrial Revolution, beginning in the late 19th century (Industrial Revolution 3.0), introduced automation to support mass production in manufacturing (Sharma et al., 2023). Technological advancements have since transformed materials procurement, production, marketing and transportation. A significant challenge in manufacturing is producing more with fewer resources, prompting investments in Research & Development (R&D) (Nie et al., 2023). High-tech sectors like pharmaceuticals, electronics, aerospace and defence components demand over 7% gross domestic product (GDP) investment in R&D to establish autonomous production systems. These systems are vital for maintaining quality, increasing productivity and meeting customer expectations. Today, automation in high-tech industries leverages cutting-edge technologies such as Artificial Intelligence (AI), Internet of Things (IoT), Cyber-Physical Systems (CPS), 5G, 3D printing, robots, drones, gene editing, big data, blockchain, nanotechnology and solar photovoltaics (PVs). These technologies are driven by agents that create a digital environment, integrating hardware with software to control manufacturing operations (UNCTAD, 2023a).

In the era of automation, multi-agent technology (MAT) is crucial across various domains. MAT enhances manufacturing by improving process quality, product quality, maintenance (Singh & Sharma, 2023b), planning, control, scheduling and supply chain management (Kim et al., 2023). In aerospace, it prevents aeroplane crashes and conducts spacecraft inspections (Choi et al., 2023). Numerous reviews have explored MAT in manufacturing: Liu et al. (2023) on distributed formation control, Hanga and Kovalchuk (2019) on machine learning and MAT in oil and gas, Bahrpeyma and Reichelt (2022) on multi-agent reinforcement learning in smart factories and Joo et al. (2024) and B. Kim et al. (2023) on MAT in manufacturing and supply chain management. However, HTM remains under-explored. While D. Chen (2015) reviewed high-tech industries in Taiwan and Zahedi et al. (2024) reviewed capacity management in high-tech industries, no comprehensive review exists on MAT trends in HTM. This review addresses this gap by examining the past, present and future trends of MAT in HTM through a state-of-the-art meta-analysis.

This article comprehensively reviews current applications of MAT in HTM. Keywords like 'Agent Technology', 'Multi-Agent Technology', 'Multi-Agent System', 'High-Tech Industries', 'High-Tech Manufacturing', and 'High-Tech Products (HTPs)' were used to find relevant articles. This research examined MAT research in manufacturing for quality improvement, scheduling, planning, computing and effective product development. MAT applications in manufacturing systems include minimizing maintenance efforts, fault identification, diagnosis, prognosis, quality checks, supply chain management and inventory management. This review identifies underexplored application scenarios and aims to enhance researchers' understanding of MAT in HTM. While various reviews exist, none comprehensively survey MAT in HTM. This review provides an overview of state-of-the-art technology in manufacturing, identifying key factors in

HTM and the role of MAT. Objectives include (1) To identify and analyze the most critical domains within HTM where MAT can be applied to achieve significant improvements, (2) To investigate and compile a list of influential publishers and journals that focus on research in MAT and HTM and (3) To specific areas for future research based on current trends of MAT research in HTM.

The rest of the article is arranged as follows: Section 2 describes the historical evolution of state-of-the-art technology and the manufacturing sector revolution. Section 3 reviews the background of MAT in HTM. Section 4 discussed the research methodology. Section 5 presents two classification schemes for agent-based research in HTM sectors. Section 6 performed a simple meta-analysis based on classification schemes, journals and publishers' published MAT and HTM research and analyzed published materials year-wise. Finally, Section 7 completed the articles with a conclusion, limitation and scope of further study.

2. LITERATURE REVIEW

The literature review explores developments in state-of-the-art technologies and the revolutionization that has occurred in the manufacturing sector, as well as reviews MAT in HTM. The detailed review is discussed below:

2.1 Evolution of State-of-the-Art Technology and Revolutions in Manufacturing Sector Revolutions

The literature on manufacturing systems highlights the evolution of state-of-the-art technology (Koren, 2000). Pre-1960s was the pre-computer numerical control (pre-CNC) period, where machines were mechanically controlled and manually operated, utilizing transfer lines and interchangeability of parts to reduce production costs. From 1960–1990, the introduction of numerical control (NC) with CNC and direct numerical control (DNC) saw hardware and software collaboration improving quality and accuracy. Techniques such as flexible manufacturing, Kaizen, just-in-time (JIT), lean manufacturing and total quality management (TQM) have become central to modern manufacturing practices. Flexible manufacturing allows for rapid adaptation to different product types and production volumes, enhancing responsiveness to market changes. Kaizen emphasizes continuous, incremental improvements involving all employees to boost efficiency and quality. JIT aims to reduce inventory costs by producing goods only as needed, minimizing waste and storage. Lean manufacturing focuses on eliminating inefficiencies and non-value-adding activities to streamline processes and increase value. TQM is a holistic approach that involves everyone in an organization working together to consistently improve product quality and customer satisfaction. Together, these techniques contribute to more agile, efficient and customer-focused manufacturing operations.

The period from 1990–1994 marked increased global competition and advancements in computer and information systems, leading to agile manufacturing or computer-integrated manufacturing in 1991 (Kumar et al., 2023). In the current era, hardware is integrated with software packages, creating autonomous production environments with flexibility, automation and reconfigurability (Upadhyay, 2014). Modern production systems leverage intelligent manufacturing (AI systems and 3D printing), cloud manufacturing (cloud computing, IoT and virtual methods) and the IoT (5G and big data analysis) (Zhong et al., 2017). These innovations have led to agents-based manufacturing systems, enhancing autonomy, flexibility, stability and reliability (Pansare et al., 2023). The development of manufacturing sectors from the 1900s to the 2000s is illustrated in Fig. 1.

From 1973 to 1992, two R&D indicators (direct and indirect intensity) and one technical intensity indicator were calculated to classify industries into higher and lower categories. In 1986, the Organization for Economic Co-operation and Development (OECD) categorized manufacturing sectors into high-tech, medium-tech and low-tech based on R&D expenditure share (Yin, 2011). This classification was refined in 1994 into four categories: high-tech, high-medium-tech, medium-low-tech and low-tech sectors. Legler and Frietsch later proposed a simplified classification based on R&D spending: high-tech (R&D $>$ 7% of turnover), medium-tech (R&D 2.5%–7%) and low-tech (R&D $<$ 2.5%) (Legler & Krawczyk, 2006). The manufacturing sector's segregation by R&D share and product association is detailed in Fig. 2.

In the 1960s, the International Standard Industrial Classification (ISIC Rev. 1, 1958–1968) categorized sectors into high-tech, medium-tech, and low-tech (United Nations, Statistical Division, 2008). The American Finance Department noted HTPs like scientific instruments, office computers, electrical machines and aeronautical equipment. Revisions in ISIC Rev. 2 (1968–1989) and Rev. 3 (1989–2006) introduced high-tech, medium-high-tech, medium-low-tech and low-tech sectors, adding new products. ISIC Rev. 4 (2006–2023) refined this further by solidifying the medium-tech sector (United Nations, Statistical Division, 2008). The detailed sector and product classifications are outlined in Fig. 2.

2.2 MAT in HTM Sector Background

HTPs are pivotal to economic growth and technological progress, significantly impacting both emerging and established economies. The relationship between technological advancement and economic growth is substantial, as breakthroughs spur GDP growth, the emergence of new services and industries, and shape economic trends. Key technologies driving HTP development include AI, 5G, 3D printing, the IoT, big data, blockchain, drones, gene editing, nanotechnology and solar PV technology. These technologies have collectively boosted GDP from $88 billion in 1980 to $350 billion in 2018, with forecasts predicting the high-tech import and export business could drive GDP growth to $3.5 trillion by 2025 (UNCTAD, 2023b).

From 1960 to 2023, the manufacturing sector evolved from traditional production methods to agile, virtual, networked, flexible and cloud manufacturing,

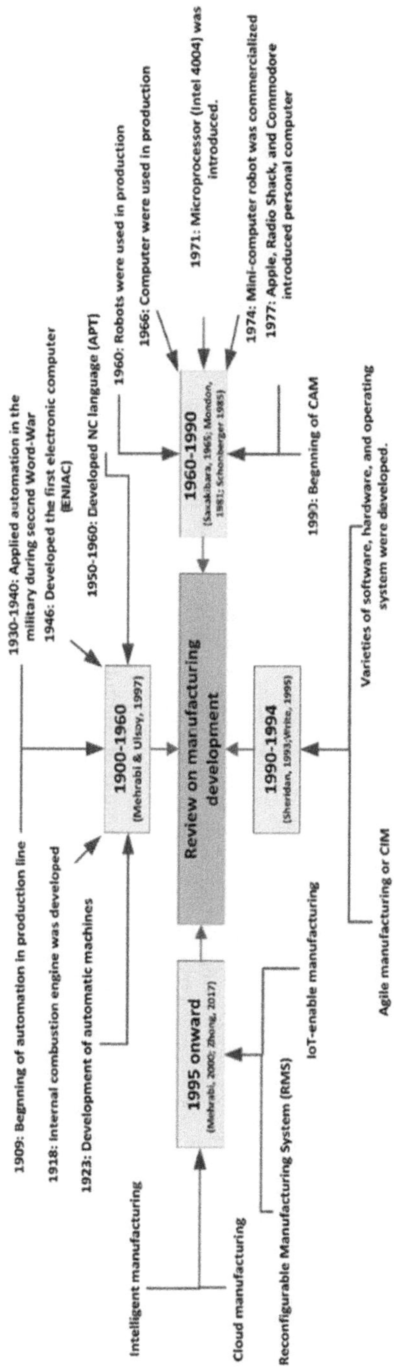

Fig. 1. Technological Evolution in the Manufacturing Sector.

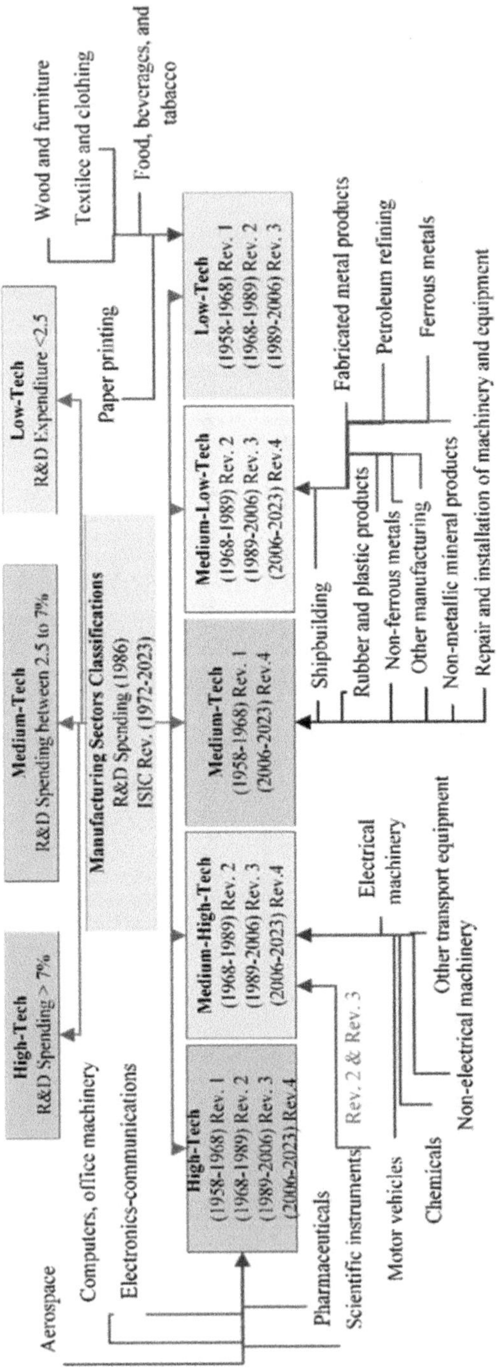

Fig. 2. Background of Manufacturing Sectors Revolution.

incorporating agent-based systems for flexibility, stability and smartness. The concept of agent technology originated from distributed AI in the 1970s, introduced by Carl Hewitt with his Actor model. This model described a self-controlled, interactive, multiprogramming entity known as an actor – essentially a computational entity or agent that shares information with other system entities, forming a multi-agent system (Jennings & Wooldridge, 1998a). Jennings and Wooldridge (1998b) provided 'weak and strong definitions' of agents. A weak definition describes an agent as a hardware and software system with social skills, responsive, predictive and autonomous abilities while a strong definition includes properties like knowledge, veracity, stability and mobility (Jennings & Wooldridge, 1998a). Agents possess features such as autonomy, reactivity, initiative, learnability and mobility. However, a single agent cannot achieve complex goals alone (Oh et al., 2015). Technological advancements have led to the development of MAT, a group of agents that enhance performance, flexibility, reliability and automation, thus increasing the likelihood of task success (Liu et al., 2023; Rasheed et al., 2022).

The applications of MAT, part of AI, began in manufacturing systems during the 1969s with the onset of the third industrial revolution (Lu et al., 2020). This revolution used computer systems and programming languages to control production and robotic systems in assembly (Pulikottil et al., 2021). Subsequent developments in AI, such as the World Wide Web (1989), Edge Computing (1990), Cloud Computing (1997), IoT (1997), CPS (2006), Big Data (2005), Deep Learning (2012), Digital Twin (2012), and 5G (2020), have marked Industrial Revolution 4.0 (Lu et al., 2020). MAT's applications have expanded beyond manufacturing to sectors like health (Park et al., 2016), supply chain management and logistics (Feizabadi, 2022), aeroplane crash prevention (Sharma & Sharma, 2022) and TQM (Atkinson et al., 2022). This study examines MAT trends in HTM. Google Scholar Trends indicate growing interest in 'MAT in manufacturing' and 'HTM' from 2010 to 2023, with 81,010 papers on MAT, including 7,544 reviews, and 6,672 papers on HTM with no review articles from SCI/Scopus in English. Fig. 3 illustrates this research trend.

This survey validates that MAT in HTM is a hot and inspiring research topic for scientific communities. Table 1 also indicates the past and present trends of MAT and HTM research in IEEE, Science Direct, Springer and Taylor & Frances digital libraries.

After reviewing trends in MAT and HTM over the past 14 years, the authors selected eight core manufacturing domains (e.g., product design, production planning and control). They identified HTM factors and MAT variables crucial for these domains. Table 2 summarises published research, aiding researchers in selecting relevant MAT variables and HTM criteria for their applications. Literature reviews have covered MAT research in supply chain management, production planning and control, cloud computing, intelligent manufacturing, maintenance and production scheduling (Kim et al., 2023; Oh et al., 2015; Shukla et al., 2020; Stornelli et al., 2021). However, there is a lack of review articles on HTM, specifically regarding MAT. This review aims to fill this research gap, providing a comprehensive overview of MAT's role in HTM. In this context, the next section outlines the research methodology.

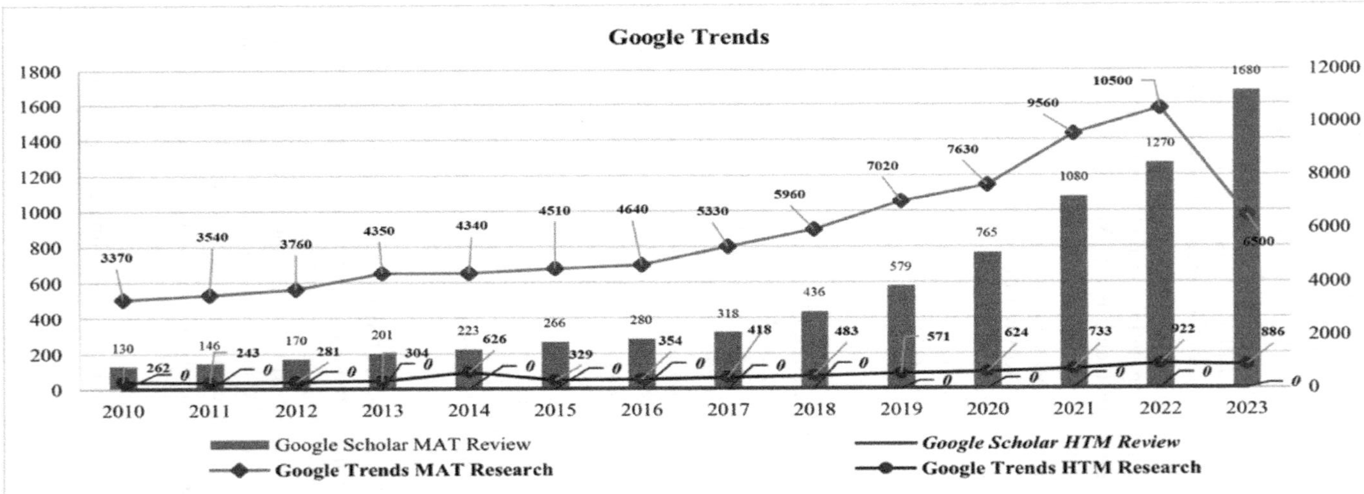

Fig. 3. Past and Present Research Google Trends From 2010 to 2023.

Table 1. Search Query of MAT and HTM Research Article From 2010 to 2023.

Search Query: Using MAT and HTM Keywords								
Year	IEEE		Springer		SD		T & F	
	MAT	HTM	*MAT*	HTM	*MAT*	HTM	*MAT*	HTM
2010	*46*	0	*82*	3	*1,314*	83	*1,537*	174
2011	*46*	0	*138*	1	*1,528*	87	*1,600*	194
2012	*44*	0	*109*	2	*1,796*	114	*1,775*	225
2013	*62*	1	*99*	2	*2,175*	100	*1,811*	224
2014	*43*	0	*89*	4	*2,254*	131	*1,838*	203
2015	*40*	0	*79*	0	*2,588*	167	*1,926*	192
2016	*36*	0	*66*	0	*2,758*	204	*2,206*	239
2017	*47*	0	*79*	2	*3,067*	227	*2,079*	252
2018	*72*	0	*84*	6	*3,750*	312	*2,231*	263
2019	*62*	0	*92*	7	*4,394*	349	*2,630*	329
2020	*58*	0	*82*	15	*5,317*	415	*2,955*	349
2021	*96*	0	*214*	65	*7,435*	571	*3,286*	386
2022	*108*	0	*288*	123	*9,033*	680	*3,130*	402
2023	*130*	0	*332*	131	*10,443*	740	*3,093*	419

3. RESEARCH METHODOLOGY

3.1 Review Framework

Fig. 4 represents the procedural steps followed to complete the review process. It consists of five stages. Stage 1 represents the source of data collection. In Stage 2, screening is performed to exclude duplicate collections, conference proceedings, book chapters and letters. In Stage 3, titles, abstracts and full texts are examined to eliminate the data that does not contain relevant information. Stage 4 contains the data for meta-analysis, and Stage 5 completes the review with a conclusion.

3.2 Data Collection and Processing for Classifications and Meta-analysis

This study reviews published research on MAT and its applications in HTM, drawing from reputable journals indexed in SCI, Scopus and Web of Science. Researchers use this literature to enhance knowledge and provide novel insights. A dataset of peer-reviewed articles on MAT and HTM was collected using the keywords 'multi-agent technology', 'multi-agent systems', 'intelligent manufacturing', 'high-tech manufacturing', 'industrial automation', 'smart manufacturing' and 'agent-based systems'. Articles were sourced from platforms like Google Scholar, PubMed, ResearchGate, IEEE and others, yielding approximately 892 articles.

Table 2. Criteria and Variables Explored From Literature, Their Research Methodology, MAT Distributions as per Classification Scheme 1.

Sr. No.	Manufacturing Domains	Criteria of HTM	Research Methodology (HTM)	HTM Reference	*Application by Constitution and Publications MAT*	*Percentage (%)*	Research Methodology (MAT)	*Variables of MAT*	*Number of Variables Selected From the Literature*	*MAT Reference*
1.	Product design & development (9 + *10*) **(18 + 10.75)%**	[High-Tech Product Features, Closely Related to Science, Nearer to Technological Development, Shorter Products Life Cycle, Closely Related to Customized Infrastructure, Feed Back Evaluation, Training and Education, Production Innovation, Technical Capabilities, R & D Expenditure, R & D Personal, Expenditure on New Product Development] = **12**	Fundamental research = **8**	Huang and Wu (2010), Jang et al. (2016), Lanza et al. (2019), Liu (2011), Sahadev and Jayachandran (2004), Wang et al. (2020), Wu and Weng (2010), Zemlickienė (2011), and Zemlickiene and Maditinos (2012)	*Multi-agent system* = ***9***	*9.70*	Fundamental research = **9**	***Autonomous agent, Production planning agent, Sales agent, Procurement agent, Design agent, Knowledge base agent, Material agent, Manufacturing capability agent, Manufacturability evaluation agent, Process planning agent, Customer agent, System design agent, Product life cycle agent, Machine agent, Material planning agent, Designing agent, Transportation agent, Forecasting agent, Maintenance agent, Negotiation agent, Dispatch agent, Competitive agent***	***22***	Baykasoglu and Gorkemli, (2017), Chien et al. (2013), Dhokia et al. (2017), Dostatni et al. (2016), Jian et al. (2010), Mishra et al. (2016), Soria Zurita et al. (2018), Sun et al. (2001), Yang et al. (2012), and Zheng et al. (2023)
			Applied research = **1**		*Virtual assistance* = ***1***	*1.08*	Applied research = **1**			

2.	Production planning and control (10 + **25**) (20 + 26.88)%	[Product Standardization and Innovation, Object Clarity, High-Tech Manufacturing Processes, Technical Convergence Trends, Operational Conditions, Firm Resources, Organization Learning, Process Innovation, Gross Industrial Output Value of Product, Production Facilities and Capacity, Material Resource Planning, Productivity, control] = **13**	Fundamental research = **9**	Borés et al. (2003), Hung et al. (2011), Kano and Nakagawa (2008), Lanza et al. (2019), Lorenz et al. (2019), MA, (2015), Ngai et al. (2012), Papadopoulos et al. (2002), Peng et al. (2010), Sharma et al. (2017), and Wu and Weng (2010)	*Multi-agent system = **19***	*20.43*	Fundamental research = **20**	***Purchase planning agent, Sales planning agent, Production agent, Resource agent, Order agent, Autonomic computing agent, Online machining processing agent, Cost estimation agent, E- resource management agent, Feature reconfiguration agent, Machining operation planning agent, Parameter selection agent, Optimization agent, Adaptive agent, Sensing agent, Digital twinning agent, Failure detection agent, Condition monitoring agent, Quality control agent, Cloud agent, System repository agent, Integration of manufacturing system with maintenance agent, Organizational productivity, Organizational control agent, Decision making***	*32*	Ansari et al. (2019), Ayhan et al. (2015), Chu et al. (2016), Dittrich and Fohlmeister (2020), Ferreira et al. (2022), Giret et al. (2017), Jana et al. (2013), Kovalenko et al. (2019), Leitão et al. (2016), Leng et al. (2023), Liu et al. (2014), López et al. (2023), Nie et al. (2022), Rolón and Martínez (2012), Scrimieri et al. (2021), Shukla et al. (2019), Singh and Sharma (2023b), Tang et al. (2020), Wu et al. (2023), Xiong et al. (2023), Zakhama et al. (2019) and Zheng et al., (2021)
			Applied research = **1**		*Multi-agent simulation = **6***	*6.45*	Applied research = **5**			

(Continued)

Table 2. *(Continued)*

Sr. No.	Manufacturing Domains	Criteria of HTM	Research Methodology (HTM)	HTM Reference	*Application by Constitution and Publications MAT*	*Percentage (%)*	Research Methodology (MAT)	*Variables of MAT*	*Number of Variables Selected From the Literature*	*MAT Reference*
								agent, Task selection agent, Order management agent, Smart workpiece agent, Intelligent agent, Managerial agent, Customer agent, Environmental agent		
3.	Production scheduling (2 + *10*) (4 + 10.75) %	[Expenditure for Technical Renovation, Break Even Time] = **2**	Fundamental research = **1**	Chen et al. (2018) and Yeh et al. (2010)	*Multi-agent system = **8***	*8.60*	Fundamental research = **7**	***Information agent, Autonomous agent, Information retrieve agent, Product agent, Order sequencing agent, Scheduling agent, Delivery agent, Process control agent, Job management agent, Optimization agent, Manager agent, Material handling agent, Inventory management agent, Resource capacity management agent, Operation agent***	*15*	Jules and Saadat (2016), Li et al. (2018), Saeidlou et al. (2019), Sahin et al. (2017), Wang et al. (2018), X. Wang et al. (2022), Zhang and Wang (2016), and Zhou et al. (2021)
			Applied research = **1**		*Multi-agent simulation = **2***	*2.15*	Applied research = **3**			

4.	Inventory control (1 + *4*) (2 + 4.30) %	[Distribution Management] = **1**	Fundamental research = **1**	Liu (2011)	*Multi-agent system = 1*	*1.08*	Fundamental research = **2**	***Warehouse agents, Trust, and reputation allow agents, Production order agents, Buffer or inventory agents, Retailor agents, Distributor agents, Analyst agents, the Learning agent***	*8*	Kim et al. (2010), Long et al. (2011), and H. Wang et al. (2022)
					Multi-agent simulation = 3	*3.23*	Applied research = **2**			
5.	Inspection and quality control (6 + *5*) (12 + 5.38) %	[Quality Management System, Quality of Design, Quality of Processes, Quality Improvement, Law and Regulations, Strategy/Policy, Quality Management Capabilities] = **7**	Fundamental research = **3**	Chen et al., (2018), Huang et al. (2019), Law and Gunasekaran (2012), Verma et al. (2022), Zhu et al. (2007), and Zu (2009)	*Multi-agent system = 5*	*5.38*	Fundamental research = **3**	***Quality control execution agent, Process data analysis agent, Central decision maker agent, QoS monitor agent, Diagnosis and decision agent, Controller agent, Hardware agent, Robotic agent, Software agent, Inspection agent, Quality control agent, Department decision maker agent***	***12***	Czimmermann et al. (2022), Priego et al. (2017), Sahebjamnia et al. (2016), and Singh and Sharma (2023a)
			Applied research = **3**				Applied research = **2**			
6.	Maintenance engineering management (6 + ***13***) (12 + 1,398)%	[Integration of Maintenance in Manufacturing Systems, Preventive Maintenance, Integrated Predictive	Fundamental research = **6**	Campos (2009), Jun (2022), Peng et al. (2010), Singh and Sharma (2023a, 2023b), and	*Multi-agent system = 7*	*7.53*	Fundamental research = **9**	***Maintenance activity agent, Computer centre agent, Reconfiguration agent, Diagnosis artificial neural networking agent,***	***15***	Brundage et al. (2019), Hedjazi et al. (2019), Kaplanoğlu (2014), Lee et al. (2020), Merdan et al. (2011), Pal
					*Multi-agent simulation = **6***	*6.45*	Applied research = **4**			

(Continued)

Table 2. *(Continued)*

Sr. No.	Manufacturing Domains	Criteria of HTM	Research Methodology (HTM)	HTM Reference	*Application by Constitution and Publications MAT*	*Percentage (%)*	Research Methodology (MAT)	*Variables of MAT*	*Number of Variables Selected From the Literature*	*MAT Reference*
		Maintenance, Condition-Based Maintenance, Maintenance cost, Quality of Maintenance Process, Health Management of Manufacturing Process] = **8**		Tortora et al. (2021)				***Interface agent, Distributed digital manufacturing agent, Diagnosis, Prognosis, Just in time, IoT, Digital twin agent, Diverter agent, Job dispatcher and resource manager agent, Monitoring agent, Job Agent***		et al. (2023), Rezki et al. (2016), Rodríguez et al. (2022), Rokhforoz et al. (2021), Sahnoun et al. (2019), Sharma et al. (2017), and Upasani et al. (2017)
7.	Shopfloor production (0 + *8*) (0 + 8.6)%	[No evidence found] = **0**	**0**	No evidence found	*Multi-agent system =* ***4***	*4.30*	Fundamental research = **5**	***Supervisor agent, Scheduling management agent, Raw material processing plan agent, Simulation agent, Production station agent, Reporting agent, Configuration agent, Traceability agent, Data mining agent, Typical shop-floor management service agent, Performance analysis agent, Capability evaluation agent***	***12***	Fang et al. (2013), Huang et al. (2019), Lou et al. (2012), Yahouni et al. (2021), and Zhang et al. (2014, 2017)
					Multi-agent simulation = ***4***	*4.30*	Applied research = **3**			

8.	Marketing and SCM (15 + ***18***) (32 + 19.35)%	[Demand Potential, High-Tech Product Market Analysis, Strategic Flexibility, Barriers and Risks Involved, Market Competition, Information Accessibility, Trade Analysis, Marketing Research, Market Potential, Marketing Strategies, Marketing Decisions, Market Entry Mode Decisions, Level of Control, Market Growth Rate, Market Attractiveness, Reputation, Sale Revenue, Export, Profit Objectives] = **18**	Fundamental research = **12**	Atkinson et al. (2022), Feng et al. (2022), Guan and Chen (2010), Huang (2002), Imiru (2022), Koch (n.d.), Li and Xiong (2022), Lin and Lee (2005), Mangla et al. (2015), Mubeen et al. (2020), Papadopoulos et al. (2002), Rana et al. (2021), Rochiyati et al. (2022), Schellenberg et al. (2018), Viswanathan and Jha (2019), and Yeh et al. (2010)	*Multi-agent system =* ***10***	*10.75*	Fundamental research = **15**	***Data Mining and Information Retrieving Agent, Capacity adjustment agent, Allocation agent, Reverse logistic agent, Supply chain configuration evaluation agent, Dispatching agent, Communication agent, Big data agent, Logistic management agent, Wrapper agent, Forecasting agent, User agent, Barge agent, Terminal agent, Mediator agent, Purchase order collection agent, Supplier selection agent, Transport agent, material collection agent, Supplier agent, Database agent, Disruptive risk management agent, Expert agent, Trading agent, Accounting agent, Producer agent***	***26***	Ameri and McArthur (2013), Belhadi et al. (2022), Du et al. (2020), Eriksson et al. (2020), Feng et al. (2017), Ghadimi et al. (2019), Giannakis and Louis (2016), Jahani et al. (2015), Kumari et al. (2015), Pino et al. (2010), Shavandi and Khedmati (2022), Shukla and Kiridena (2016), and Wu et al. (2013)
			Applied research = **3**		*Multi-agent simulation = 7*	*7.53*				
					Artificial intelligence = ***1***	*1.08*	Applied research = **3**			

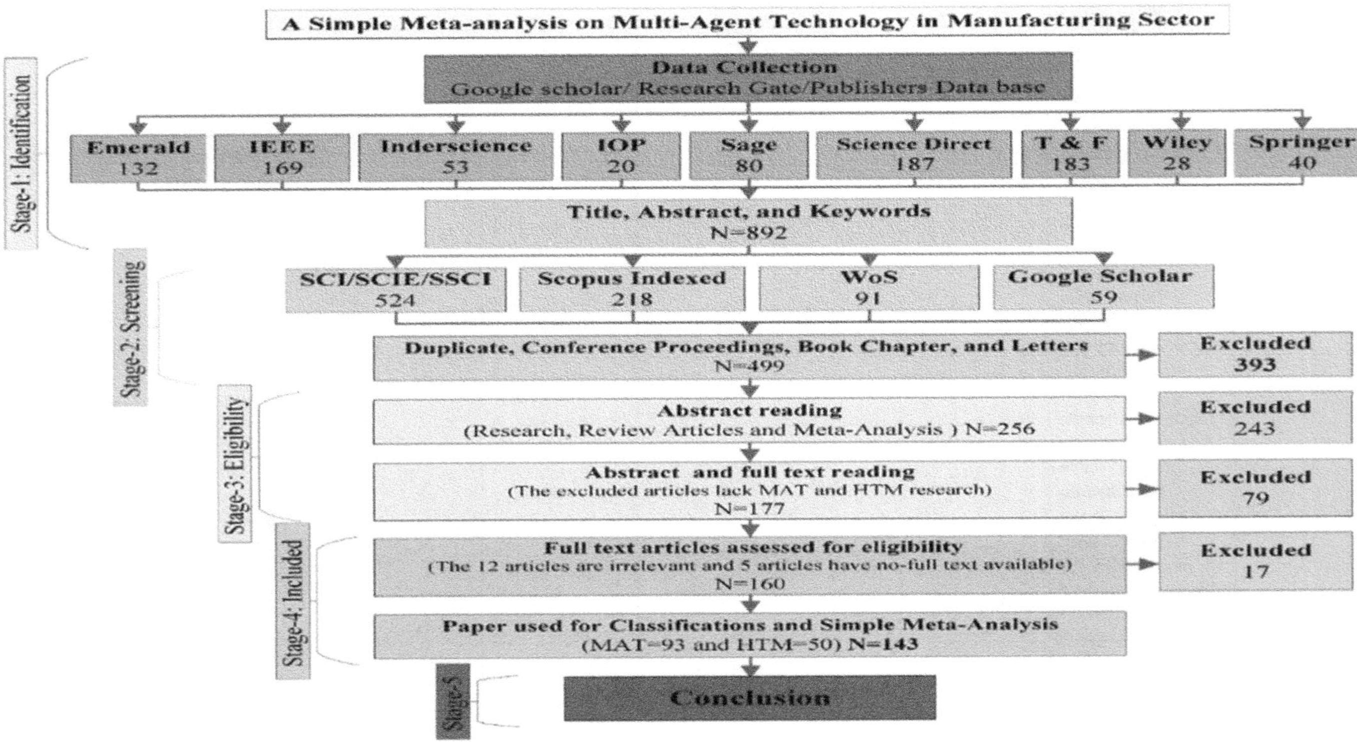

Fig. 4. Review Methodology.

A total of 892 collected articles were initially reviewed to remove duplicates, conference papers, lecture notes and book chapters, resulting in the exclusion of 349 items. The remaining articles were then screened by examining abstracts and keywords to identify those related to MAT and HTM. Afterwards, 160 eligible articles were reviewed in full to assess their relevance to MAT or HTM, eliminating those that lacked relevance or full-text availability. This systematic process ensured that the final 143 articles (93 on MAT and 50 on HTM) articles were highly relevant and credible for meta-analysis. This review focuses on journals in areas like product design, production planning, scheduling, maintenance, quality management, inventory control and marketing. It offers a meta-analysis to understand past, present, and future trends, capturing the evolution of MAT in HTM and suggesting future research topics. The findings, presented through tables and figures, provide a comprehensive overview of MAT's growth and impact in HTM.

4. CLASSIFICATION METHOD

Based on the literature screened and the nature of research conducted on MAT and HTM research. This review article introduced two classification schemes to organize published manuscripts systematically. The schemes are discussed below.

4.1 Classification Scheme Based on MAT and HTM Research

MAT and HTP manufacturing research is categorized by manufacturing domains and MAT applications (Fig. 5). Classification Scheme 1 organizes MAT into eight domains and four application categories (multi-agent systems, simulations, virtual assistance and AI). This creates 24 MAT research categories and eight HTM research domains. Fig. 5 and Table 3 illustrate and reference these categories.

Table 2 summarizes published research on MAT and HTM by domain and MAT application by constitution. The highest number of HTM articles are in 'marketing and SCM' (18) and 'production planning and control' (10), followed by 'product design and development' and 'inspection and quality control.' For MAT, 'production planning and control' (25) and 'marketing and SCM' (18) have the most publications while 'product design and development,' 'inventory control,' and 'inspections and quality control' have the fewest. Regarding MAT applications,

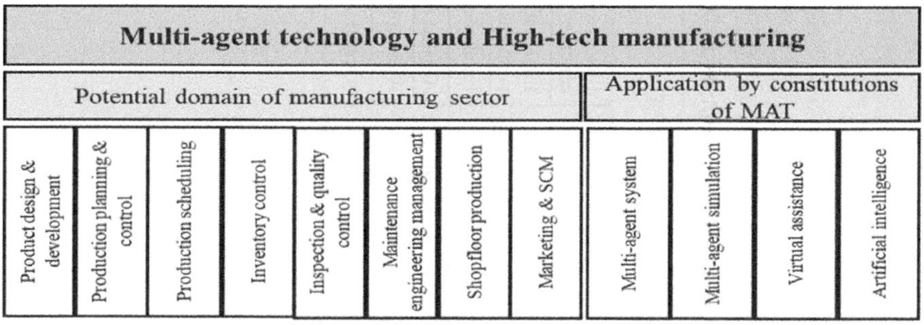

Fig. 5. Classification of MAT and HTM Research.

Table 3. Distribution of MAT According to Classification Scheme 2.

Research Methodology		HTM	Total HTM	Age HTM (%)	*MAT*	*MA Simulation*	*Virtual Assistance*	*AI*	*Total MAT*		*Age MAT (%)*	
Fundamental research	Fundamental conceptual	37	41	82	*24*	*5*			*29*	*71*	*31.18*	*75.27*
	Fundamental mathematical	4			*25*	*12*			*37*		*39.78*	
	Fundamental statistical				*4*		*1*		*5*		*5.38*	
Applied research	Applied experimental	2	9	18	*2*	*7*			*9*	*22*	*9.68*	*24.73*
	Applied statistical							*1*	*1*		*1.07*	
	Applied case study	7			*8*	*4*			*12*		*12.90*	

'production planning and control' (19) has the most 'multi-agent system' publications, followed by 'marketing and SCM' (10). 'Multi-agent simulation' is prominent in 'marketing and SCM' (7) and 'production planning and control' (6). 'Virtual assistance' appears in 'production planning and control' (1) and 'artificial intelligence' in 'marketing and SCM' (1). After implementing Classification Scheme 1, which categorizes HTM research by domain and MAT research by the application of constitutions, the literature review conducted on MAT and HTM research has led us to classify the research methodologies discussed in the following sub-section.

4.2 Classification Scheme Based on Research Methodology

The classification based on research methodologies followed so far is explored in this review and is arranged into fundamentals and applied research (Fig. 6). The complete classification is called Classification Scheme 2.

The arrangement of MAT and HTM research concerning research methodologies, publication details and references is shown in Table 2. The table indicates that both fundamental and applied research methodologies were utilized in the research of MAT and HTM.

The classified data using Schemes 1 and 2 are further analyzed using a simple meta-analysis and discussed in the next section.

5. A SIMPLE META-ANALYSIS

In this study, summary counts were employed to analyze key factors and methods used in reviewed studies related to MAT and HTM. This descriptive meta-analysis aims to enhance understanding of MAT's development in HTM, identify potential research areas and categorize findings by publication years and journal publishers.

5.1 A Simple Meta-analysis Using Classification Scheme – 1

Table 2 breaks down MAT and HTM research based on Classification Scheme 1, detailing frequencies and percentages across eight manufacturing domains and MAT applications. Fig. 7 (a) visually represents these findings. HTM research (in bold) shows a significant focus on 'marketing and SCM' (32%) and 'production planning and control' (20%), followed by 'product design and development' (18%), 'inspection and quality control' (12%), 'maintenance engineering management' (12%), 'production scheduling' (4%), 'inventory control' (2%) and 'shopfloor' (0%). In contrast, MAT research (in regular font) indicates the highest publications in 'production planning and control' (26.88%), 'marketing and supply chain management' (19.35%), 'maintenance engineering management' (13.98%) and 'production scheduling' (10.75%). 'Product design and development' and 'inventory control' have lower percentages (4.30%).

Fig. 7 (b) depicts the breakdown of MAT applications by constitutions according to Classification Scheme 1. 'Multi-agent system' is most utilized (67.74%), followed by 'multi-agent simulation' (30.11%), and least by 'virtual assistance' and 'artificial intelligence' (1.08%). Table 5 shows that 'multi-agent

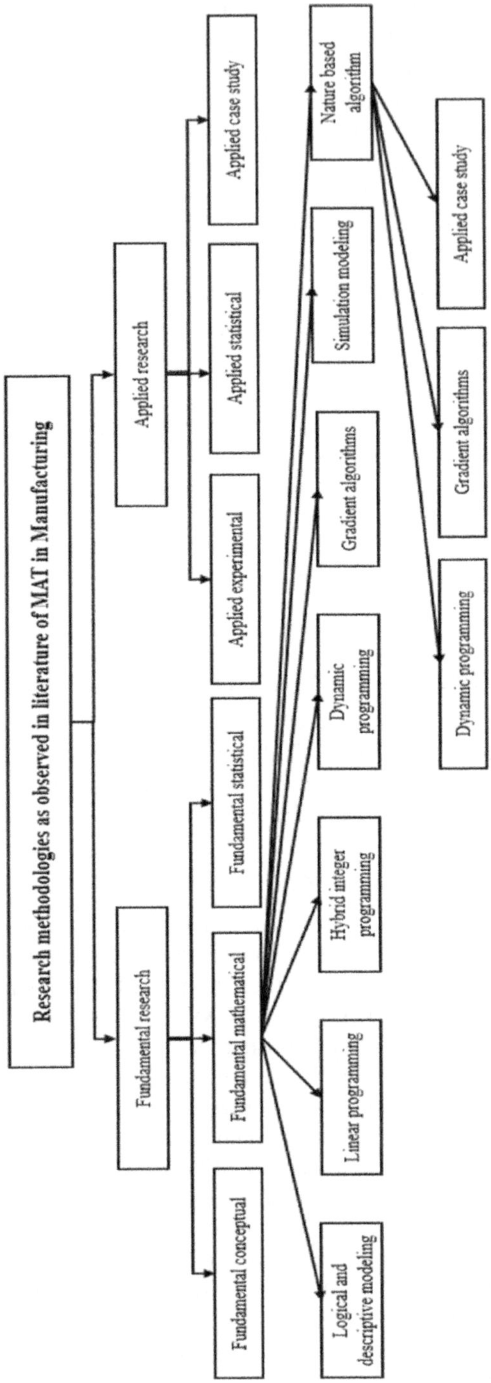

Fig. 6. Classification Based on Research Methodology.

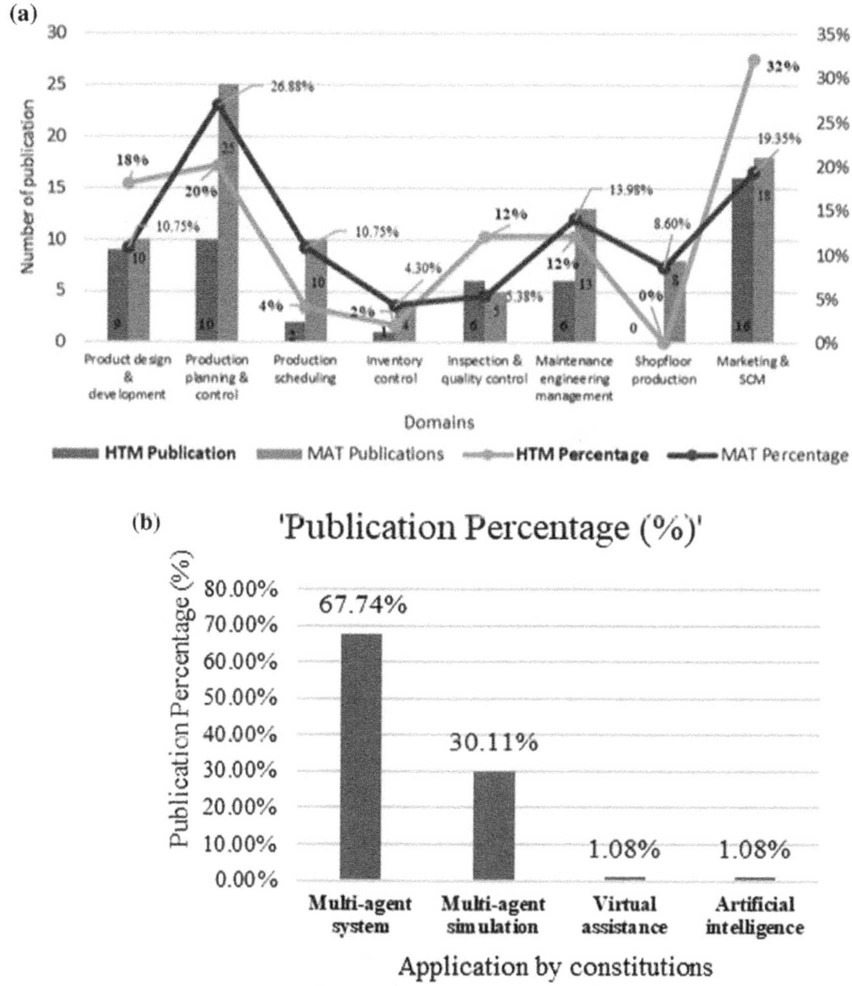

Fig. 7. (a) MAT Application by Domain. (b) Application by Constitution.

system' is predominantly applied in production planning & control (20.43%) while 'multi-agent simulation' is prominent in marketing and SCM (7.53%). This analysis suggests potential for future research focusing on virtual assistance and AI within MAT applications.

5.2 A Simple Meta-analysis Using Classification Scheme – 2

Segregation of research articles according to the proposed Classification Scheme 2 is listed in Table 3, based on the solution methodology used to complete the selected published articles. This indicates that most articles utilized 'fundamental

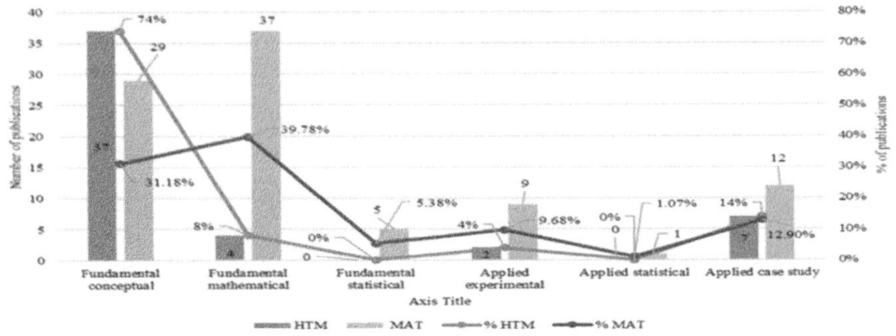

Fig. 8. Research Methodology in MAT Constitutions.

research' about 82% (HTM) and 75.27% (MAT); the remaining used applied research. This table is proposed to give more profound knowledge about the methodology used in HTM research and the application of MAT by constitutions. Accordingly, Fig. 7 is prepared.

Fig. 8 illustrates that in fundamental research, conceptual, mathematical and statistical techniques were predominantly employed across articles on multi-agent systems (24, 25 and 4 articles respectively), followed by multi-agent simulation (5, 12 and 0 articles), virtual assistance (0, 0 and 1 article) and with no articles using AI. In applied research, case studies accounted for 12.90% of articles, experimental studies for 9.68% and the rest were statistical.

5.3 Publisher and Journal-Wise Distribution of Articles

The number of articles published on MAT and HTM research by journals along with their publisher are listed in Table 4. It is seen from the table that in MAT research, there are 7 publishers with 43 journals and in HTM research, the table indicates 8 publishers with 30 journals. This table also represents a list of published articles in different journals and publishers.

Fig. 9 analyzes the distribution of articles across 7 publishers and 43 journals for MAT research, and 8 publishers and 30 journals for HTM research. ScienceDirect leads in MAT research with 39.78% of articles, followed by Springer (21.51%), Taylor & Francis (20.43%), IEEE (9.68%), Emerald (4.30%), ASME (3.23%) and Sage (1.08%). In HTM research, ScienceDirect also leads with 42% of articles, followed by Emerald (18%), Taylor & Francis (16%), Springer (12%) and others (2%). This insight aids researchers in selecting journals aligned with their interests and informs decisions on journal subscriptions and article submissions.

5.4 Articles Distribution as per Publication Year

Table 5 illustrates the publication trends of MAT and HTM research by various publishers from 2009 to 2023. Science Direct, Springer, Taylor & Francis and

Table 4. Publisher and Journal-Based Distribution of Material.

Publisher	Name of the Journal	No. of Articles	Total	Percentage (%)
ASME (MAT)	*Journal of Computing and Information Science in Engineering*	*1*	*3*	*3.23*
	Journal of Manufacturing Science and Engineering	*2*		
Emerald (MAT)	*The Total Quality Management Journal*	*1*	*4*	*4.30*
	Strategic Outsourcing: An International Journal	*1*		
	Journal of Enterprise Information Management	*1*		
	Journal of Advances in Management Research	*1*		
Emerald (HTM)	Management Decision	2	9	18
	European Journal of Marketing	1		
	Benchmarking: An International Journal	1		
	International Journal of Quality & Reliability Management	2		
	Marketing Intelligence & Planning	2		
	International Journal of Emerging Markets	1		
IEEE (MAT)	*IEEE Internet of Things Journal*	*1*	*9*	*9.68*
	IEEE Systems Journal	*1*		
	IEEE Transactions on Automation Science and Engineering	*1*		
	IEEE Transactions on Engineering Management	*2*		
	IEEE Transactions on Industrial Informatics	*2*		
	IEEE Transactions on Systems, Man, and Cybernetics: Systems	*1*		
	IEEE Transactions on Systems, Man, and Cybernetics - Part A: Systems and Humans	*1*		
IEEE (HTM)	IEEE Transactions on Engineering Management	1	1	
Sage (MAT)	*International Journal of Advanced Robotic Systems*	*1*	*1*	*1.08*
ScienceDirect (MAT)	*Advanced Engineering Informatics*	*1*	*37*	*39.78*
	Applied Soft Computing	*2*		
	CIRP Annals - Manufacturing Technology	*3*		
	Computers & Industrial Engineering	*6*		
	Computers and Electrical Engineering	*1*		
	Computers and Operations Research	*1*		
	Computers in Industry	*4*		
	Control Engineering Practice	*1*		
	Engineering Applications of Artificial Intelligence	*1*		

(Continued)

Table 4. *(Continued)*

Publisher	Name of the Journal	No. of Articles	Total	Percentage (%)
	Expert Systems with Applications	*3*		
	International Journal of Computer Integrated Manufacturing	*1*		
	International Journal of Production Research	*1*		
	Journal of Cleaner Production	*1*		
	Journal of Intelligent Manufacturing	*1*		
	Journal of Manufacturing Systems	*7*		
	Robotics and Computer-Integrated Manufacturing	*3*		
ScienceDirect (HTM)	Socio-Economic Planning Sciences	1	21	42
	Tech novation	1		
	International Business Review	2		
	Computers and Chemical Engineering	4		
	Journal of Engineering and Technology Management (JET-M)	3		
	International Journal of Production Economics	1		
	Resources, Conservation, and Recycling	2		
	Arabian Journal for Science and Engineering	1		
	Information Systems Frontiers	2		
	International Journal of Advanced Manufacturing Technology	1		
	Journal of Industrial Engineering International	2		
	Journal of Intelligent Manufacturing	1		
Springer (MAT)	*Journal of Central South University*	*1*	*20*	*21.51*
	Soft Computing	*1*		
	The Journal of Technology Transfer	*9*		
	Quality & Quantity	*2*		
	Cogent Engineering	*3*		
	Journal of Industrial and Production Engineering	*1*		
	Technology Analysis & Strategic Management	*1*		
	Total Quality Management & Business Excellence	*2*		
Springer (HTM)	International Journal of Computer Integrated Manufacturing	2	6	12
	Journal of Strategic Marketing	3		
	Applied Sciences	1		

Table 4. *(Continued)*

Publisher	Name of the Journal	No. of Articles	Total	Percentage (%)
Taylor & Francis (MAT)	*Sustainability*	*1*	*19*	*20.43*
	Frontiers in Manufacturing Technology	*4*		
	Sciendo (Journal name needed – may need clarification, as this is a platform)	*13*		
	Management Decision	*1*		
Taylor & Francis (HTM)	European Journal of Marketing	2	8	16
	Benchmarking: An International Journal	3		
	International Journal of Quality & Reliability Management	2		
	Marketing Intelligence & Planning	1		
MDPI (HTM)	International Journal of Emerging Markets	1	3	6
	IEEE Internet of Things Journal	2		
Frontiers (HTM)	IEEE Systems Journal	1	1	2
Sciendo (HTM)	IEEE Transactions on Automation Science and Engineering	1	1	2

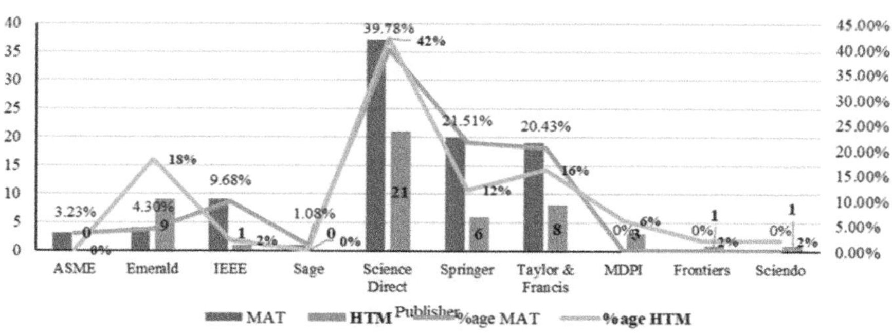

Fig. 9. Publisher–Article Distribution.

IEEE consistently published MAT research throughout this period, with Science Direct being the most active. Emerald contributed minimally while ASME and Sage had no publications in MAT during the specified years. In HTM research, Science Direct, Emerald, Springer and Taylor & Francis were actively publishing while IEEE and Sage had limited involvement, and ASME had no publications.

Fig. 10 depicts significant fluctuations in publications between 2010 and 2014, with MAT articles decreasing from nine to three and HTM articles declining from five to one. A slight uptick occurred in 2014–2015, followed by a notable increase in

Table 5. Bi-annually Distribution of Articles.

Year	ASME	Emerald		IEEE		Sage	SD		Springer		T&F		Other	Total		Percentage (%)	
	MAT	*MAT*	HTM	*MAT*	HTM	*MAT*	*MAT*	HTM	*MAT*	HTM	*MAT*	HTM	HTM	*MAT*	HTM	*MAT*	HTM
2009–2010		*1*	2	*1*			*2*	2	*1*	1	*4*	1		*9*	5	*9.68*	10
2010–2011							*1*	3	*2*	1	*4*			*7*	4	*7.53*	8
2011–2012			2	*1*			*1*	3	*3*	1	*1*			*6*	6	*6.45*	12
2012–2013				*1*			*1*		*1*		*2*	1		*5*	1	*5.38*	2
2013–2014							*2*	1	*1*					*3*	1	*3.23*	2
2014–2015		*1*	2	*1*			*2*	1	*2*			1		*6*	4	*6.45*	8
2015–2016		*1*		*1*			*3*	2	*3*		*3*	1		*11*	3	*11.83*	6
2016–2017	*1*			*1*			*4*		*2*	2				*8*	2	*8.60*	4
2017–2018	*1*						*3*	2				1		*4*	3	*4.30*	6
2018–2019						*1*	*5*	2	*3*		*1*		1	*10*	3	*10.75*	6
2019–2020	*1*	*1*		*1*			*1*	2				1	1	*4*	4	*4.30*	8
2020–2021			1				*3*		*1*		*2*		1	*6*	2	*6.45*	4
2021–2022			1	*1*			*4*	1	*1*		*1*		3	*7*	5	*7.53*	10
2022–2023			1	*1*	1		*5*	2		1	*1*	2		*7*	7	*7.53*	14

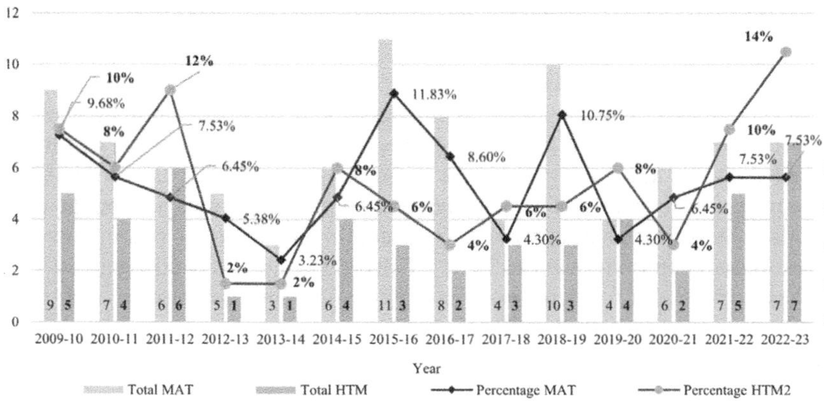

Fig. 10. Distribution of Articles w.r.t. Publisher for the Period 2009–2023.

MAT articles in 2015–2016 to 11 while HTM articles saw a steady decline until 2019. Similar fluctuations continued in MAT research until 2019, after which both domains showed a continuous rise. These fluctuations reflect technological advancements and global market demands for HTPs. The recent uptrend since 2019 underscores organizations' efforts to automate systems with innovations like MAT to meet consumer demands. This analysis aids researchers in understanding the trends in MAT and HTM research over the past 14 years, encouraging deeper exploration and potential integrated studies in these evolving domains.

6. IMPLICATIONS

The findings of this review on MAT and HTM have significant implications across theoretical, practical and social dimensions. These contributions enhance the broader understanding and application of MAT in various manufacturing contexts.

6.1 Theoretical Implications

This research enhances the theoretical framework surrounding MAT by providing a comprehensive meta-analysis of existing literature. It identifies key trends and gaps in the current body of knowledge, particularly in areas like shopfloor production and inventory control, which have received limited attention in previous studies. By proposing two classification schemes, the study lays the groundwork for future theoretical explorations, encouraging researchers to develop more nuanced models that can better explain the dynamics of MAT in HTM. This theoretical advancement can lead to the formulation of new hypotheses and research questions, driving further academic inquiry into the integration of MAT with emerging technologies such as AI and machine learning, which are currently underexplored.

6.2 Practical Implications

The findings of this study have significant implications for industry practitioners. The review highlights the importance of MAT in enhancing various manufacturing processes, including quality control, maintenance and supply chain management. By understanding the trends and applications of MAT, manufacturers can make informed decisions about adopting these technologies to improve operational efficiency and product quality. The identification of active journals and publication trends also serves as a valuable resource for practitioners seeking to stay updated on the latest research and innovations in MAT. Furthermore, the study suggests that future research should focus on practical applications in underrepresented areas, providing a roadmap for industry stakeholders to explore new opportunities for implementing MAT in their operations.

6.3 Social Implications

As MAT continues to evolve and integrate into HTM, it has the potential to transform the workforce landscape. The automation and efficiency brought about by MAT can lead to job displacement in certain areas; however, it can also create new opportunities for skilled labour in technology management and system integration. The study emphasizes the need for a balanced approach to workforce development, where training and education programs are aligned with the technological advancements in MAT. This alignment can help mitigate the negative impacts of automation while fostering a workforce that is equipped to thrive in a technology-driven environment. Additionally, the research study underscores the importance of collaboration between academia and industry to ensure that the social implications of MAT are addressed, promoting a sustainable and inclusive approach to technological advancement.

7. CONCLUSION, LIMITATIONS AND FUTURE SCOPES

This comprehensive literature review focuses on exploring MAT in the context of HTM, aiming to uncover past, present and future trends through classification schemes and a simple meta-analysis of 143 identified articles published between 2009 and 2023. The review began with a detailed examination of MAT and HTM research across various journals, identifying and scrutinizing articles that contributed to understanding eight major domains within manufacturing organizations: product design and development, production planning and control, production scheduling, inventory control, inspection and quality control, maintenance engineering management, shopfloor production and marketing and supply chain management. This categorization was pivotal in structuring the subsequent analysis. Two classification schemes were applied to these articles. Scheme 1 focused on the application of MAT across different domains and identified the distribution of articles published in MAT and HTM research. It highlighted that 'production planning and control' and 'marketing & supply chain management' were the most researched domains in MAT and HTM, respectively, whereas domains like 'inventory control' and 'shopfloor production' had fewer publications, indicating potential areas for future research.

Scheme 2 analyzed the methodologies employed in MAT and HTM research. It found that conceptual and mathematical approaches were more prevalent than applied research techniques such as case studies and experimental studies. This suggests an opportunity for more applied research to complement the foundational studies in MAT and HTM. The meta-analysis based on these schemes revealed that multi-agent systems and simulations were predominantly used in MAT research, with limited utilization of virtual assistance and AI. This underscores a potential for future studies to explore the applications of these lesser-utilized methodologies. Examining publication trends from 2009 to 2023, fluctuations were observed in MAT and HTM research outputs until around 2019, followed by a notable increase in publications thereafter. The spike in publications from 2022 to 2023 compared to 2019–2020 reflects heightened interest and activity in MAT and HTM, likely driven by technological advancements and increasing global demand for HTPs. The review's implications extend to organizational management, suggesting a focus on domains with fewer publications and aiding in journal subscription decisions. It also serves researchers by identifying underexplored areas and guiding future research directions in MAT and HTM. Additionally, it provides a time-saving resource for scholars engaged in literature review and article submissions within these domains. In conclusion, this review article provides valuable insights into the evolving landscape of MAT and HTM research, offering a foundation for researchers, scholars and practitioners to deepen their understanding, pursue innovative research avenues and contribute to advancing knowledge in these dynamic fields.

Despite its contributions, this review acknowledges limitations such as its focus on English-language peer-reviewed journals and exclusion of conferences and non-English publications. Future researchers should focus on exploring the under-researched areas of 'shopfloor' operations and 'inventory control,' which currently have minimal publications (0% and 2%). Additionally, integrating AI with MAT remains a significant gap that warrants investigation. Researchers should also analyze the factors contributing to the recent increase in research trends over the past three years, aiming to develop more comprehensive classification schemes for MAT applications in HTM.

REFERENCES

Ameri, F., & McArthur, C. (2013). A multi-agent system for autonomous supply chain configuration. *International Journal of Advanced Manufacturing Technology*, *66*(5–8), 1097–1112. https://doi.org/10.1007/s00170-012-4392-9

Ansari, F., Glawar, R., & Nemeth, T. (2019). PriMa: A prescriptive maintenance model for cyber-physical production systems. *International Journal of Computer Integrated Manufacturing*, *32*(4–5), 482–503. https://doi.org/10.1080/0951192X.2019.1571236

Atkinson, P., Hizaji, M., Nazarian, A., & Abasi, A. (2022). Attaining organisational agility through competitive intelligence: The roles of strategic flexibility and organisational innovation. *Total*

Quality Management and Business Excellence, *33*(3–4), 297–317. https://doi.org/10.1080/14783363.2020.1842188

Ayhan, M. B., Aydin, M. E., & Öztemel, E. (2015). A multi-agent based approach for change management in manufacturing enterprises. *Journal of Intelligent Manufacturing*, *26*(5), 975–988. https://doi.org/10.1007/s10845-013-0794-2

Bahrpeyma, F., & Reichelt, D. (2022). A review of the applications of multi-agent reinforcement learning in smart factories. In *Frontiers in robotics and AI* (Vol. 9). Frontiers Media S.A. https://doi.org/10.3389/frobt.2022.1027340

Baykasoglu, A., & Gorkemli, L. (2017). Dynamic virtual cellular manufacturing through agent-based modelling. *International Journal of Computer Integrated Manufacturing*, *30*(6), 564–579. https://doi.org/10.1080/0951192X.2016.1187294

Belhadi, A., Kamble, S., Fosso Wamba, S., & Queiroz, M. M. (2022). Building supply-chain resilience: An artificial intelligence-based technique and decision-making framework. *International Journal of Production Research*, *60*(14), 4487–4507. https://doi.org/10.1080/00207543.2021.1950935

Borés, C., Saurina, C., & Torres, R. (2003). Technological convergence: A strategic perspective. *Technovation*, *23*(1), 1–13. https://doi.org/10.1016/S0166-4972(01)00094-3

Brundage, M. P., Sexton, T., Hodkiewicz, M., Morris, K. C., Arinez, J., Ameri, F., Ni, J., & Xiao, G. (2019). Where do we start? Guidance for technology implementation in maintenance management for manufacturing. *Journal of Manufacturing Science and Engineering, Transactions of the ASME*, *141*(9). https://doi.org/10.1115/1.4044105

Campos, J. (2009). Development in the application of ICT in condition monitoring and maintenance. *Computers in Industry*, *60*(1), 1–20. https://doi.org/10.1016/j.compind.2008.09.007

Chen, D. (2015). We have never been latecomers: A critical review of high-tech industry and social studies of technology in Taiwan. *East Asian Science, Technology and Society: An International Journal*, *9*(4), 381–396. https://doi.org/10.1215/18752160-3142998

Chen, X., Liu, Z., & Zhu, Q. (2018). Performance evaluation of China's high-tech innovation process: Analysis based on the innovation value chain. *Technovation*, *74–75*, 42–53. https://doi.org/10.1016/j.technovation.2018.02.009

Chien, T. H., Lin, Y. I., & Tien, K. W. (2013). Agent-based negotiation mechanism for multi-project human resource allocation. *Journal of Industrial and Production Engineering*, *30*(8), 518–527. https://doi.org/10.1080/21681015.2013.861521

Choi, C., Nakka, Y. K., Rahmani, A., & Chung, S. J. (2023, March). Resilient multi-agent collaborative spacecraft inspection. In *IEEE aerospace conference proceedings*. https://doi.org/10.1109/AERO55745.2023.10115886

Chu, W., Li, Y., Liu, C., Mou, W., & Tang, L. (2016). Collaborative manufacturing of aircraft structural parts based on machining features and software agents. *International Journal of Advanced Manufacturing Technology*, *87*(5–8), 1421–1434. https://doi.org/10.1007/s00170-013-4976-z

Czimmermann, T., Chiurazzi, M., Milazzo, M., Roccella, S., Barbieri, M., Dario, P., Oddo, C. M., & Ciuti, G. (2022). An autonomous robotic platform for manipulation and inspection of metallic surfaces in Industry 4.0. *IEEE Transactions on Automation Science and Engineering*, *19*(3), 1691–1706. https://doi.org/10.1109/TASE.2021.3122820

Dhokia, V., Essink, W. P., & Flynn, J. M. (2017). A generative multi-agent design methodology for additively manufactured parts inspired by termite nest building. *CIRP Annals - Manufacturing Technology*, *66*(1), 153–156. https://doi.org/10.1016/j.cirp.2017.04.039

Dittrich, M. A., & Fohlmeister, S. (2020). Cooperative multi-agent system for production control using reinforcement learning. *CIRP Annals*, *69*(1), 389–392. https://doi.org/10.1016/j.cirp.2020.04.005

Dostatni, E., Diakun, J., Grajewski, D., Wichniarek, R., & Karwasz, A. (2016). Multi-agent system to support decision-making process in design for recycling. *Soft Computing*, *20*(11), 4347–4361. https://doi.org/10.1007/s00500-016-2302-z

Du, J., Jing, H., Choo, K.-K. R., Sugumaran, V., & Castro-Lacouture, D. (2020). An ontology and multi-agent based decision support framework for prefabricated component supply chain. *Information Systems Frontiers*, *22*(6), 1467–1485. https://doi.org/10.1007/s10796-019-09941-x

Eriksson, T., Bigi, A., & Bonera, M. (2020). Think with me, or think for me? On the future role of artificial intelligence in marketing strategy formulation. *TQM Journal*, *32*(4), 795–814. https://doi.org/10.1108/TQM-12-2019-0303

Fang, J., Huang, G. Q., & Li, Z. (2013). Event-driven multi-agent ubiquitous manufacturing execution platform for shop floor work-in-progress management. *International Journal of Production Research*, *51*(4), 1168–1185. https://doi.org/10.1080/00207543.2012.693644

Feizabadi, J. (2022). Machine learning demand forecasting and supply chain performance. *International Journal of Logistics Research and Applications*, *25*(2), 119–142. https://doi.org/10.1080/13675567.2020.1803246

Feng, F., Pang, Y., Lodewijks, G., & Li, W. (2017). Collaborative framework of an intelligent agent system for efficient logistics transport planning. *Computers & Industrial Engineering*, *112*, 551–567. https://doi.org/10.1016/j.cie.2016.12.044

Feng, Y., Akram, R., Hieu, V. M., & Tien, N. H. (2022). The impact of corporate social responsibility on the sustainable financial performance of Italian firms: Mediating role of firm reputation. *Economic Research-Ekonomska Istrazivanja*, *35*(1), 4740–4758. https://doi.org/10.1080/1331677X.2021.2017318

Ferreira, W. d. P., Armellini, F., Santa-Eulalia, L. A. d., & Thomasset-Laperrière, V. (2022). Extending the lean value stream mapping to the context of Industry 4.0: An agent-based technology approach. *Journal of Manufacturing Systems*, *63*, 1–14. https://doi.org/10.1016/j.jmsy.2022.02.002

Ghadimi, P., Wang, C., Lim, M. K., & Heavey, C. (2019). Intelligent sustainable supplier selection using multi-agent technology: Theory and application for Industry 4.0 supply chains. *Computers & Industrial Engineering*, *127*, 588–600. https://doi.org/10.1016/j.cie.2018.10.050

Giannakis, M., & Louis, M. (2016). A multi-agent based system with big data processing for enhanced supply chain agility. *Journal of Enterprise Information Management*, *29*(5), 706–727. https://doi.org/10.1108/JEIM-06-2015-0050

Giret, A., Trentesaux, D., Salido, M. A., Garcia, E., & Adam, E. (2017). A holonic multi-agent methodology to design sustainable intelligent manufacturing control systems. *Journal of Cleaner Production*, *167*, 1370–1386. https://doi.org/10.1016/j.jclepro.2017.03.079

Guan, J., & Chen, K. (2010). Measuring the innovation production process: A cross-region empirical study of China's high-tech innovations. *Technovation*, *30*(5–6), 348–358. https://doi.org/10.1016/j.technovation.2010.02.001

Hanga, K. M., & Kovalchuk, Y. (2019). Machine learning and multi-agent systems in oil and gas industry applications: A survey. In *Computer science review* (Vol. 34). Elsevier Ireland Ltd. https://doi.org/10.1016/j.cosrev.2019.08.002

Hedjazi, D., Layachi, F., & Boubiche, D. E. (2019). A multi-agent system for distributed maintenance scheduling. *Computers & Electrical Engineering*, *77*, 1–11. https://doi.org/10.1016/j.compeleceng.2019.04.016

Huang, H.-H. (2002). Autonomous behaviour in automated manufacturing systems. *International Journal of Advanced Manufacturing Technology*, *20*, 381–389.

Huang, Y. C., & Wu, Y. C. J. (2010). The effects of organizational factors on green new product success: Evidence from high-tech industries in Taiwan. *Management Decision*, *48*(10), 1539–1567. https://doi.org/10.1108/00251741011090324

Huang, Z., Kim, J., Sadri, A., Dowey, S., & Dargusch, M. S. (2019). Industry 4.0: Development of a multi-agent system for dynamic value stream mapping in SMEs. *Journal of Manufacturing Systems*, *52*, 1–12. https://doi.org/10.1016/j.jmsy.2019.05.001

Hung, R. Y. Y., Lien, B. Y. H., Yang, B., Wu, C. M., & Kuo, Y. M. (2011). Impact of TQM and organizational learning on innovation performance in the high-tech industry. *International Business Review*, *20*(2), 213–225. https://doi.org/10.1016/j.ibusrev.2010.07.001

Imiru, G. A. (2022). Determinants of multinational companies' choice of market-entry mode for operating in Ethiopia: An empirical study. *European Journal of Management and Marketing Studies*, *7*(4). https://doi.org/10.46827/ejmms.v7i4.1296

Jahani, A., Azmi Murad, M. A., bin Sulaiman, M. N., & Selamat, M. H. (2015). An agent-based supplier selection framework: Fuzzy case-based reasoning perspective. *Strategic Outsourcing*, *8*(2–3), 180–205. https://doi.org/10.1108/SO-01-2015-0003

Jana, T. K., Bairagi, B., Paul, S., Sarkar, B., & Saha, J. (2013). Dynamic schedule execution in an agent based holonic manufacturing system. *Journal of Manufacturing Systems*, *32*(4), 801–816. https://doi.org/10.1016/j.jmsy.2013.07.004

Jang, H., Lee, S., & Suh, E. (2016). A comparative analysis of the change in R& D efficiency: A case of R& D leaders in the technology industry. *Technology Analysis & Strategic Management*, *28*(8), 886–900. https://doi.org/10.1080/09537325.2016.1180354

Jennings, N. R., & Wooldridge, M. (1998a). A roadmap of agent research and development. *Autonomous Agents and Multi-Agent Systems*, *1*, 7–38.

Jennings, N. R., & Wooldridge, M. J. (1998b). *Agent technology: Foundations, applications and markets*. Springer.

Jian, G., Gao, J., & Wang, Y. (2010). A multi-agent based knowledge search framework to support the product development process. *International Journal of Computer Integrated Manufacturing*, *23*(3), 237–247. https://doi.org/10.1080/09511920903529222

Joo, J., Kim, J., Yang, S. M., Park, H. W., & Kim, D. Y. (2024). Tool wear evolution and chip formation of the Ti-6Al-4V end milling under cryogenic cooling and minimum quantity lubrication conditions. *International Journal of Advanced Manufacturing Technology*, *130*(1–2). https://doi.org/10.1007/s00170-023-12704-3

Jules, G., & Saadat, M. (2016). Agent cooperation mechanism for decentralized manufacturing scheduling. *IEEE Transactions on Systems, Man, and Cybernetics: Systems*, *47*(12), 3351–3362. https://doi.org/10.1109/tsmc.2016.2578879

Jun, H.-B. (2022). A review on the advanced maintenance approach for achieving the zero-defect manufacturing system. *Frontiers in Manufacturing Technology*, *2*. https://doi.org/10.3389/fmtec.2022.920900

Kano, M., & Nakagawa, Y. (2008). Data-based process monitoring, process control, and quality improvement: Recent developments and applications in steel industry. *Computers & Chemical Engineering*, *32*(1–2), 12–24. https://doi.org/10.1016/j.compchemeng.2007.07.005

Kaplanoğlu, V. (2014). Multi-agent based approach for single machine scheduling with sequence-dependent setup times and machine maintenance. *Applied Soft Computing Journal*, *23*, 165–179. https://doi.org/10.1016/j.asoc.2014.06.020

Kim, B., Kim, J. G., & Lee, S. (2023). A multi-agent reinforcement learning model for inventory transshipments under supply chain disruption. *IISE Transactions*, 1–14. https://doi.org/10.1080/24725854.2023.2217248

Kim, C. O., Kwon, I. H., & Kwak, C. (2010). Multi-agent based distributed inventory control model. *Expert Systems with Applications*, *37*(7). https://doi.org/10.1016/j.eswa.2009.12.073

Koch, A. J. (n.d.). *Factors influencing market and entry mode selection: Developing the MEMS model*. https://www.emerald.com/insight

Koren, Y. (2000). Reconfigurable manufacturing systems: Key to future manufacturing. *Journal of Intelligent Manufacturing*, *11*(4), 403–419.

Kovalenko, I., Tilbury, D., & Barton, K. (2019). The model-based product agent: A control oriented architecture for intelligent products in multi-agent manufacturing systems. *Control Engineering Practice*, *86*, 105–117. https://doi.org/10.1016/j.conengprac.2019.03.009

Kumar, R., Singh, K., & Jain, S. K. (2023). A tactical three-phase implementation model for agile manufacturing. *International Journal of Business Excellence*, *30*(3), 383–412. https://doi.org/10.1504/IJBEX.2023.132639

Kumari, S., Singh, A., Mishra, N., & Garza-Reyes, J. A. (2015). A multi-agent architecture for outsourcing SMEs manufacturing supply chain. *Robotics and Computer-Integrated Manufacturing*, *36*, 36–44. https://doi.org/10.1016/j.rcim.2014.12.009

Lanza, G., Ferdows, K., Kara, S., Mourtzis, D., Schuh, G., Váncza, J., Wang, L., & Wiendahl, H. P. (2019). Global production networks: Design and operation. *CIRP Annals*, *68*(2), 823–841. https://doi.org/10.1016/j.cirp.2019.05.008

Law, K. M. Y., & Gunasekaran, A. (2012). Sustainability development in high-tech manufacturing firms in Hong Kong: Motivators and readiness. *International Journal of Production Economics*, *137*(1), 116–125. https://doi.org/10.1016/j.ijpe.2012.01.022

Lee, J., Ni, J., Singh, J., Jiang, B., Azamfar, M., & Feng, J. (2020). Intelligent maintenance systems and predictive manufacturing. *Journal of Manufacturing Science and Engineering, Transactions of the ASME*, *142*(11). https://doi.org/10.1115/1.4047856

Legler, H., & Krawczyk, O. (2006). *The global distribution of R&D activities*. Springer.

Leitão, P., Colombo, A. W., & Karnouskos, S. (2016). Industrial automation based on cyber-physical systems technologies: Prototype implementations and challenges. *Computers in Industry*, *81*, 11–25. https://doi.org/10.1016/j.compind.2015.08.004

Leng, J., Sha, W., Lin, Z., Jing, J., Liu, Q., & Chen, X. (2023). Blockchained smart contract pyramid-driven multi-agent autonomous process control for resilient individualised manufacturing towards Industry 5.0. *International Journal of Production Research*, *61*(13). https://doi.org/10.1080/00207543.2022.2089929

Li, K. S., & Xiong, Y. Q. (2022). Host country's environmental uncertainty, technological capability, and foreign market entry mode: Evidence from high-end equipment manufacturing MNEs in emerging markets. *International Business Review*, *31*(1). https://doi.org/10.1016/j.ibusrev.2021.101900

Li, K., Zhou, T., Liu, B. h., & Li, H. (2018). A multi-agent system for sharing distributed manufacturing resources. *Expert Systems with Applications*, *99*, 32–43. https://doi.org/10.1016/j.eswa.2018.01.027

Lin, H. F., & Lee, G. G. (2005). Impact of organizational learning and knowledge management factors on e-business adoption. *Management Decision*, *43*(2). https://doi.org/10.1108/00251740510581902

Liu, P. L. (2011). Empirical study on influence of critical success factors on ERP knowledge management on management performance in high-tech industries in Taiwan. *Expert Systems with Applications*, *38*(8), 10696–10704. https://doi.org/10.1016/j.eswa.2011.02.045

Liu, C., Li, Y., & Shen, W. (2014). Integrated manufacturing process planning and control based on intelligent agents and multi-dimension features. *International Journal of Advanced Manufacturing Technology*, *75*(9–12), 1457–1471. https://doi.org/10.1007/s00170-014-6246-0

Liu, Y., Liu, J., He, Z., Li, Z., Zhang, Q., & Ding, Z. (2023). A survey of multi-agent systems on distributed formation control. *Unmanned Systems*, 1–14. https://doi.org/10.1142/s2301385024500274

Long, Q., Lin, J., & Sun, Z. (2011). Modeling and distributed simulation of supply chain with a multi-agent platform. *International Journal of Advanced Manufacturing Technology*, *55*(9–12), 1241–1252. https://doi.org/10.1007/s00170-010-3148-7

López, A., Casquero, O., Estévez, E., Armentia, A., Orive, D., & Marcos, M. (2023). An industrial agent-based customizable platform for I4.0 manufacturing systems. *Computers in Industry*, *146*. https://doi.org/10.1016/j.compind.2023.103859

Lorenz, A., Raven, M., & Blind, K. (2019). The role of standardization at the interface of product and process development in biotechnology. *The Journal of Technology Transfer*, *44*, 1097–1133. https://doi.org/10.1007/s10961-017-9644-2

Lou, P., Liu, Q., Zhou, Z., Wang, H., & Sun, S. X. (2012). Multi-agent-based proactive-reactive scheduling for a job shop. *International Journal of Advanced Manufacturing Technology*, *59*(1–4), 311–324. https://doi.org/10.1007/s00170-011-3482-4

Lu, Y., Xu, X., & Wang, L. (2020). Smart manufacturing process and system automation – a critical review of the standards and envisioned scenarios. *Journal of Manufacturing Systems*, *56*, 312–325. https://doi.org/10.1016/j.jmsy.2020.06.010

MA, J. (2015). A two-stage DEA model considering shared inputs and free intermediate measures. *Expert Systems with Applications*, *42*(9), 4339–4347. https://doi.org/10.1016/j.eswa.2015.01.040

Mangla, S. K., Kumar, P., & Barua, M. K. (2015). Risk analysis in green supply chain using fuzzy AHP approach: A case study. *Resources, Conservation and Recycling*, *104*, 375–390. https://doi.org/10.1016/j.resconrec.2015.01.001

Merdan, M., Vallee, M., Lepuschitz, W., & Zoitl, A. (2011). Monitoring and diagnostics of industrial systems using automation agents. *International Journal of Production Research*, *49*(5), 1497–1509. https://doi.org/10.1080/00207543.2010.526368

Mishra, N., Singh, A., Kumari, S., Govindan, K., & Ali, S. I. (2016). Cloud-based multi-agent architecture for effective planning and scheduling of distributed manufacturing. *International Journal of Production Research*, *54*(23), 7115–7128. https://doi.org/10.1080/00207543.2016.1165359

Mubeen, R., Han, D., Abbas, J., & Hussain, I. (2020). The effects of market competition, capital structure, and CEO duality on firm performance: A mediation analysis by incorporating the GMM model technique. *Sustainability*, *12*(8). https://doi.org/10.3390/SU12083480

Ngai, E. W. T., Chau, D. C. K., Poon, J. K. L., Chan, A. Y. M., Chan, B. C. M., & Wu, W. W. S. (2012). Implementing an RFID-based manufacturing process management system: Lessons learned and success factors. *Journal of Engineering and Technology Management*, *29*(1), 112–130. https://doi.org/10.1016/j.jengtecman.2011.09.009

Nie, Q., Tang, D., Liu, C., Wang, L., & Song, J. (2023). A multi-agent and cloud-edge orchestration framework of digital twin for distributed production control. *Robotics and Computer-Integrated Manufacturing*, *82*. https://doi.org/10.1016/j.rcim.2023.102543

Nie, Q., Tang, D., Zhu, H., & Sun, H. (2022). A multi-agent and internet of things framework of digital twin for optimized manufacturing control. *International Journal of Computer Integrated Manufacturing*, *35*(10–11), 1205–1226. https://doi.org/10.1080/0951192X.2021.2004619

Oh, K. K., Park, M. C., & Ahn, H. S. (2015). A survey of multi-agent formation control. *Automatica*, *53*, 424–440. https://doi.org/10.1016/j.automatica.2014.10.022

Pal, M., Mittal, M. l., Soni, G., & Chouhan, S. S. (2023). A multi-agent system for integrated scheduling and maintenance planning of the flexible job shop. *Computers & Operations Research*, *159*, 106365. https://doi.org/10.1016/j.cor.2023.106365

Pansare, R., Yadav, G., & Nagare, M. R. (2023). Reconfigurable manufacturing system: A systematic review, meta-analysis and future research directions. *Journal of Engineering, Design and Technology*, *21*(1), 228–265. https://doi.org/10.1108/JEDT-05-2021-0231

Papadopoulos, N., Chen, H., & Thomas, D. R. (2002). Toward a tradeoff model for international market selection. *International Business Review*, *11*, 165–192. www.elsevier.com/locate/ibusrev

Park, H. S., Cho, H., & Kim, H. S. (2016). Development of a multi-agent M-health application based on various protocols for chronic disease self-management. *Journal of Medical Systems*, *40*(1). https://doi.org/10.1007/s10916-015-0401-5

Peng, Y., Dong, M., & Zuo, M. J. (2010). Current status of machine prognostics in condition-based maintenance: A review. *International Journal of Advanced Manufacturing Technology*, *50*(1–4), 297–313. https://doi.org/10.1007/s00170-009-2482-0

Pino, R., Fernández, I., de la Fuente, D., Parreño, J., & Priore, P. (2010). Supply chain modelling using a multi-agent system. *Journal of Advances in Management Research*, *7*(2), 149–162. https://doi.org/10.1108/09727981011084968

Priego, R., Iriondo, N., Gangoiti, U., & Marcos, M. (2017). Agent-based middleware architecture for reconfigurable manufacturing systems. *International Journal of Advanced Manufacturing Technology*, *92*(5–8), 1579–1590. https://doi.org/10.1007/s00170-017-0154-z

Pulikottil, T., Estrada-Jimenez, L. A., Rehman, H. U., Barata, J., Nikghadam-Hojjati, S., & Zarzycki, L. (2021, September). Multi-agent based manufacturing: Current trends and challenges. In *IEEE international conference on emerging technologies and factory automation, ETFA*. https://doi.org/10.1109/ETFA45728.2021.9613555

Rana, S., Prashar, S., Barai, M. K., & Hamid, A. B. A. (2021). Determinants of international marketing strategy for emerging market multinationals. *International Journal of Emerging Markets*, *16*(2), 154–178. https://doi.org/10.1108/IJOEM-09-2019-0742

Rasheed, A. A. A., Abdullah, M. N., & Al-Araji, A. S. (2022). A review of multi-agent mobile robot systems applications. *International Journal of Electrical and Computer Engineering*, *12*(4), 3517–3529. https://doi.org/10.11591/ijece.v12i4.pp3517-3529

Rezki, N., Kazar, O., Mouss, L. H., Kahloul, L., & Rezki, D. (2016). On the use of multi-agent systems for the monitoring of industrial systems. *Journal of Industrial Engineering International*, *12*(1), 111–118. https://doi.org/10.1007/s40092-015-0133-7

Rochiyati, M., Herning, I., & Jati, K. (2022). Information accessibility and market responsiveness: The mediating relational capability to enhance business performance. *Studies in Business and Economics*, *17*(1), 41–51. https://doi.org/10.2478/sbe-2022-0003

Rodríguez, M. L. R., Kubler, S., de Giorgio, A., Cordy, M., Robert, J., & Traon, Y. L. (2022). Multi-agent deep reinforcement learning based Predictive Maintenance on parallel machines. *Robotics and Computer-Integrated Manufacturing*, *78*. https://doi.org/10.1016/j.rcim.2022.102406

Rokhforoz, P., Gjorgiev, B., Sansavini, G., & Fink, O. (2021). Multi-agent maintenance scheduling based on the coordination between central operator and decentralized producers in an electricity market. *Reliability Engineering & System Safety*, *210*. https://doi.org/10.1016/j.ress.2021.107495

Rolón, M., & Martínez, E. (2012). Agent-based modeling and simulation of an autonomic manufacturing execution system. *Computers in Industry*, *63*(1), 53–78. https://doi.org/10.1016/j.compind.2011.10.005

Saeidlou, S., Saadat, M., Amini Sharifi, E., & Jules, G. D. (2019). Agent-based distributed manufacturing scheduling: An ontological approach. *Cogent Engineering*, *6*(1), 1–23. https://doi.org/10.1080/23311916.2019.1565630

Sahadev, S., & Jayachandran, S. (2004). Managing the distribution channels for high-technology products: A behavioural approach. *European Journal of Marketing*, *38*(1–2), 121–149. https://doi.org/10.1108/03090560410511159

Sahebjamnia, N., Tavakkoli-Moghaddam, R., & Ghorbani, N. (2016). Designing a fuzzy Q-learning multi-agent quality control system for a continuous chemical production line – A case study. *Computers & Industrial Engineering*, *93*, 215–226. https://doi.org/10.1016/j.cie.2016.01.004

Sahin, C., Demirtas, M., Erol, R., Baykasoğlu, A., & Kaplanoğlu, V. (2017). A multi-agent based approach to dynamic scheduling with flexible processing capabilities. *Journal of Intelligent Manufacturing*, *28*(8), 1827–1845. https://doi.org/10.1007/s10845-015-1069-x

Sahnoun, M., Baudry, D., Mustafee, N., Louis, A., Smart, P. A., Godsiff, P., & Mazari, B. (2019). Modelling and simulation of operation and maintenance strategy for offshore wind farms based on multi-agent system. *Journal of Intelligent Manufacturing*, *30*(8), 2981–2997. https://doi.org/10.1007/s10845-015-1171-0

Schellenberg, M., Harker, M. J., & Jafari, A. (2018). International market entry mode–a systematic literature review. *Journal of Strategic Marketing*, *26*(7), 601–627. https://doi.org/10.1080/0965254X.2017.1339114

Scrimieri, D., Afazov, S. M., & Ratchev, S. M. (2021). Design of a self-learning multi-agent framework for the adaptation of modular production systems. *International Journal of Advanced Manufacturing Technology*, *115*(5–6), 1745–1761. https://doi.org/10.1007/s00170-021-07028-z

Sharma, A., & Sharma, S. K. (2022). Analyzing the role of multiagent technology in preventing airplane crash using AHP and DEMATEL approach. *International Journal of Crashworthiness*, *27*(6), 1753–1769. https://doi.org/10.1080/13588265.2021.2008739

Sharma, M., Raut, R. D., Sehrawat, R., & Ishizaka, A. (2023). Digitalisation of manufacturing operations: The influential role of organisational, social, environmental, and technological impediments. *Expert Systems with Applications*, *211*, 118501. https://doi.org/10.1016/j.eswa.2022.118501

Sharma, S. K., Vishwakarma, S., & Jha, N. (2017). Prognosis agent technology: Influence on manufacturing organizations. *International Journal of Advanced Manufacturing Technology*, *92*(1–4), 435–446. https://doi.org/10.1007/s00170-017-0025-7

Shavandi, A., & Khedmati, M. (2022). A multi-agent deep reinforcement learning framework for algorithmic trading in financial markets. *Expert Systems with Applications*, *208*. https://doi.org/10.1016/j.eswa.2022.118124

Shukla, N., & Kiridena, S. (2016). A fuzzy rough sets-based multi-agent analytics framework for dynamic supply chain configuration. *International Journal of Production Research*, *54*(23), 6984–6996. https://doi.org/10.1080/00207543.2016.1151567

Shukla, O. J., Joshi, A., Soni, G., & Kumar, R. (2019). Analysis of critical drivers affecting implementation of agent technology in a manufacturing system. *Journal of Industrial Engineering International*, *15*(2), 303–313. https://doi.org/10.1007/s40092-018-0293-3

Shukla, O. J., Soni, G., Kumar, R., & Ahluwalia, R. S. (2020). A review of multi agent-based production scheduling in manufacturing system. *Recent Patents on Engineering*, *15*(5). https://doi.org/10.2174/1872212114999200423112955

Singh, V., & Sharma, S. K. (2023a). Applying hybrid approach of AHP, DEMATEL, and TOPSIS to study the impact of multiagent technology on the performance of manufacturing organizations. In *IEEE transactions on engineering management*. https://doi.org/10.1109/TEM.2023.3293948

Singh, V., & Sharma, S. K. (2023b). Critical factors of multi-agent technology influencing manufacturing organizations: An AHP and DEMATEL-oriented analysis. *International Journal of Computer Integrated Manufacturing*. https://doi.org/10.1080/0951192X.2023.2209857

Soria Zurita, N. F., Colby, M. K., Tumer, I. Y., Hoyle, C., & Tumer, K. (2018). Design of complex engineered systems using multi-agent coordination. *Journal of Computing and Information Science in Engineering*, *18*(1). https://doi.org/10.1115/1.4038158

Stornelli, A., Ozcan, S., & Simms, C. (2021). Advanced manufacturing technology adoption and innovation: A systematic literature review on barriers, enablers, and innovation types. *Research Policy*, *50*(6). https://doi.org/10.1016/j.respol.2021.104229

Sun, J., Zhang, Y. F., & Nee, A. Y. C. (2001). A distributed multi-agent environment for product design and manufacturing planning. *International Journal of Production Research*, *39*(4), 625–645. https://doi.org/10.1080/00207540010004340

Tang, H., Li, D., Wan, J., Imran, M., & Shoaib, M. (2020). A reconfigurable method for intelligent manufacturing based on industrial cloud and edge intelligence. *IEEE Internet of Things Journal*, *7*(5), 4248–4259. https://doi.org/10.1109/JIOT.2019.2950048

Tortora, A. M. R., Di Pasquale, V., Franciosi, C., Miranda, S., & Iannone, R. (2021). The role of maintenance operator in industrial manufacturing systems: Research topics and trends. *Applied Sciences*, *11*(7). https://doi.org/10.3390/app11073193

UNCTAD. (2023a). *Catching technological waves innovation with equity*. UNCTAD.

UNCTAD. (2023b). *Technology and Innovation Report 2023*. UNCTAD. https://shop.un.org/

United Nations, Statistical Division. (2008). *International Standard industrial classification of all economic activities (ISIC)*. United Nations.

Upadhyay, D. B. (2014). A review paper on Multi agent base intelligent manufacturing system. *International Journal of Advanced Engineering Research and Science*, *1*(3).

Upasani, K., Bakshi, M., Pandhare, V., & Lad, B. K. (2017). Distributed maintenance planning in manufacturing industries. *Computers & Industrial Engineering*, *108*, 1–14. https://doi.org/10.1016/j.cie.2017.03.027

Verma, P., Kumar, S., & Sharma, S. K. (2022). Evaluating the total quality and its role in measuring consumer satisfaction with e-healthcare services using the 5Qs model: A structure equation modeling approach. *Benchmarking: An International Journal*, *29*(1), 22–46. https://doi.org/10.1108/BIJ-09-2020-0467

Viswanathan, S. K., & Jha, K. N. (2019). Factors influencing international market selection for Indian construction firms. *Journal of Management in Engineering*, *35*(5). https://doi.org/10.1061/(asce)me.1943-5479.0000703

Wang, H., Tao, J., Peng, T., Brintrup, A., Kosasih, E. E., Lu, Y., Tang, R., & Hu, L. (2022). Dynamic inventory replenishment strategy for aerospace manufacturing supply chain: Combining reinforcement learning and multi-agent simulation. *International Journal of Production Research*, *60*(13). https://doi.org/10.1080/00207543.2021.2020927

Wang, X., Zhang, L., Liu, Y., Li, F., Chen, Z., Zhao, C., & Bai, T. (2022). Dynamic scheduling of tasks in cloud manufacturing with multi-agent reinforcement learning. *Journal of Manufacturing Systems*, *65*. https://doi.org/10.1016/j.jmsy.2022.08.004

Wang, Z., Hu, H., Gong, J., & Ma, X. (2018). Synchronizing production scheduling with resources allocation for precast components in a multi-agent system environment. *Journal of Manufacturing Systems*, *49*, 131–142. https://doi.org/10.1016/j.jmsy.2018.09.004

Wang, Y., Pan, J. f., Pei, R. m., Yi, B. W., & Yang, G. l. (2020). Assessing the technological innovation efficiency of China's high-tech industries with a two-stage network DEA approach. *Socio-Economic Planning Sciences*, *71*. https://doi.org/10.1016/j.seps.2020.100810

Wu, M. Y., & Weng, Y. C. (2010). A study of supplier selection factors for high-tech industries in the supply chain. *Total Quality Management and Business Excellence*, *21*(4), 391–413. https://doi.org/10.1080/14783361003606662

Wu, T., Huang, S., Blackhurst, J., Zhang, X., & Wang, S. (2013). Supply chain risk management: An agent-based simulation to study the impact of retail stockouts. *IEEE Transactions on Engineering Management*, *60*(4), 676–686. https://doi.org/10.1109/TEM.2012.2190986

Wu, W., Lu, J., & Zhang, H. (2023). A fractal-theory-based multi-agent model of the cyber physical production system for customized products. *Journal of Manufacturing Systems*, *67*. https://doi.org/10.1016/j.jmsy.2023.01.008

Xiong, J., Guo, P., Wang, Y., Meng, X., Zhang, J., Qian, L., & Yu, Z. (2023). Multi-agent deep reinforcement learning for task offloading in group distributed manufacturing systems. *Engineering Applications of Artificial Intelligence*, *118*. https://doi.org/10.1016/j.engappai.2022.105710

Yahouni, Z., Ladj, A., Belkadi, F., Meski, O., & Ritou, M. (2021). A smart reporting framework as an application of multi-agent system in machining industry. *International Journal of Computer Integrated Manufacturing*, *34*(5), 470–486. https://doi.org/10.1080/0951192X.2021.1901312

Yang, H.-D., Jia-Qiang (鄂加强), E., & Ting, Q. U. (2012). Multidisciplinary design optimization for air-condition production system based on multi-agent technique. *Journal of Central South University*, *19*, 527–536. https://doi.org/10.1007/s11771-012-1036-z

Yeh, T. M., Pai, F. Y., & Yang, C. C. (2010). Performance improvement in new product development with effective tools and techniques adoption for high-tech industries. *Quality and Quantity*, *44*(1), 131–152. https://doi.org/10.1007/s11135-008-9186-7

Yin, R. (2011). Notice of Retraction: Defining standards of high, medium and low-tech industries. In *2011 2nd International conference on artificial intelligence, management science and electronic commerce (AIMSEC)* (pp. 1042–1045). https://doi.org/10.1109/AIMSEC.2011.6010741

Zahedi, M. R., Naghdi Khanachah, S., & Papoli, S. (2024). Identifying and prioritizing the factors affecting the knowledge flow in high-tech industries. *Journal of Science and Technology Policy Management*, *15*(5), 895–925. https://doi.org/10.1108/JSTPM-01-2021-0011

Zakhama, A., Charrabi, L., & Jelassi, K. (2019). Intelligent Selective Compliance Articulated Robot Arm robot with object recognition in a multi-agent manufacturing system. *International Journal of Advanced Robotic Systems*, *16*(2). https://doi.org/10.1177/1729881419841145

Zemlickienė, V. (2011). Analysis of high-technology product development models. *Intellectual Economics*, *5*(2), 283–297.

Zemlickiene, V., & Maditinos, D. I. (2012). Marketing strategy formulation for innovative product development process. *Business: Theory and Practice*, *13*(4), 365–374. https://doi.org/10.3846/btp.2012.38

Zhang, J., & Wang, X. (2016). Multi-agent-based hierarchical collaborative scheduling in re-entrant manufacturing systems. *International Journal of Production Research*, *54*(23), 7043–7059. https://doi.org/10.1080/00207543.2016.1194535

Zhang, Y., Huang, G. Q., Sun, S., & Yang, T. (2014). Multi-agent based real-time production scheduling method for radio frequency identification enabled ubiquitous shopfloor environment. *Computers & Industrial Engineering*, *76*(1), 89–97. https://doi.org/10.1016/j.cie.2014.07.011

Zhang, Y., Qian, C., Lv, J., & Liu, Y. (2017). Agent and cyber-physical system based self-organizing and self-adaptive intelligent shopfloor. *IEEE Transactions on Industrial Informatics*, *13*(2), 737–747. https://doi.org/10.1109/TII.2016.2618892

Zheng, C., Du, Y., Sun, T., Eynard, B., Zhang, Y., Li, J., & Zhang, X. (2023). Multi-agent collaborative conceptual design method for robotic manufacturing systems in small- and mid-sized enterprises. *Computers & Industrial Engineering*, *183*, 109541. https://doi.org/10.1016/j.cie.2023.109541

Zheng, P., Xia, L., Li, C., Li, X., & Liu, B. (2021). Towards Self-X cognitive manufacturing network: An industrial knowledge graph-based multi-agent reinforcement learning approach. *Journal of Manufacturing Systems*, *61*, 16–26. https://doi.org/10.1016/j.jmsy.2021.08.002

Zhong, R. Y., Xu, X., Klotz, E., & Newman, S. T. (2017). Intelligent manufacturing in the context of Industry 4.0: A review. *Engineering*, *3*(5), 616–630. https://doi.org/10.1016/J.ENG.2017.05.015

Zhou, T., Tang, D., Zhu, H., & Zhang, Z. (2021). Multi-agent reinforcement learning for online scheduling in smart factories. *Robotics and Computer-Integrated Manufacturing*, *72*. https://doi.org/10.1016/j.rcim.2021.102202

Zhu, Y. M., Alard, R., & Schoensleben, P. (2007). *Advances in production management systems* (Vol. 246, pp. 133–141). Springer. https://doi.org/10.1007/978-0-387-74157-4

Zu, X. (2009). Infrastructure and core quality management practices: How do they affect quality? *International Journal of Quality & Reliability Management*, *26*(2), 129–149. https://doi.org/10.1108/02656710910928789

Adoption of Green Banking and Finance: A Systematic Review and Future Research Directions

Anshul Jain[a], Biswajit Behera[b] and Khyati Kochhar[a]

[a]*Banasthali Vidyapith, India*
[b]*National Institute of Technology, Rourkela, India*

ABSTRACT

The objective of this chapter is to perform a systematic literature review (SLR) of the academic research on green banking and finance adoption and suggest areas of research that require further exploration. Using the POWER and Theory, Characteristics, Context and Methodology (TCCM) frameworks, the 51 relevant articles from Scopus database (2005–2023) were reviewed, with a focus on bibliometric insights and a framework-based review. The findings reveal a significant surge in publications after 2020, with India, China and Pakistan emerging as the top contributors. The stakeholder theory emerged as the most commonly applied framework for studying green banking and finance adoption intentions. The study further classified the various factors affecting the adoption of green banking under three categories: customer-related, employee-related and industry-related. Based on these insights, a comprehensive conceptual framework and substantial directions for subsequent empirical studies are proposed. The study also emphasizes the need to incorporate more environmental theories into banking sector research and calls for more extensive empirical studies to explore domain-specific services. The findings are crucial for customers, policymakers and financial institutions, aiding efforts to mitigate climate-related risks and enhance sustainability in banking sector.

Keywords: Adoption intentions; banking sector; bibliometric analysis; green banking; POWER framework; systematic literature review; TCCM framework

Reviewing the Latest Trends in Management Literature
Review of Management Literature, Volume 4B, 91–123

Published under exclusive licence by Emerald Publishing Limited
ISSN: 2754-5865/doi:10.1108/S2754-58652025000004B004

1. INTRODUCTION

Climate change is a worldwide issue affecting business operations (Iqbal et al., 2018). As concern pertaining to the environment grows, businesses are becoming more environmentally friendly to achieve Sustainable Development Goals (Akomea-Frimpong et al., 2021). The two biggest obstacles currently faced by the countries include protecting the ecosystem and mitigating the adverse impact of carbon dioxide emissions (Aslam & Jawaid, 2023a). Consequently, there has been an expansion in academic study on environmentally friendly techniques. However, most past research has primarily concentrated on the manufacturing industry while largely neglecting the service sector (Tara et al., 2019). The current state of environmental degradation has reached such a level of urgency that the financial sector must confront this problem (Aracil et al., 2021; Debrah et al., 2022). This is so because financial organizations, especially banks, assume a critical role within a nation's economic framework and fundamentally impact all forms of businesses by allocating monetary resources (Nisha et al., 2020; Sardana et al., 2014; Sarker & Rashid, 2015). Thus, banks must significantly contribute to preserving natural surroundings by incorporating environmental factors into their credit and investment guidelines and adopting green banking practices (Hang, 2022; Okyere-Kwakye & Nor, 2021).

Green banking supports mitigating climate-related damage and protects the environment through internal procedures and diverse financial goods and services (Iqbal et al., 2018; Rehman et al., 2021). The transition towards sustainable banking offers competitive advantages to financial institutions and clients (Okyere-Kwakye & Nor, 2021). Green banking reduces the carbon footprint, enables easy business transactions with minimal exertion and facilitates quick access to funds. Due to their intermediary function in absorbing and distributing surplus funds within society, banks must incorporate environmentally friendly attributes into their financing practices (Javier & Aracil, 2021). This necessitates extending financial resources towards safeguarding the environment, promoting clean energy, constructing eco-friendly buildings, addressing climate change, fostering social inclusivity and upholding corporate governance across all economic areas (Zhu et al., 2023). Previously, extensive investigations have been carried out on the subject of adopting green measures, such as green finance, within banking establishments (Ibe-enwo et al., 2019; Kumar & Prakash, 2020; Pawar & Munuswamy, 2022; Thistlethwaite, 2014). However, there is a lack of in-depth reviews addressing the perception and acceptance of green banking and finance. Moreover, the findings of these studies reveal discrepancies and multiple diversions, hindering a comprehensive understanding of the factors impacting the adoption of green banking and finance.

The prior studies regarding the adoption of green banking and finance have utilized a variety of foundational theories, demonstrating that theoretical viewpoints within this area are fragmented and still in the process of development. Consequently, synthesizing the theories and models utilized in green banking research will enhance the existing literature and promote its advancement. Moreover, the fragmented literature on green banking and finance could be addressed through a thorough examination of research within this realm and an evaluation of its present dynamics. The research study would be enhanced by integrating the variables that influence the decision to adopt green banking, the theoretical frameworks supported in the literature and the recognized sub-domains within this field. Consequently, Paul and Criado (2020) suggest conducting a systematic literature review (SLR) to integrate the growing and scattered knowledge within the domain.

Table 1 shows that prior researchers have conducted a thorough examination of sustainable banking literature using the bibliometric method, network analysis and content analysis (Agrawal et al., 2023; Akomea-Frimpong et al., 2021; Aslam & Jawaid, 2023b; Debrah et al., 2022). However, it has been noted that these reviews failed to delve into the concepts, contexts, frameworks and approaches related to understanding and accepting green banking and finance to a satisfactory extent and failed to propose a definitive direction for future researchers. Aracil et al. (2021) have undertaken a bibliometric analysis of studies related to sustainable banking. However, their research has neglected the qualitative dimension and is primarily centred on delivering quantitative metrics. Mustaffa et al. (2021), in their thematic analysis, have focused on the barriers concerning green finance while ignoring the drivers and other factors influencing green finance adoption. Moreover, a study by Aslam and Jawaid (2023b) has made a great contribution to the literature on green banking adoption. However, the present literature review diverges from their investigation, as it solely considers the facilitators of green banking adoption from the viewpoints of employees and customers and has merely addressed a limited number of pertinent theories. Additionally, their research lacks explicit future directions for the field.

Due to the limited investigation on the perception and adoption of green banking, a comprehensive evaluation of existing literature is done using the SLR technique.

Table 1. Past Literature on Green Banking and Finance.

Source	Literature Review Method	Number of Papers	Focus Research Field	Type of Papers Considered	Year Range
Akomea-Frimpong et al. (2021)	Content analysis	46	Green finance products	Only journal articles	1990–2019
Aracil et al. (2021)	Bibliometric review	676	Sustainable banking	Peer-reviewed articles	1995–2019
Mustaffa et al. (2021)	Thematic analysis	19	Green financing	Barriers in green financing	2016–2020
Debrah et al. (2022)	Systematic scoping review	28	Green buildings investment	Academic publications and policy reports	NA
Aslam and Jawaid (2023b)	Systematic review and meta-analysis	51	Green banking adoption	Only journal articles	Till April 2022
Agrawal et al. (2023)	Bibliometric and Systematic literature evolution	85	Green finance and innovation	Peer-reviewed journal articles	2016–2023

Source: The researcher's own work.

The significance of SLR lies in their ability to uncover a range of research approaches related to various aspects, such as data collection methods, sizes of samples, countries involved, and the methodologies utilized (Dhiman et al., 2023). Farrukh and Sajjad (2023) and Paul et al. (2021) indicated that numerous methods exist for undertaking SLR. However, the framework-based review suggested by Paul and Rosado-serrano (2019) has been employed in the present review. The TCCM framework utilizes literature analysis and focuses on Theory, Characteristics, Context and Methodology within the subject area. Moreover, it thoroughly examines research on important subjects, identifying areas that need further exploration (Chauhan et al., 2021; Ganti & Singhania, 2024). Throughout this course, the researcher has not encountered any studies that have effectively utilized the TCCM framework to analyze the existing literature. This study also examines the patterns of publication and identifies the most influential authors, journals, nations and affiliations in this research field through bibliometric analysis. Thus, the current study proposed two major research objectives to bridge this gap. The first objective is to understand the contribution of existing literature in the evolution of theories, contextual understanding, characteristics and research methodologies in green banking and finance. The second objective is to suggest future directions in response to the TCCM framework.

This review carries both theoretical and practical importance. Analyzing how this field has progressed over time helps researchers understand the current state of research, including the underlying theories, the geographical focus and the various domains within the subject area. This integration provides a clearer picture of where the literature stands and what gaps still exist. Moreover, based on the synthesis of the literature, the review proposes a comprehensive conceptual framework that outlines the antecedents, mediators and moderators of green banking and finance adoption intention. This framework serves as a guide for forthcoming empirical investigations, offering a systematic approach for the examination of green banking and finance adoption. The systematic review also highlights neglected areas within the green banking and finance literature. By identifying these gaps, the review encourages further exploration and research in under-researched aspects of the field, thereby advancing the academic discourse and contributing to a more complete understanding of the topic.

The subsequent sections describe the methodology used in this study, followed by a descriptive analysis showing the annual trend in publications and most prominent authors and journals. The subsequent section presents the analysis of TCCM framework-based green banking and finance literature. Finally, future research avenues are proposed, preceded by theoretical and practical implications, leading to a conclusion.

2. RESEARCH METHODOLOGY

The objective of this manuscript is to perform a SLR regarding the adoption of green banking and finance literature, pinpointing areas of research that require further exploration and suggesting potential paths for future research endeavours.

For conducting an SLR, the research study utilized the POWER framework guideline proposed by Rana et al. (2022, 2023). The POWER framework comprises five components: Planning, Operationalizing, Writing, Embedding and Reflecting, which must be considered when formulating an effective review paper.

The Planning phase underscores the necessity for authors to establish a clear understanding of the concepts, themes and theories to be addressed at the outset of the review process. The review of existing literature on green banking and finance shows that the research study in this area is fragmented, and there is a need to thoroughly identify the theoretical frameworks supported in the literature, integrate the variables that influence the decision to adopt green banking and the recognized sub-domains within this field.

The phase of operationalization places importance on gathering pertinent literature from diverse sources, eliminating duplications and determining which materials to include and which to exclude. Thus, to conduct an SLR, the exploration of literature was carried out in January 2024, utilizing the extensive Scopus database. Scopus stands out as the most extensive citation database encompassing peer-reviewed literature within the realm of social sciences (Ferreira, 2018). Furthermore, Scopus encompasses a wider array of subject areas and classifications in comparison to the Web of Science and is similar to Google Scholar in terms of comprehensiveness; it surpasses Google Scholar in the aspect of filtering out articles from predatory publications (Paul et al., 2021). Moreover, for deciding the relevant document, Fig. 1 shows the steps employed in filtering and obtaining the final set of 51 journal articles. During the phase of document screening, a variety of keywords such as 'green banking', 'sustainable banking', 'green finance', and 'sustainable finance' in conjunction with 'perception', 'intention' and 'adoption' were utilized to search for documents on Scopus, resulting in 283 documents. The choice of suitable keywords was influenced by the past literature (Aracil et al., 2021; Aslam & Jawaid, 2023b). Subsequently, specific inclusion and exclusion criteria were applied to further refine the search process. The criteria for inclusion and exclusion were derived from previous research studies (Paul et al., 2021; Paul & Rosado-serrano, 2019; Rosado-Serrano et al., 2018). Initially, the subject area was restricted to 'economics, econometrics and finance' and 'business, management and accounting', leading to 144 documents. Second, documents other than journal articles, such as editorials, conference proceedings and book chapters, were eliminated. This exclusion criterion reduced the documents to 110. Finally, only English journal articles were included as per the criteria, resulting in 108 documents. After applying these filters, 108 journal articles were retrieved and scrutinized in the next phase. During the initial screening phase, 108 documents were evaluated based on their title, abstract and keywords, resulting in the exclusion of 43 documents that did not align with the study's objective. Following this, 14 documents were eliminated from the review due to their non-empirical nature. Therefore, this systematic review examines 51 papers published from 2005 to 2023. Further, the complete textual content of each article was acquired and assessed to fulfil the objectives of this review article. The selection of 2005 as the base year is justified by the emergence of significant initiatives in the early 2000s, including the

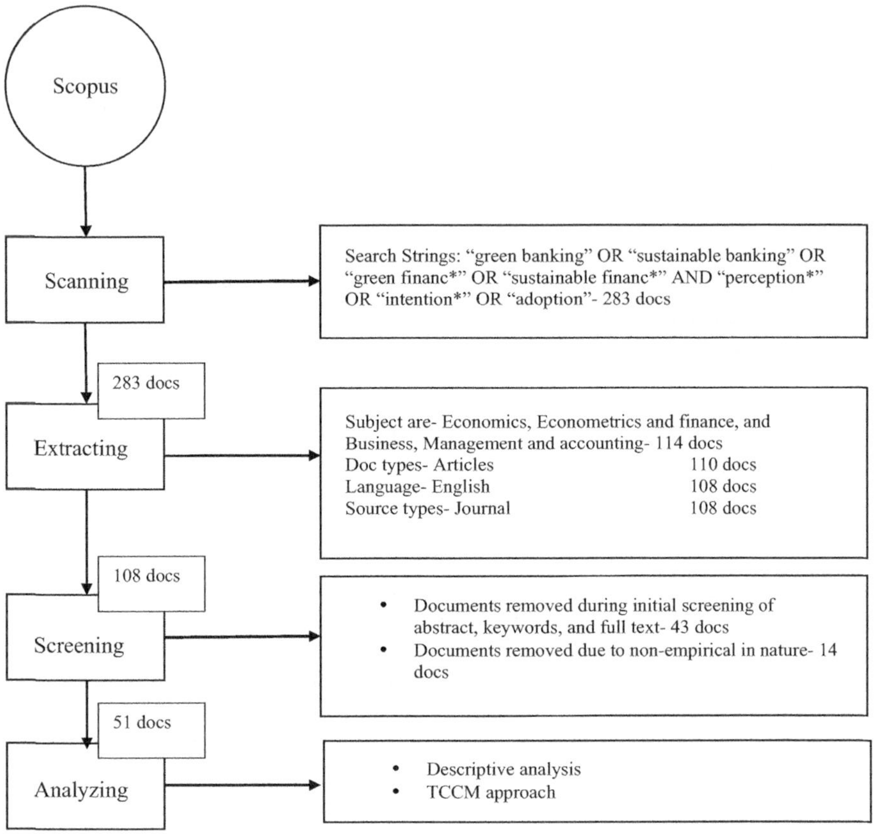

Fig. 1. Stages of Bibliometric Analysis. *Source:* The researcher's own work.

Equator Principles (2003), the revised United Nations Environment Programme Finance Initiative guidelines (2003) and the World Summit on Sustainable Development (2002). These initiatives established a framework for the incorporation of sustainability within the financial sector.

The writing phase is highly subjective and reliant on the expertise and familiarity of the authors. Therefore, to ensure that each and every aspect of the reviewed studies will be analyzed in this review paper, the authors have adopted a blend of framework-based review and bibliometric analysis to accomplish their research objectives. The systematic review is structured based on the TCCM framework, which identifies the commonly used theories (T), contexts (C), characteristics (C) and methods (M) within a particular research area (Chen et al., 2021; Rosado-Serrano et al., 2018). The TCCM framework illuminates both the theoretical and empirical dimensions of a research field, which removes the limitations of traditional systematic reviews (Chen et al., 2021). The selection of this methodology for this review was made as the synthesis of previous literature reviews in this field (see Table 1), indicating a lack of thorough exploration of the concepts, contexts, frameworks and methodologies associated with understanding and embracing green banking and finance to a satisfactory extent and a failure to propose a clear path for future researchers.

In the embedding phase, the collected documents are then thoroughly analyzed. First, a descriptive analysis of selected papers is presented, showing the annual trend in publications, most relevant sources, authors and their corresponding countries. Subsequently, the first objective is evaluated, showing a detailed analysis of papers using the TCCM framework. Lastly, future directions are suggested to accomplish the second objective of this study.

Lastly, in the reflecting phase, the implications of this study for users, policymakers and financial institutions are presented, and suggestions are made to improve the prospects of green banking and finance adoption among various stakeholders.

3. DESCRIPTIVE ANALYSIS

In this section, a descriptive analysis of the shortlisted articles for evaluation is presented. The trend of publications is discussed by considering the year of the selected studies. A bibliometric analysis highlights the most influential authors, journals and countries. Additionally, a co-occurrence analysis of keywords is performed to determine the words or phrases that are utilized most frequently.

3.1 Annual Scientific Production

Fig. 2 shows the quantity of articles disseminated within this particular domain. Despite being in its early stages of expansion, there has been a significant increase in published articles after 2020. Prior to 2019, the number of published documents

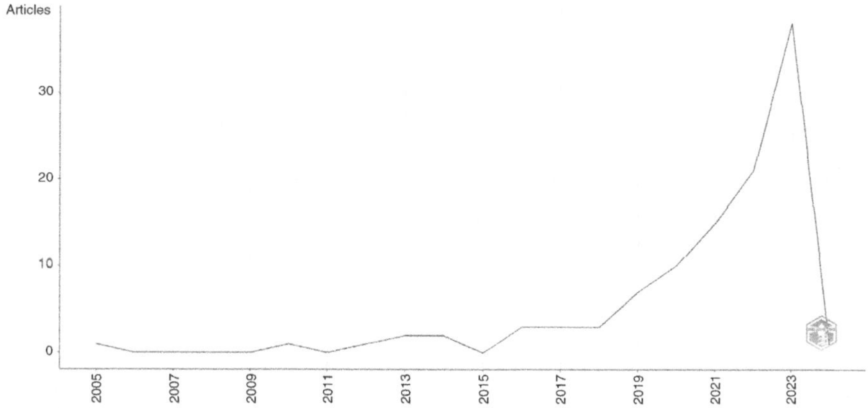

Fig. 2. Annual Trend in Publication. *Source:* The researcher's own work.

was less than 10 per year. The majority of articles were published in 2023 (36.54%), followed by 2022 (20.19%) and 2021 (14.42%). Moreover, the observed decline following 2023 does not imply that the number of publications has diminished to zero; rather, it indicates that this review has exclusively taken into account articles published up to the year 2023.

3.2 Most Relevant Sources

Fig. 3 displays the top 10 sources that have produced the most articles in the field of green banking and finance. Among the articles analyzed, the highest number ($N = 8$) were published in the 'Resources Policy' journal, followed by 'Environment, Development and Sustainability' and 'International Journal of Ethics and Systems' with five articles each.

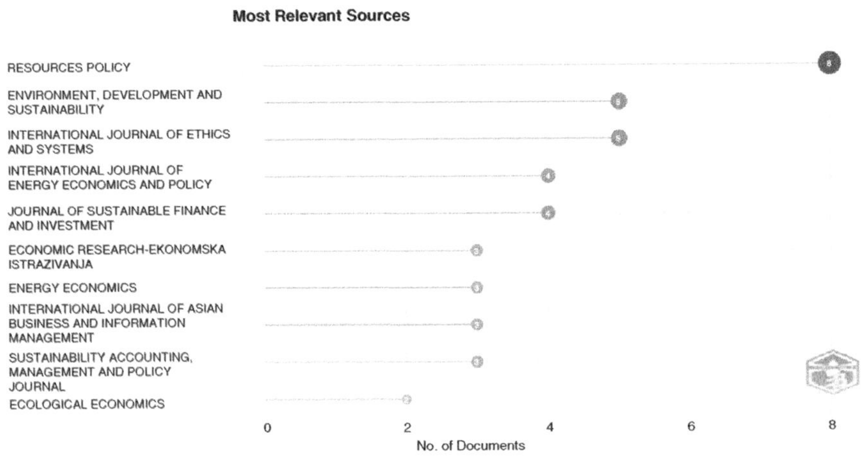

Fig. 3. Most Relevant Sources. *Source:* The researcher's own work.

3.3 Most Prominent Authors

Fig. 4 presents the publications authored by the top 10 scholars who have made significant additions to the literature on green banking and finance. Notably, Bukhari SAA and Hashim F have both contributed five publications with an article fractionalized score of 1.58. Other prominent authors in the field include Amran A ($N = 4$), Aslam W ($N = 3$), Jawaid ST ($N = 3$), Li X ($N = 3$) and Nisha N ($N = 3$).

3.4 Corresponding Author's Countries

In Fig. 5, the geographical origins of the articles authored by the researchers were indicated. The data reveal that the majority of corresponding authors were predominantly affiliated with China. India ($N = 15$), Malaysia ($N = 12$), Indonesia

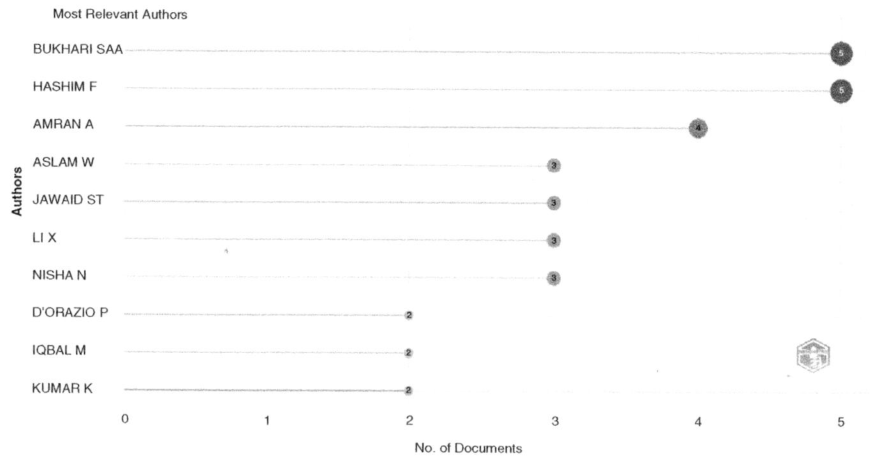

Fig. 4. Most Prominent Authors. *Source:* The researcher's own work.

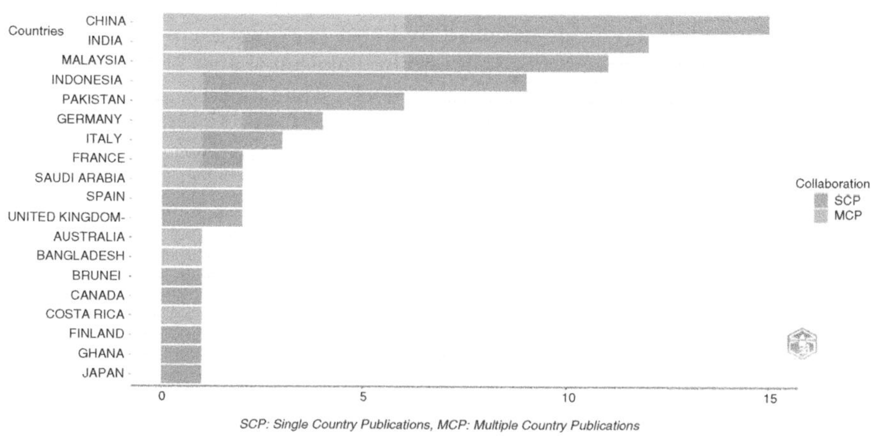

Fig. 5. Corresponding Author's Countries. *Source:* The researcher's own work.

(N = 11), and Pakistan (N = 9) were under the top five corresponding geographical origins of authors.

When the country of the corresponding author was examined, China was ranked first with a total of 25 articles (f = 0.231). As per Table 2, in China, the majority of authors wrote their articles while being affiliated with institutions in their country itself, but six studies involved collaboration between authors from different countries. It can be observed that the frequency of single-country publications is prominent across almost all countries, indicating a limited amount of collaborative work.

Table 2. List of Corresponding Author's Countries.

Country	Documents	SCP	MCP	Frequency
China	25	19	6	0.231
India	15	9	6	0.139
Malaysia	12	10	2	0.111
Indonesia	11	5	6	0.102
Pakistan	9	8	1	0.083
Germany	6	5	1	0.056
Italy	4	2	2	0.037
France	3	2	1	0.028
Saudi Arabia	2	1	1	0.019
Spain	2	0	2	0.019

Source: The researcher's own work.

Note: SCP, Single Country Publications; MCP, Multiple Country Publication.

Fig. 6 depicts the spatial distribution of all participating countries, where the top 10 participating countries are labelled in the figure. It is worth noting that India, China and Malaysia (represented by Label 1) exhibit the most substantial contributions with 40 documents, followed by Pakistan (Label 2) and Indonesia (Label 3) with 27 and 25 documents, respectively. The United States of America (Label 4) with 11 documents, Bangladesh and Italy (Label 5) with 9 documents, and Germany and Saudi Arabia (Label 6) with 8 documents.

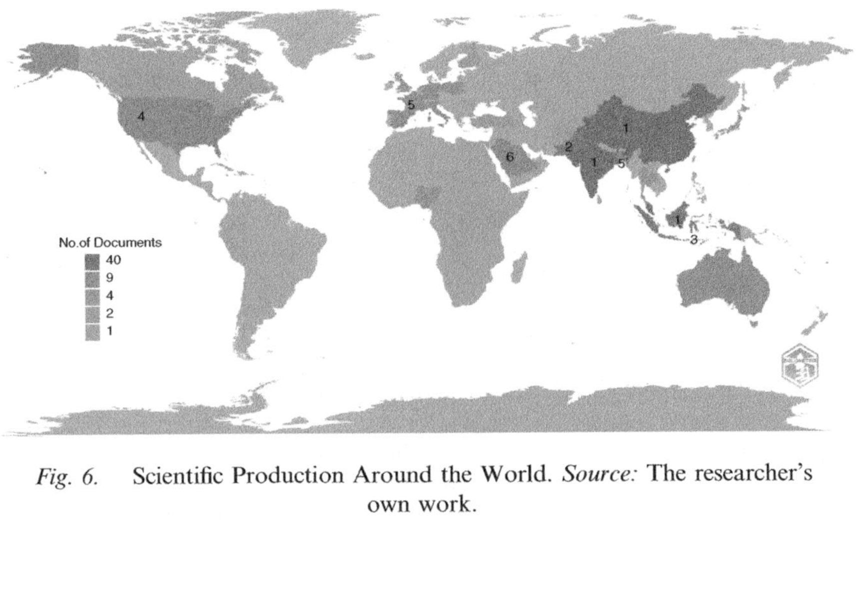

Fig. 6. Scientific Production Around the World. *Source:* The researcher's own work.

4. THEORY (T), CONTEXT (C), CHARACTERISTICS (C) AND METHODOLOGY (M) ANALYSIS

4.1 Theories (T)

As demonstrated in Table 3, numerous theories have been identified in the selected studies. A total of 27 studies have been discovered, all of which utilized at least one theory. Furthermore, this section will delve into an analysis of the prevalent theories in the field of intention and adoption of green banking and green finance.

4.1.1 Stakeholder Theory

According to stakeholder theory, any individual or entity that experiences the influence of the organization or its operations in any capacity is regarded as a stakeholder (Lin et al., 2014). These stakeholders include employees, clients, suppliers, local communities, environmental organizations, government entities and additional parties. This theory is frequently observed in research examining

Table 3. Theories Identified in the Literature.

Theory	No. of Documents	Source
Stakeholder theory	6	Nisha (2020), Bukhari et al. (2022), Pawar and Munuswamy (2022), Anis et al. (2023), Khan et al. (2023), and Saif-Alyousfi et al. (2023)
Unified theory of acceptance and use of technology	5	Rifat et al. (2016), Iqbal et al. (2018), Oseni et al. (2018), Bouteraa et al. (2022), and Chen and Zhao (2023)
Theory of planned behaviour	4	Bryson et al. (2016), Burhanudin et al. (2021), Taneja and Ali (2021), and Rasheed and Siddiqui (2022)
Legitimacy theory	3	Contreras et al. (2019), Björkholm and Lehner (2021), and Rehman et al. (2021)
Socially responsible investment theory	2	Escrig-Olmedo et al. (2013) and Rehman et al. (2021)
Technology acceptance model	2	Malik and Singh (2022) and Nisha (2020)
Resource-based view theory	2	Aslam and Jawaid (2022, 2023a)
Agency theory	1	Amidjaya and Widagdo (2020)
Trade-off theory	1	Saif-Alyousfi et al. (2023)
Theory of self-congruity	1	Bukhari et al. (2020)
Sustainability theory	1	Rehman et al. (2021)
Perceived risk theory	1	Iqbal et al. (2021)
Attractiveness theory	1	Iqbal et al. (2021)
Institutional theory	1	Dong et al. (2021)
Social identity theory	1	Rubel et al. (2020)
Self-regulation theory	1	Burhanudin et al. (2021)
Tripple bottom line theory	1	Aslam and Jawaid (2023a)
Theory of ethical decision-making	1	Bayer et al. (2019)

Source: The researcher's own work.

the adoption and intention of stakeholders towards green banking and finance. As stakeholders become more engaged, there is a growing recognition of banks' accountability for environmental degradation (Pawar & Munuswamy, 2022). Consequently, banks take necessary actions to mitigate environmental effects and contribute to a sustainable economy. Stakeholders' theory can drive green innovation in banking by exerting pressure that influences the development of greening behavior (Lin et al., 2014). Moreover, it is assumed that the expansion of sustainable banking is contingent upon the inclination and concerns of the parties involved. Stakeholders' viewpoints regarding the sustainable behaviour of banks enhance their financial reputation (Khan et al., 2023).

4.1.2 Unified Theory of Acceptance and Use of Technology (UTAUT)

Venkatesh et al. (2003) postulate that four factors (performance expectancy, effort expectancy, social influence and facilitating condition) dictate behavioural intention to utilize technology. It has wide applicability in research pertaining to emerging information technology. Earlier studies have used this model as the fundamental framework to tackle concerns that impact customers' inclination towards adopting green banking services (Bouteraa et al., 2022; Chen & Zhao, 2023; Iqbal et al., 2018; Oseni et al., 2018).

Performance expectancy, the first factor in the UTAUT model, represents how users perceive the usefulness of a technology (Venkatesh et al., 2003). If individuals perceive green banking services to align with their perceptions, they are more inclined to embrace this technology. The second significant factor, effort expectancy, elucidates the anticipated complexity of employing technologies. Considering the prominence of sustainable practices within the banking sector, the level of effort involved in their implementation becomes crucial for the parties involved. The third factor, social influence, as per Venkatesh et al. (2003), describes how much a person believes significant others in their life should use a particular technology. The concept of social influence posits that people would still employ new technologies, like green banking, even if they personally disagree with them because they think it will improve their standing in their social group. Lastly, facilitating conditions refer to the resources and technical setup that an individual perceives necessary to facilitate the adoption of a specific technology (Rifat et al., 2016). These conditions serve as a significant determinant of user adoption of environmentally friendly banking technologies, as the absence of these resources and conditions may hinder the embracing of sustainable technologies within the banking sector.

4.1.3 Theory of Planned Behaviour (TPB)

The theory of planned behaviour (TPB) model, put forth by Ajzen (1991), is widely regarded as an invaluable framework for assessing the behaviour of individuals across various domains and circumstances. The TPB postulates that an individual's behaviour is influenced by three distinct categories of beliefs, which subsequently contribute to the formation of subjective norms, perceived behavioural control and attitude towards the specific behaviour, respectively (Taneja & Ali, 2021).

The TPB model has been extensively applied to comprehend the behavioural inclination of adopting green banking. The model was utilized by Burhanudin et al. (2021) in their analysis to examine the bearing of customer guilt on the attitude towards endorsing banking services that are conducive to preserving the environment. The attitude, commonly known as a person's affirmative or unfavourable emotional assessment of engaging in a behaviour, is also impacted by different external factors such as environmental concern, perceived environmental integrity and collectivism, which in turn determine the person's inclination towards utilizing green banking services (Bryson et al., 2016). The model is examined in the framework of small and medium-sized enterprises (SMEs) as well in order to scrutinize the intentions of Islamic users in adopting Islamic green finance services (Rasheed & Siddiqui, 2022).

4.1.4 Legitimacy Theory

Legitimacy pertains to a broad perception that an organization's actions are commendable or fit in a socially formulated framework of values, norms, beliefs and explanations (Suchman, 1995). Burlea-schiopoiu and Popa (2013) stated that the concept of legitimacy is a tool through which organizations accept and promote voluntary social and environmental disclosures. This, in turn, enables them to fulfil their societal responsibilities, thereby making it easier for their objectives to be recognized and guarantee that they thrive in a dynamic and unpredictable environment. The legitimacy theory of a firm is one of the prevailing hypotheses that effectively elucidate the environmental behaviour of banks (Miah et al., 2021). This theory has served as the basis of many studies focusing on social and environmental disclosure of bank activities (Björkholm & Lehner, 2021; Contreras et al., 2019; Rehman et al., 2021). Banks with higher visibility disclose environmental information to gain legitimacy. Moreover, they must be accountable for disclosing their carbon emissions (Patten, 1991).

4.1.5 Socially Responsible Investment (SRI) Theory

According to Escrig-Olmedo et al. (2013), the rise of socially responsible investment (SRI) results from investors' increasing focus on and incorporation of ecological and socio-economic criteria into their investment strategies. The SRI theory advocates the adoption of financial and well-being objectives, particularly among financial establishments and socially motivated companies, to address the escalating ecological challenges, generate employment opportunities and foster rural and urban development (Escrig-Olmedo et al., 2013). Moreover, it employs finance to achieve both social and financial values and objectives, with a particular emphasis on the social dimension. Certain authors have argued that banks hinder responsible investment due to limited access to information concerning investments in green projects (Panda, 2017). This constraint arises from various obstacles, such as inadequate documentation and environmentally friendly energy utilization. However, it has been seen that banks investing in environmentally viable projects create a good brand image and wins customers' trust, which in turn influences the customers' loyalty and behaviour (Ibe-enwo et al., 2019; Sharma & Choubey, 2022).

4.1.6 Technology Acceptance Model (TAM)

The technology acceptance model (TAM) model, projected by Davis (1989), is a widely utilized framework that elucidates the rationale behind adopting a specific innovation. As per the TAM, a person's propensity for technology, including their perceived usefulness (PU) and perceived ease of use (PEU), has an impact on their behavioural intention. The model has undergone numerous revisions in various studies to align with the specific technological context being examined. The two prominent factors of TAM have been extensively employed in previous scholarly works to explore the behavioural intentions of users towards environmentally friendly technology and products (Venkatesh et al., 2012). Nisha (2020) employed the TAM model to ascertain the inclination of central bank personnel towards eco-friendly banking services. This was done by positing that both PU and PEU exert a notable influence on attitude towards utilization, which ultimately affects the behavioural intentions of the employees. Similarly, Malik and Singh (2022) present an all-encompassing framework that merges the 'big five' personality traits with the TAM model. They examined the effect of personality traits on the perception of usefulness, subsequently shaping users' persistent inclination towards utilizing the green banking channel.

4.1.7 Resource-Based View Theory (RBVT)

The resource-based view theory (RBVT) posits that companies may create and preserve a competitive edge by obtaining and utilizing resources that are uncommon, precious, distinctive and irreplaceable (Sirmon et al., 2011). This particular theory holds significant importance in the domain of strategic management and is steadily acquiring acceptance in related fields as well. The theory is widely recognized for its ability to clarify the interaction between a firm's resources, abilities and inclusive performance (Sirmon et al., 2011). According to Ryszko (2016), this theory emerges as the most suitable theory to elucidate the correlation between pro-environmental strategies and firm performance. Aslam and Jawaid (2023a), in their study, applied the understanding of the RBVT to comprehend the association between green banking adoption practices and customers' continued relationship with the banks, in which customer green trust, green perceived quality, customer green satisfaction and environment friendliness act as the mediating variables. In their other research, they scrutinize the impact of green banking adoption strategies on the financial, operational and environmental performance of banks (Aslam & Jawaid, 2022).

4.1.8 Other Theories

Various other theories are employed in the literature that influence individuals' acceptance and inclination towards green banking and finance. These include perceived risk and attractiveness theory (Iqbal et al., 2021), in which risk and attractiveness are located at opposite ends of a continuum that impacts the decision-making process. Uncertainties indicate risk while attractiveness can be assessed. The self-regulation theory states that the capacity of self can influence an individual's behaviour (Burhanudin et al., 2021). The social identity theory (Rubel et al., 2020) contends that an individual's conception of their own personal identity is shaped by their involvement in social interactions and their relationships with others. The institutional theory (Dong et al., 2021) has been widely used to study the institution's sustainability disclosure. The theory of self-congruity (Bukhari et al., 2020) links product or service alignment to customer satisfaction, loyalty and emotional connection. The sustainability theory (Rehman et al., 2021), first conceptualized in 1972, serves as a fundamental and universally accepted framework for implementing sustainable business strategies on a global scale. The triple bottom line theory (Aslam & Jawaid, 2023a) emphasizes the examination of the overall performance and endurance of an organization through the assessment of social, environmental and financial factors. Lastly, the ethical decision-making theory (Bayer et al., 2019) guides individuals and organizations to make ethical and moral choices when facing ethical dilemmas.

4.2 Context (C)

This section explores the countries and green banking products and services that have received significant attention in the existing body of research on adopting and intention towards sustainable banking and finance. The country-wise article contribution is presented in Table 4, and the description of studies focusing on various green banking products and services is presented in Table 5.

4.2.1 Countries

The investigation shows that Asian nations made a 70.59% contribution to the body of scholarly publications. These nations include India (Bryson et al., 2016; Maheswari et al., 2017; Malik & Singh, 2022; Wasan et al., 2021), China (Chen &

Table 4. Countries' Contribution to the Literature.

Countries	No. of Documents	% of Documents
Asia	36	70.59
Europe	5	9.80
Africa	2	3.92
OECD counties	1	1.96
Islamic counties	1	1.96
G20 countries	1	1.96
Worldwide	2	3.92
Country not identified	3	5.88

Source: The researcher's own work.

Table 5. Domain in Green Banking Services Identified in the Literature.

Domain of Green Banking Service	No. of Documents	% of Documents
Green finance	20	38.46
Digital and online banking	7	13.46
Green bonds	2	3.85
Sustainable reporting and disclosure	6	11.54
Green internal operations	7	13.46
Green technology	3	5.77
ESG strategies	2	3.85
General	5	9.61

Source: The researcher's own work.

Zhao, 2023; Li et al., 2023; Qian & Yu, 2023; Xiliang et al., 2023), Indonesia (Anis et al., 2023; Burhanudin et al., 2021), Pakistan (Ellahi et al., 2021; Khan et al., 2023; Rasheed & Siddiqui, 2022), Bangladesh (Rubel et al., 2020; Iqbal et al., 2021), Vietnam (Moslehpour et al., 2023; Phuong, 2020), Malaysia (Oseni et al., 2018; Pek et al., 2019) and United Arab Emirates (Bouteraa et al., 2022). Among all the Asian nations, India has made a substantial contribution to this research area by contributing 10 publications. After extensive research conducted in Asia, the European continent made a significant scholarly contribution of 9.80%. These European nations include Germany (Bayer et al., 2019), Spain (Escrig-Olmedo et al., 2013), Switzerland (Strauß et al., 2023) and a group of Nordic countries (Björkholm & Lehner, 2021). Nearly 9.80% of studies were conducted in multiple countries, such as OECD countries (Cantero-Saiz et al., 2023), G20 countries (D'Orazio & Popoyan, 2023), Islamic countries (Bukhari et al., 2020) and countries worldwide (Contreras et al., 2019; Saif-Alyousfi et al., 2023). However, Australia and the United States have made a negligible contribution to the literature as no articles were found from these countries. Moreover, three articles failed to specify the country of origin. For instance, Thistlethwaite (2014) and Metawa et al. (2022) have utilized secondary sources to gather quantitative data, with no specific emphasis on any particular nation.

4.2.2 Domains in Green Banking Service

The analysis shows that 38.46% of the literature focuses on the green financing aspect of environmentally friendly banking practices. The objective of green finance (such as green loans or green credits) is to distribute financial resources to endeavours that yield favourable environmental and societal outcomes while also promoting economic growth and financial stability (Bukhari et al., 2020; Burhanudin et al., 2021; Strauß et al., 2023). Meanwhile, 13.46% of the literature discusses the connection between green banking and digital and online practices, allowing customers to use banking services via the internet (Maheswari et al., 2017; Oseni et al., 2018; Okyere-Kwakye & Nor, 2021). Nearly 11.54% of the studies consider sustainability reporting as a crucial aspect of green banking, as it allows financial institutions to establish their obligation to environmental and social responsibility (Amidjaya & Widagdo, 2020; Awawdeh et al., 2021; Bryson et al., 2016). Moreover, green banking also encompasses environmentally conscious practices within the internal operations of a financial institution, such as paperless transactions and the use of energy-efficient and renewable resources. Nearly 13.46% of the literature studied has considered green internal operations of banks as a component of green banking (Aslam & Jawaid, 2023a; Iqbal et al., 2018; Rifat et al., 2016). However, only 3.85% of the studies focus on green bonds as eco-friendly financing products (Björkholm & Lehner, 2021; Prajapati et al., 2021). Moreover, 9.61% of studies have not specifically focused on one area of green services or products.

4.3 Characteristics (C)

This section explores the diverse characteristics of literature on the adoption of green banking and finance. Table 6 presents the various factors identified in the reviewed studies. These factors are grouped under three categories: customer-related, employee-related and industry-related. Based on these factors, the present investigation proposes a theoretical framework for the factors strongly associated with the inclination to adopt green banking and finance. The framework was established through a dual-phase approach (Fig. 7), showcasing the conceptualization of the framework's structure. The first phase delineates the antecedents and outcome variables, and the second phase concentrates on the mediators and moderators between the drivers and customers' adoption and intention.

Table 6. Characteristics Identified in the Literature.

Variables	Examples	Source
Antecedents		
Customer-related factors	Guilt, ease and convenient to use, perceived risk, trust, personality traits, performance expectancy, social influence, perceived advantage, environmental concern, perceived behavioural control, effort expectancy, technology innovations, economic factors, social factors, environmental factors and financial factor, facilitating condition, knowledge barrier, economic barrier, policy barrier, moral awareness.	Maheswari et al. (2017), Burhanudin et al. (2021), Iqbal et al. (2021), Taneja and Ali (2021), Bouteraa et al. (2022), Aslam and Jawaid (2023a), and Strauß et al. (2023)
Employee-related factors	Customer pressure, management pressure, competitors' pressure, perceived ease of use, susceptibility, financial knowledge, religious belief, capacity of bank officials, green HRM, government supportive policies, financial capacity of banks, perceived risk.	Contreras et al. (2019), Bukhari et al. (2020), Nisha (2020), Okyere-Kwakye and Nor (2021), Rehman et al. (2021), and Khan et al., (2023)

(Continued)

Table 6. *(Continued)*

Variables	Examples	Source
Industry-related factors	Firm size and location, green financial regulation, environmental policy, sustainability reporting, state influence, political connectedness, technology advancement, company structure, market barriers, ESG factors, private environmental governance (PEG).	Tara et al. (2019), Kumar and Prakash (2020), Dong et al. (2021), Zhang (2022), Anis et al. (2023), Cantero-Saiz et al. (2023), and Qian and Yu (2023)
Outcome variables		
Customer-related factors	Intention to adopt, behavioural intention, likeliness to invest, usage intention, willingness to accept, risk and return in investment	Kumar and Prakash (2020), Awawdeh et al. (2021), Burhanudin et al. (2021), Iqbal et al. (2021), Prajapati et al. (2021), and Taneja and Ali (2021)
Employee-related factors	Intention to adopt, green service behaviour, attitude, behavioural intention, green loyalty, green bank development, bank daily operations	Tara et al. (2019), Rubel et al. (2020), Okyere-Kwakye and Nor (2021), and Aslam and Jawaid (2022)
Industry-related factors	Greenwash, adoption of climate related policies, green finance disclosure, bank profitability, sustainable and financial development, bank diversification	Amidjaya and Widagdo (2020), D'Orazio and Popoyan (2023), Mirza et al. (2023), and Zhang (2022)
Mediators		
Customer-related factors	Attitude, attractiveness, green trust, green image, sustainable finance literacy, moral judgement	Aslam and Jawaid (2023a), Bryson et al. (2016), Iqbal et al. (2018, 2021), and Malik and Singh (2022)
Employee-related factors	Green knowledge, perceived usefulness, subjective norms, attitude, perceived behavioural control	Nisha (2020), Rubel et al. (2020), Rehman et al. (2021), and Rasheed and Siddiqui (2022)
Industry-related factors	Operational efficiency, liquidity, financial position, capitalization, clean technology	D'Orazio and Popoyan (2023) and Zhang (2022)
Moderators		
Employee-related factors	Environmental awareness, top management support	Bukhari et al. (2020) and Khan et al. (2023)
Industry-related factors	Foreign ownership and family ownership	Amidjaya and Widagdo (2020)

Source: The researcher's own work.

4.3.1 Antecedents and Outcomes

Customer-related factors are those that significantly influence the behaviour and intention of users and investors to adopt green banking and finance. It has been seen that societal norms, facilitating conditions (such as technical support), performance expectancy (users' view of the usefulness of technology), effort expectancy (efforts required to use the technology) and environmental concern favourably influence the user's behaviour intention towards green banking (Bouteraa et al., 2022; Chen & Zhao, 2023; Iqbal et al., 2018; Oseni et al., 2018). Similarly, perceived trust is significant in making decisions about

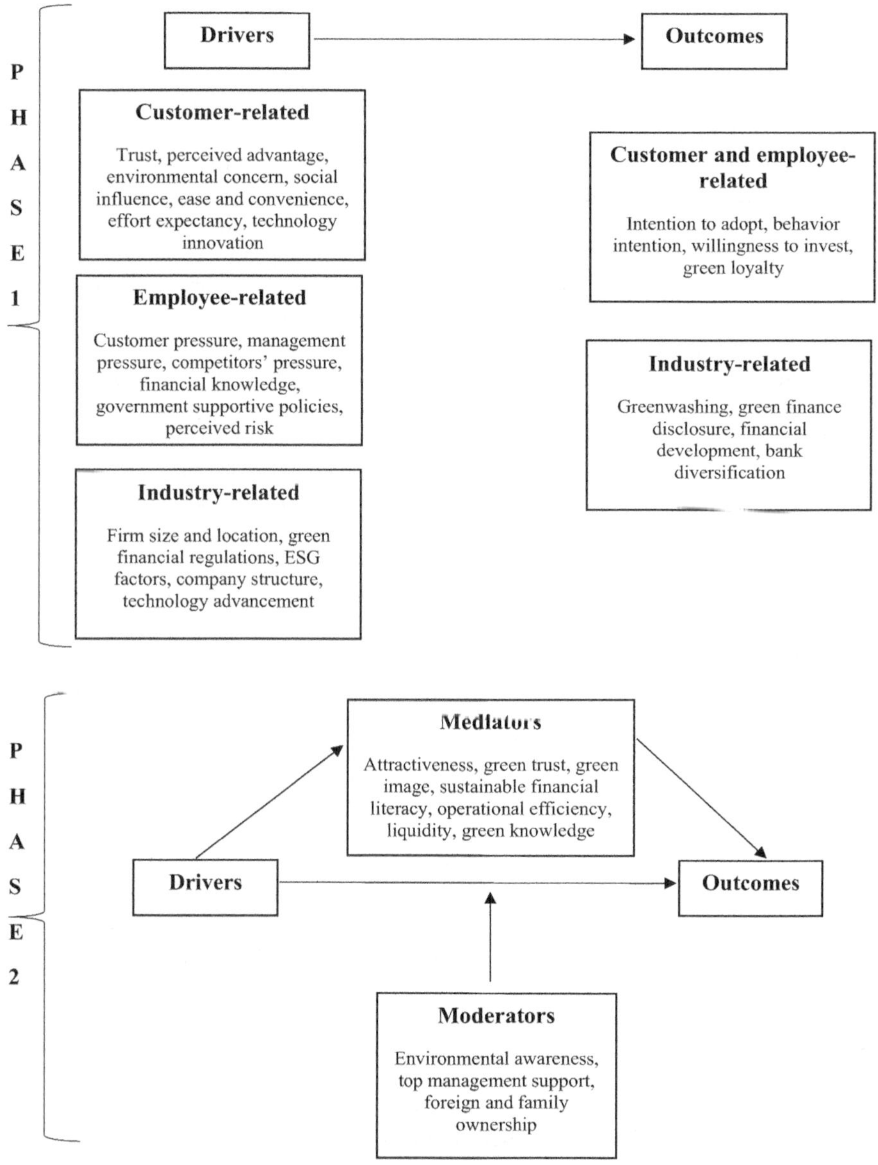

Fig. 7. Framework for Green Banking and Finance. *Source:* The researcher's own work.

green investments, as it pertains to an individual's inclination to depend on an entity based on their expectations of its competence, honesty and dependability (Chen & Zhao, 2023; Oseni et al., 2018; Strauß et al., 2023; Taneja & Ali, 2021). The significant variables of the TPB model, such as attitude, which is linked to cognitive beliefs and the evaluation of potential consequences of engaging in a behaviour, and perceived behavioural control, which is defined as the perceived level of simplicity or complexity associated with executing a specific behaviour, also influence the customer's behaviour towards green banking and finance (Bryson et al., 2016; Taneja & Ali, 2021). Moreover, Burhanudin et al. (2021) stated that the experience of guilt among customers also influences their attitude towards green banking, as guilt arises when they perceive that their ethical principles have been violated. Apart from this, Wasan et al. (2021) have identified knowledge, policy and economic barriers that negatively influence the adoption of green finance among individuals.

Various employee-related factors have been identified that influence the employee's behaviour and attitude towards green banking and finance. As per stakeholder theory (Contreras et al., 2019; Okyere-Kwakye & Nor, 2021; Nisha, 2020), the bank workers' attitudes and intentions to implement green banking are greatly influenced by pressure from stakeholders, including consumers, management and competition. However, apart from external party pressure, the employees' financial knowledge, religious beliefs, self-efficacy and evaluation capacity relating to green financial projects also significantly influence their adoption intention and green bank development (Phuong, 2020; Rasheed & Siddiqui, 2022). Additionally, the green finance-related policies and regulations from the central bank favourable influence the bank's financial performance and the employee's usage behaviour of green banking services (Rehman et al., 2021; Rifat et al., 2016; Xiliang et al., 2023). Moreover, authors like Rubel et al. (2020) came out with different perspectives and identified the effect of green human resource management (HRM) on green values, which ultimately influences their green service behaviour.

The industry-related factors that are uncontrollable affect the green and sustainable behaviour of the entire financial industry. According to the literature, the location, size, and capital structure of the financial institution have an important bearing on their profitability and sustainability disclosure (Björkholm & Lehner, 2021; Dong et al., 2021; Mirza et al., 2023; Tara et al., 2019). The bigger the firm size, the more it will indulge in green financial practices. Moreover, sustainability governance practices and green finance policies significantly influence the overall sustainability reporting and ESG performance of financial institutions (Amidjaya & Widagdo, 2020; Anis et al., 2023; Qian & Yu, 2023; Saif-Alyousfi et al., 2023). Good corporate governance includes independent board members and a strong audit committee for transparency in sustainability disclosures. However, various factors restricting banks' involvement in green practices are also identified. These factors include market barriers, political constraints, environmental factors, social factors and economic policy uncertainties (Dong et al., 2021; Li et al., 2022; Mirza et al., 2023; Saif-Alyousfi et al., 2023).

4.3.2 Mediating and Moderating Variables

Several customer-related factors mediate the association between antecedents and the intention to adopt green banking. The attitude works as a robust mediator that connects environmental concerns and collectivism to behavioural intentions (Bryson et al., 2016). Moreover, green trust, green image and moral judgement can also act as mediating factors (Aslam & Jawaid, 2023a; Iqbal et al., 2018, 2021; Malik & Singh, 2022). Subjective norms, attitude and perceived behavioural control similarly act as mediators linking religious beliefs, self-efficacy and perceived risk to the intention of employers to adopt green banking (Rasheed & Siddiqui, 2022). Similarly, possessing green knowledge among banking staff significantly influences in-role green service behaviour (Rubel et al., 2020). Delving into industry-related factors, liquidity and financial position of the firm, capitalization, clean technology and operational efficiency also impact green financing adoption (D'Orazio & Popoyan, 2023; Zhang, 2022).

In examining the identified literature, only a few moderating variables were recognized. The concept of environmental awareness, which pertains to the employees' understanding of the regulations and guidelines related to environmental policies in the banking sector, is highlighted as a moderating factor in the research led by Khan et al. (2023). Additionally, foreign ownership and family ownership emerge as significant determinants, as companies with varying degrees of foreign and family ownership exhibit discrepancies in their adoption of corporate governance practices (Amidjaya & Widagdo, 2020).

4.4 Methodology (M)

This section offers a thorough examination of the evaluation of the methodologies and research strategies utilized in the articles chosen for the reviews. Tables 7 and 8 present the specific methodologies and techniques used for data analysis in the studies.

As per the analysis, out of the 51 reviewed papers, 38 (or 74.51%) used the quantitative method in their studies. Among all the quantitative techniques of data analysis, structural equation modelling (SEM) using AMOS (Bryson et al., 2016; Rehman et al., 2021) and Smart PLS (Bayer et al., 2019; Iqbal et al., 2018; Rifat et al., 2016) has been used by the maximum number of researchers. This is because SEM possesses the statistical capability to examine the causal associations among variables that encompass multiple measurement items (Hair et al., 2011). After SEM, many authors have used various regression models as well, such as multiple regression (Okyere-Kwakye & Nor, 2021), ordinary least square regression (Strauß et al., 2023), cox regression (Contreras et al., 2019) and many other. At the same time, many authors have also used basic data analysis

Table 7. Survey Methods Used in the Literature.

Method	No. of Documents	% of Documents
Quantitative	38	74.51
Qualitative	5	9.80
Mixed	8	15.68

Source: The researcher's own work.

Table 8. Data Analysis Techniques Used in the Literature.

Data Analysis Technique	No. of Documents	Source
Quantitative		
Structural equation modelling	21	Bryson et al. (2016), Rubel et al. (2020), Iqbal et al. (2021), Rehman et al. (2021), and Khan et al. (2023)
Regression	10	Contreras et al. (2019) and Strauß et al. (2023)
Econometric	3	Metawa et al. (2022) and Saif-Alyousfi et al. (2023)
Difference-in-difference method	2	Qian and Yu (2023) and Zhang (2022)
ANOVA	1	Maheswari et al. (2017)
Correlation analysis	1	Phuong (2020)
Percentage analysis	1	Escrig-Olmedo et al. (2013)
Qualitative		
Interview method	2	Björkholm and Lehner (2021)
Literature review method	2	Kumar & Prakash (2020) and Wasan et al. (2021)
Data triangulation	1	Bukhari et al. (2020)
Delphi technique	1	Wasan et al. (2021)
Best–worst technique	1	Wasan et al. (2021)

Source: The researcher's own work.

techniques such as ANOVA, correlation and regression analysis. However, a few studies (9.80%) have adopted the qualitative data analysis method. The qualitative techniques used include semi-structured or unstructured interviews, literature review method, data triangulation, Delphi technique and best–worst technique.

The mixed method, which accounted for 15.68 % of the total studies, encompassed a combination of experimental and survey-based techniques. For instance, the integration of focus group discussion with questionnaire research method (Burhanudin et al., 2021), content analysis with survey analysis (Dong et al., 2021), face-to-face interview method with regression models (Pek et al., 2019) and thematic content analysis with SEM (Bouteraa et al., 2022). The mixed method approach is now increasingly used as researchers posit that studies employing a combination of methods get a deeper knowledge of the phenomenon than studies that solely employ a quantitative or qualitative method (Mckim, 2017).

5. FUTURE RESEARCH DIRECTIONS

The growing trend of sustainable banking and financial services can aid policymakers and regulators in understanding the intentions and actions of stakeholders. The present section guides future research endeavours within this field, drawing upon the TCCM framework (refer Table 9).

Table 9. Future Research Directions in Green Banking and Finance Adoption.

Theory development	• Stakeholder theory can be applied to study the perception and behavior of different stake parties, which will help them easily adopt green banking facilities. • Develop a combined model by studying multiple variables simultaneously from two or more frameworks, such as combining UTAUT and TPB frameworks • Integrate more environmental theories in the financing sector by exploring sustainability and ethical decision-making theories
Context	• Compare the green financing practices of two or more nations, as there is a dearth of comparative analysis studies • Study the adoption of domain-specific green banking services, such as green technologies, green bonds and sustainability reporting in the banking sector • Countries like China, Indonesia and India are leading in green banking and financing research. Therefore, more empirical studies in domain-specific services can be explored in these countries.
Characteristics	• Explore the influence of negative factors, such as barriers in knowledge, policy and economics, on the customer adoption of green finance • Explore the mediating and moderating role of various personality factors in green banking adoption, as understanding the human element is crucial in behavioural research • Integrate demographic factors, namely gender, age and experience, as moderators to provide a more extensive perspective of customer behaviour • Investigate greenwashing in the sustainable banking sector • Identify more industry-related factors that impact the adoption of green policies on the bank's overall profitability
Methods	• Conduct a longitudinal study to understand the users' continued usage behaviour of green banking services • Integrate mixed methodologies to better understand the relationship between the two concepts • Examine the factors that influence customers' involvement in sustainable financing by employing experimental and field-based methods • Employ large-scale research to develop a standard measurement scale to measure factors affecting customer adoption of green banking

Source: The researcher's own work.

5.1 Theories

Future researchers can employ stakeholder theory to investigate stakeholders' adoption and inclination towards the green banking and finance domain. Furthermore, they may align their methodologies with the works of Nisha (2020) and Khan et al. (2023) to observe the impact of stakeholder pressure on the employees' conduct and banks' reputation. It is important to highlight that previous studies only focused on customer perspectives, top management and competitors as stakeholders, so future research should also consider other entities like investors, regulators and governmental bodies. Moreover, it has been identified that many authors have applied the UTAUT model in examining behaviour. However, Venkatesh et al. (2012) have extended the UTAUT model by adding three additional variables that influence the user's behaviour intentions. Therefore, future researchers can empirically apply the extended UTAUT model in understanding an individual's behaviour.

Also, while examining the sustainability disclosure and overall performance of institutions, future research can employ the triple bottom line theory and legitimacy theory. These theoretical frameworks allow for the analysis of the financial, social and environmental dimensions of green financing activities (Aslam & Jawaid, 2023a; Rehman et al., 2021). Moreover, to provide a more comprehensive picture of an individual's inclination towards green banking and finance, future investigations could combine two or three frameworks, such as the TPB model and the UTAUT model, while incorporating certain societal and ecological aspects, such as moral awareness and environmental concern (Bayer et al., 2019; Taneja & Ali, 2021).

5.2 Context

Based on the current analysis, future researchers can align with the work of Indian authors as India is the only Asian nation that has contributed the maximum number of articles in this research domain (Bryson et al., 2016; Prajapati et al., 2021; Taneja & Ali, 2021). However, it was found that there is a dearth of studies identifying adoption and behaviour intention towards green banking in the United States and Australian countries. Consequently, an immense potential exists for both empirical and conceptual studies in these aforementioned nations. Additionally, future researchers can compare the adoption practices of green banking in two or more countries and sectors to understand the cultural differences between the two areas. Moreover, investigation can be carried out regarding adopting other aspects of green banking, for instance, green loans and mortgages, green disclosure and green building, across various banking systems in diverse economies (Bukhari et al., 2020). This particular field of study also lacks substantial academic work in comparative analyses between traditional and green banks and the banking sectors of different nations. This research endeavour can provide valuable insights into the subject mentioned above, as the adoption of green banking has been observed to depend on specific contexts.

5.3 Characteristics

The existing body of literature focuses on various factors related to customers, employees and the industry. In future, these studies will be extremely helpful in understanding the various factors influencing customer and employee behaviour, as well as overall industrial performance. However, some factors are not properly researched and may impact behaviour differently when combined with already described factors. For instance, customer guilt influences attitude and behaviour towards green banking but has not been studied holistically in relation to green financing behaviour (Burhanudin et al., 2021). Moreover, various prior research highlights the importance of customer ethics and morals in shaping eco-friendly behaviour (Bayer et al., 2019; Lu et al., 2015). Therefore, these moral factors must be studied within the green banking and finance context. Besides, there is a dearth of researchers studying industry-related factors. Certain factors, such as sustainability governance practices, economic policy uncertainty, lack of green financing policies and technological innovations, also influence the progress of a green banking system (Anis et al., 2023; Awawdeh et al., 2021; Moslehpour et al., 2023). In future, efforts can be made to study the effect of these factors within the framework of green banking and finance.

Furthermore, future studies can include other mediating and moderating variables that impact the adoption and intention to behave of both customers and employees. For instance, green values (Al-Ghazali, 2020) and cultural profile (Rosado-Serrano et al., 2018) always remain the neglecting variable even though they may influence the attitude and behaviour of a person. Moreover, certain personality traits (such as individualism, openness and loyalty) can also act as a mediating variable in influencing a customer's green behaviour (Lu et al., 2015). Also, integrating demographic factors, namely gender, age, and experience, as moderators with pre-defined models would provide a more comprehensive view of customer behaviour.

5.4 Methods

The current examination of literature has led to the identification of prospects for assessing adoption and inclination towards green finance. Given that the majority of contemporary literature has employed SEM, forthcoming studies may endeavour to develop more intricate SEM analyses by incorporating a diverse range of theories and variables, thereby facilitating a more comprehensive comprehension of user behaviour. Moreover, longitudinal studies can be beneficial in understanding user intention over time in green banking (Kim et al., 2021; Zhao et al., 2018). A longitudinal investigation can be beneficial in the realm of green banking since it offers a thorough examination of the user's continuous behaviour, trends and effectiveness of eco-friendly banking initiatives. The studies using the Delphi method had a limited number of experts, so future research should involve a wider range of specialists (Wasan et al., 2021). Since few studies use a mixed method approach, future research can integrate mixed methodologies to better understand the relationship between the two concepts. The data triangulation method can be used to explore the effect of bank resilience on the profitability of banks (Anis et al., 2023). Moreover, future research should include more real-world data or conduct experiments to identify obstacles in implementing green banking practices (Wasan et al., 2021).

6. DISCUSSION

This study aimed to comprehensively examine the perception and intentions to adopt green banking and finance using a framework-based review strategy. It analyzed existing research and provided guidance for future studies. The observations suggest that changes in environmental concern and increased knowledge have primarily influenced adoption and behaviour. The percentage of research publications in this field has improved substantially since 2020, and more growth is expected. This study adds to existing knowledge by combining factors influencing individuals' inclination towards environmentally-conscious banking and finance. It also suggests new areas for future research. Future researchers can focus on empirical investigations to address gaps in theoretical frameworks, contextual circumstances, characteristics and methodological approaches.

6.1 Theoretical Implications

This investigation incorporated a systematic evolution and bibliometric analysis to understand individuals' perceptions and behaviour concerning green banking and finance. This analysis results in numerous theoretical implications. Primarily, it reveals that research on green banking and finance adoption is fragmented due to its shift from a conventional banking setting. As a result, the literature on green banking is still evolving and needs to be more consistent, underscoring the necessity for a comprehensive SLR. Therefore, based on the TCCM framework, this review offered an outline of prior investigations in this area, making it beneficial for academics.

Second, a comprehensive conceptual framework has been formulated grounded in the synthesis of the literature, delving into the antecedents, mediators and moderators of green banking adoption. While a few previous reviews touch upon green banking and finance (e.g., Akomea-Frimpong et al., 2021; Aslam & Jawaid, 2023b), they lack an extensive conceptual framework like the one presented here. Consequently, this study introduces a conceptual model wherein factors are classified into customer-related, employee-related and industry-related factors, facilitating researchers and educators to understand and put them into practice.

Third, this review drives the theoretical foundation of research on green banking and finance adoption forward. It integrates the theoretical frameworks utilised in prior research. The literature on green banking has advanced significantly through the utilization of various theoretical frameworks. Stakeholder theory, the UTAUT model, the TPB model and the legitimacy theory are widely employed theoretical frameworks in this field. Nonetheless, this systematic review advocates for future researchers to explore green banking adoption intention by blending two or more theories. Overall, this research endeavour enhances the theoretical foundation of literature in this area.

Lastly, this review pinpoints neglected areas within green banking and finance adoption and suggests specific directions for future research in this domain. Overall, examining the future research paths outlined in this review will enrich the knowledge base and enhance the existing body of literature.

6.2 Practical Implications

The findings from the review possess some crucial managerial implications for users, policymakers and financial institutions interested in adopting green banking and finance. First, this review classified factors into three sub-categories, i.e., customer-related, employee-related and industry-related, and discussed the importance of these factors. Thus, practitioners (i.e., the customers, banking employees and industrialists) who seek to adopt green banking and finance in their daily operations should consider these factors while developing the intention to adopt these practices.

Second, the literature synthesis shows that firm size and location, ESG disclosure and sustainability reporting are some of the crucial industrial factors that impact the adoption of green finance. This is because ESG disclosures attract investors with a strong emphasis on sustainability whereas sustainability reporting can strengthen a firm's position and trustworthiness among its stakeholders. Thus, financial institutions must focus on these factors and advocate the formulation of policy guidelines and governance frameworks towards green financing. This necessitates regulations at both national and international levels that can enhance public trust in green financial services.

Third, establishing trust in banking services is essential to actively engage customers physically and mentally in adopting green banking practices, particularly in emerging economies. This objective can be achieved by disseminating information via marketing campaigns, delivering suitable customer support and extending green financing options with reduced interest rates.

Finally, it is important to understand that all parties, i.e. customers, banking employees and financial regulators, are interrelated. Customers represent the ultimate users of financial services, and in order to translate their intention to embrace green banking into tangible actions, it is imperative for banking staff and financial regulators to grasp the factors influencing each stakeholder and subsequently devise suitable policies and services.

7. CONCLUSION

Conclusively, this investigation aimed to systematically examine the past studies concerning the adoption of green banking and financial practices on a global scale, as well as to pinpoint research gaps and forthcoming avenues of research within this field. The primary objectives of this analysis were effectively achieved through the integration of available studies on green banking and finance, which were examined in relation to theories, contexts, characteristics and methodologies. Furthermore, a theoretical framework was formulated, illustrating the antecedents, intermediate factors and moderating variables commonly utilized in studies on this subject. This framework serves as a valuable tool for guiding future research and deepening the understanding of the dynamics within this critical area. Corresponding with the secondary objective, insightful suggestions were put forth for prospective research endeavours in the realm of green banking and finance, employing the TCCM framework. This approach not only highlights neglected areas in the literature but also offers precise directions for scholars to explore new avenues, ensuring that the field continues to evolve in response to emerging challenges and opportunities.

While this review significantly advances the academic discourse on green banking and finance, it is essential to recognize certain discrepancies, which also present promising opportunities for future studies. For instance, the scope of this study was intentionally confined to empirical studies, allowing for a focused and detailed analysis. However, this leaves room for future research to incorporate conceptual studies that can enrich theoretical perspectives and offer novel insights. Moreover, expanding the scope to include other databases such as Web of Science may uncover additional studies and enhance the comprehensiveness of the review. The current study also underscores the potential for future research to explore a broader range of sources, including conference papers, theses and non-English publications, which may provide unique perspectives and findings that are currently underrepresented.

Overall, this review establishes a strong foundation for subsequent research in green banking and finance. It not only addresses existing gaps but also opens new pathways for exploration, ensuring that both scholars and practitioners are well-equipped to tackle the pressing environmental and financial challenges of the current era.

REFERENCES

Agrawal, R., Agrawal, S., Samadhiya, A., Kumar, A., Luthra, S., & Jain, V. (2023). Geoscience Frontiers Adoption of green finance and green innovation for achieving circularity: An exploratory review and future directions. *Geoscience Frontiers*, 101669. https://doi.org/10.1016/j.gsf.2023.101669

Ajzen, I. (1991). The theory of planned behavior. *Organizational Behavior and Human Decision Processes, 50*(2), 179–211. https://doi.org/10.1016/0749-5978(91)90020-T

Akomea-Frimpong, I., Adeabah, D., Ofosu, D., & Tenakwah, E. J. (2021). A review of studies on green finance of banks, research gaps and future directions and future directions. *Journal of Sustainable Finance & Investment, 12*(4), 1241–1264. https://doi.org/10.1080/20430795.2020.1870202

Al-Ghazali, B. M. (2020). Green human resource management and employees' green creativity: The roles of green behavioral intention and individual green values. *Corporate Social Responsibility and Environmental Management, 28*(1), 1–18. https://doi.org/10.1002/csr.1987

Amidjaya, P. G., & Widagdo, A. K. (2020). Sustainability reporting in Indonesian listed banks. *Journal of Applied Accounting Research, 21*(2), 231–247. https://doi.org/10.1108/JAAR-09-2018-0149

Anis, I., Gani, L., Fauzi, H., Hermawan, A. A., & Adhariani, D. (2023). The sustainability awareness of banking institutions in Indonesia , its implication on profitability by the mediating role of operational efficiency. *Asian Journal of Accounting Research*. https://doi.org/10.1108/AJAR-06-2022-0179

Aracil, E., Nájera-Sánchez, J. J., & Forcadell, F. J. (2021). Sustainable banking: A literature review and integrative framework. *Finance Research Letters, 42*(July 2020). https://doi.org/10.1016/j.frl.2021.101932

Aslam, W., & Jawaid, S. T. (2022). Green banking adoption practices: Improving environmental, financial, and operational performance. *International Journal of Ethics and Systems*. https://doi.org/10.1108/IJOES-06-2022-0125

Aslam, W., & Jawaid, S. T. (2023a). Let's go green: Achieving consumer-related performance outcomes in banks. *International Journal of Ethics and Systems*. https://doi.org/10.1108/IJOES-01-2023-0019

Aslam, W., & Jawaid, S. T. (2023b). Systematic review of green banking adoption: Following PRISMA protocols. *IIM Kozhikode Society & Management Review, 12*(2), 213–233. https://doi.org/10.1177/22779752231168169

Awawdeh, A. E., Ananzeh, M., El-khateeb, A. I., & Aljumah, A. (2021). Role of green financing and corporate social responsibility (CSR) in technological innovation and corporate environmental performance: A COVID-19 perspective. *China Finance Review International, 12*(2), 297–316. https://doi.org/10.1108/CFRI-03-2021-0048

Bayer, S., Gimpel, H., & Sarikaya, S. (2019). Bank customers' decision-making process in choosing between ethical and conventional banking: A survey-based examination. *Journal of Business Economics*, *89*(6). Springer Berlin Heidelberg. https://doi.org/10.1007/s11573-019-00934-5

Björkholm, L., & Lehner, O. M. (2021). Nordic green bond issuers' views on the upcoming EU Green Bond Standard. *ACRN Journal of Finance and Risk Perspectives*, *10*, 222–279. https://doi.org/10.35944/jofrp.2021.10.1.012

Bouteraa, M., Raja Hisham, R. R. I., & Zainol, Z. (2022). Challenges affecting bank consumers' intention to adopt green banking technology in the UAE: A UTAUT-based mixed-methods approach. *Journal of Islamic Marketing*, (November). https://doi.org/10.1108/JIMA-02-2022-0039

Bryson, D., Atwal, G., & Dave, K. (2016). Antecedents of intention to use green banking. *Strategic Change*, *25*, 551–567. https://doi.org/10.1002/jsc.2080

Bukhari, S. A. A., Hashim, F., & Amran, A. (2022). Pathways towards green banking adoption: Moderating role of top management commitment. *International Journal of Ethics and Systems*, *38*(2), 286–315. https://doi.org/10.1108/IJOES-05-2021-0110

Bukhari, S. A. A., Hashim, F., Amran, A. B., & Hyder, K. (2020). Green banking and Islam: Two sides of the same coin. *Journal of Islamic Marketing*, *11*(4), 977–1000. https://doi.org/10.1108/JIMA-09-2018-0154

Burhanudin, B., Ronny, R., & Theresia, E. (2021). Consumer guilt and green banking services. *International Journal of Consumer Studies*, *45*(1), 38–53. https://doi.org/10.1111/ijcs.12602

Burlea-schiopoiu, A., & Popa, I. (2013). Legitimacy theory. In *Encyclopedia of corporate social responsibility* (pp. 1579–1584). https://doi.org/10.1007/978-3-642-28036-8

Cantero-Saiz, M., Torre-Olmo, B., & Sanfilippo-Azofra, S. (2023). Sustainable banking , financial strength and the bank lending channel of monetary policy. *E&M Economics and Management*, *26*(1), 165–185. https://doi.org/10.15240/tul/001/2023-1-010

Chauhan, S., Akhtar, A., & Gupta, A. (2021). Gamification in banking: A review , synthesis and setting research agenda. *Young Consumers*, *22*(3). https://doi.org/10.1108/YC-10-2020-1229

Chen, Y., Mandler, T., & Meyer-Waarden, L. (2021). Three decades of research on loyalty programs: A literature review and future research agenda. *Journal of Business Research*, *124*(December 2020), 179–197. https://doi.org/10.1016/j.jbusres.2020.11.057

Chen, H., & Zhao, X. (2023).Use intention of green financial security intelligence service based on UTAUT. *Environment, Development and Sustainability*, *25*(10). https://doi.org/10.1007/s10668-022-02501-5

Contreras, G., Bos, J. W. B., & Kleimeier, S. (2019). Self-regulation in sustainable finance: The adoption of the Equator Principles. *World Development*, *122*, 306–324. https://doi.org/10.1016/j.worlddev.2019.05.030

Davis, F. D. (1989). Perceived usefulness, perceived ease of use, and user acceptance of information technology. *MIS Quarterly: Management Information Systems*, *13*(3), 319–339. https://doi.org/10.2307/249008

Debrah, C., Ping, A., Chan, C., & Darko, A. (2022). Green finance gap in green buildings: A scoping review and future research needs. *Building and Environment*, *207*, 108443. https://doi.org/10.1016/j.buildenv.2021.108443

Dhiman, R., Srivastava, V., Srivastava, A., Rajni, & Uppal, A. (2023). How to plan and write for systematic literature review papers in management domain. In S. Rana, J. Singh, & S. Kathuria (Eds.), *Advancing methodologies of conducting literature review in management domain (Review of management literature)* (Vol. 2, pp. 37–55). https://doi.org/10.1108/s2754-58652023 0000002003

Dong, S., Xu, L., & McIver, R. (2021). China's financial sector sustainability and "green finance" disclosures. *Sustainability Accounting, Management and Policy Journal*, *12*(2), 353–384. https://doi.org/10.1108/SAMPJ-10-2018-0273

D'Orazio, P., & Popoyan, L. (2023). Do monetary policy mandates and financial stability governance structures matter for the adoption of climate-related financial policies? *International Economics*, *173*, 284–295. https://doi.org/10.1016/j.inteco.2023.01.004

Ellahi, A., Jillani, H., & Zahid, H. (2021). Customer awareness on Green banking practices. *Journal of Sustainable Finance and Investment*, *0*(0), 1–17. https://doi.org/10.1080/20430795.2021.1977576

Escrig-Olmedo, E., Muñoz-Torres, M. J., & Fernández-Izquierdo, M. Á. (2013). Sustainable development and the financial system: Society's perceptions about socially responsible investing. *Business Strategy and the Environment*, *22*(6), 410–428. https://doi.org/10.1002/bse.1755

Farrukh, A., & Sajjad, A. (2023). A critical review of literature review methodologies. In S. Rana, J. Singh, & S. Kathuria (Eds.), *Advancing methodologies of conducting literature review in management domain (Review of management literature)* (Vol. 2, pp. 103–123). https://doi.org/10.1108/S2754-586520230000002006

Ferreira, F. A. F. (2018). Mapping the field of arts-based management: Bibliographic coupling and co-citation analyses. *Journal of Business Research*, *85*(September 2015), 348–357. https://doi.org/10.1016/j.jbusres.2017.03.026

Ganti, A., & Singhania, S. (2024). Integration of game theory optimization in financial markets: A systematic literature review based on TCCM framework. *Journal of Modelling in Management*. https://doi.org/10.1108/JM2-04-2024-0114

Hair, J. F., Ringle, C., & Sarstedt, M. (2011). PLS-SEM: Indeed a silver bullet. *Journal of Marketing Theory and Practice*, *19*(2), 139–151. https://doi.org/10.2753/MTP1069-6679190202

Hang, N. P. T. (2022). Policy implications for the green bank development in the context of global policy. *Emerging Science Journal*, *6*(4). https://doi.org/10.28991/ESJ-2022-06-04-011

Ibe-enwo, G., Igbudu, N., Garanti, Z., & Popoola, T. (2019). Assessing the relevance of green banking practice on bank loyalty: The mediating effect of green image and bank trust. *Sustainability*, *11*(17). https://doi.org/10.3390/su11174651

Iqbal, M., Nisha, N., Rifat, A., & Panda, P. (2018). Exploring client perceptions and intentions in emerging economies: The case of green banking technology. *International Journal of Asian Business and Information Management*, *9*(3), 14–34. https://doi.org/10.4018/IJABIM.2018070102

Iqbal, M., Rifat, A., & Nisha, N. (2021). Evaluating attractiveness and perceived risks: The case of green banking services in Bangladesh. *International Journal of Asian Business and Information Management*, *12*(1), 1–23. https://doi.org/10.4018/IJABIM.20210101.oa1

Javier, F., & Aracil, E. (2021). Sustainable banking: A literature review and integrative framework. *Finance Research Letters*, *42*(July 2020). https://doi.org/10.1016/j.frl.2021.101932

Khan, I. U., Hameed, Z., Khan, S. U., & Khan, M. A. (2023). Green banking practices, bank reputation, and environmental awareness: Evidence from Islamic banks in a developing economy. *Environment, Development and Sustainability*, 1–21. https://doi.org/10.1007/s10668-023-03288-9

Kim, S. T., Lee, H., & Lim, S. (2021). The effects of green SCM implementation on business performance in SMEs: A longitudinal study in electronics industry. *Sustainability*, *13*. https://doi.org/10.3390/su132111874

Kumar, K., & Prakash, A. (2020). Managing sustainability in banking: Extent of sustainable banking adaptations of banking sector in India. *Environment, Development and Sustainability*, *22*(6), 5199–5217. https://doi.org/10.1007/s10668-019-00421-5

Li, H., Usman, N., Coulibay, M. H., Phiri, R., & Tang, X. (2022). Does the resources curse hypothesis exist in China? What is the dynamic role of fiscal decentralization, economic policy uncertainty, and technology innovation for sustainable financial development? *Resources Policy*, *79*. https://doi.org/10.1016/j.resourpol.2022.103002

Li, X., Wu, G., & Lin, J. H. (2023). Enhancing borrowing-firm equity through renewable energy adoption, consumer green awareness, and insurer sustainable finance. *Energy Economics*, *126*, 106937. https://doi.org/10.1016/j.eneco.2023.106937

Lin, H., Zeng, S. X., Ma, H. Y., Qi, G. Y., & Tam, V. W. Y. (2014). Can political capital drive corporate green innovation? Lessons from China. *Journal of Cleaner Production*, *64*, 63–72.

Lu, L.-C., Chang, H.-H., & Chang, A. (2015). Consumer personality and green buying intention: The mediate role of consumer ethical beliefs. *Journal of Business Ethics*, *127*, 205–219. https://doi.org/10.1007/s10551-013-2024-4

Maheswari, G. U., Sundaram, N., & Rengasamy, D. (2017). Green banking initiatives as catalyst for demonetization chaos – A study with reference to ICICI Bank. *International Journal of Applied Business and Economic Research*, *15*(21).

Malik, G., & Singh, D. (2022). Personality matters: Does an individual's personality affect adoption and continued use of green banking channels? *International Journal of Bank Marketing*, *40*(4), 746–772. https://doi.org/10.1108/IJBM-04-2021-0133

Mckim, C. A. (2017). The value of mixed methods research: A mixed methods study. *Journal of Mixed Methods Research*, *11*(2), 202–222. https://doi.org/10.1177/1558689815607096

Metawa, N., Dogan, E., & Taskin, D. (2022). Analyzing the nexus of green economy, clean and financial technology. *Economic Analysis and Policy*, *76*, 385–396. https://doi.org/10.1016/j.eap.2022.08.023

Miah, M. D., Rahman, S. M., & Mamoon, M. (2021). Green banking: The case of commercial banking sector in Oman. *Environment, Development and Sustainability*, *23*(2), 2681–2697. https://doi.org/10.1007/s10668-020-00695-0

Mirza, N., Umar, M., Afzal, A., & Firdousi, S. F. (2023). The role of fintech in promoting green finance, and profitability: Evidence from the banking sector in the euro zone. *Economic Analysis and Policy*, *78*, 33–40. https://doi.org/10.1016/j.eap.2023.02.001

Moslehpour, M., Aldeehani, T. M., Sibghatullah, A., & Tai, T. D. (2023). Dynamic association between technological advancement, green finance, energy efficiency and sustainable development: Evidence from Vietnam. *Economic Research-Ekonomska Istraživanja*, *36*(3). https://doi.org/10.1080/1331677X.2023.2190796

Mustaffa, A. H., Ahmad, N., & Bahrudin, N. Z. (2021). A systematic literature review on barriers to green financing participation worldwide. *Global Business and Management Research: International Journal*, *13*(4), 66–79.

Nisha, N. (2020). Can Central Bank survive the green banking revolution? A case of Bangladesh bank. *International Journal of Asian Business and Information Management*, *11*(3). https://doi.org/10.4018/IJABIM.2020070104

Nisha, N., Iqbal, M., & Rifat, A. (2020). Green banking adoption: An examination of state-owned. *International Journal of Technology and Human Interaction*, *16*(2). https://doi.org/10.4018/IJTHI.2020040106

Okyere-Kwakye, E., & Nor, K. (2021). The intention of banks to adopt green banking in an emerging market: The employees' perspective. *Economic and Political Studies*, *9*(4), 497–504. https://doi.org/10.1080/20954816.2021.1899621

Oseni, U. A., Adewale, A. A., & Omoola, S. O. (2018). The feasibility of online dispute resolution in the Islamic banking industry in Malaysia: An empirical legal analysis. *International Journal of Law and Management*, *60*(1), 34–54. https://doi.org/10.1509/jim.14.0065

Panda, P. (2017). Green bond: A socially responsible investment (SRI) instrument. *Research Bulletin*, *14*(1), 97–113.

Patten, D. M. (1991). Exposure, legitimacy, and social disclosure. *Journal of Accounting and Public Policy*, *10*, 297–308. https://doi.org/10.1016/0278-4254(91)90003-3

Paul, J., & Criado, A. R. (2020). The art of writing literature review: What do we know and what do we need to know? *International Business Review*, *29*(4). https://doi.org/10.1016/j.ibusrev.2020.101717

Paul, J., Lim, W. M., Bresciani, S., Cass, A. O., & Hao, A. W. (2021). Scientific procedures and rationales for systematic literature. *International Journal of Consumer Studies*, *45*, 1–16. https://doi.org/10.1111/ijcs.12695

Paul, J., & Rosado-serrano, A. (2019). Gradual Internationalization vs Born-Global/International new venture models: A review and research agenda. *International Marketing Review*, *36*(6), 830–858. https://doi.org/10.1108/IMR-10-2018-0280

Pawar, D. S., & Munuswamy, J. (2022). The linkage between green banking practices and green loyalty: A customer perspective. *Banks and Bank Systems*, *17*(3), 201–212. https://doi.org/10.21511/bbs.17(3).2022.17

Pek, C. K., Tan, H. B., Kim, R. C., & Ang, P. M. M. (2019). Industry lessons for green banking in Malaysia. *International Journal of Green Economics*, *13*(3–4), 167–186. https://doi.org/10.1504/IJGE.2019.104506

Phuong, N. A. (2020). Factors affecting the development of green banks in Vietnam. *Accounting*, *6*(6), 1001–1006. https://doi.org/10.5267/j.ac.2020.7.020

Prajapati, D., Paul, D., Malik, S., & Mishra, D. K. (2021). Understanding the preference of individual retail investors on green bond in India: An empirical study. *Investment Management and Financial Innovations*, *18*(1), 177–189. https://doi.org/10.21511/imfi.18(1).2021.15

Qian, S., & Yu, W. (2023). Green finance and environmental, social, and governance performance. *International Review of Economics & Finance*, *89*(A), 1185–1202. https://doi.org/10.1016/j.iref.2023.08.017

Rana, S., Sakshi, & Singh, J. (2022). Presenting the POWER framework of conducting literature review. In *Exploring the latest trends in management literature review of management literature* (Vol. 1, pp. 1–13). https://doi.org/10.1108/s2754-586520220000001001

Rana, S., Singh, J., & Kathuria, S. (2023). Parameters and decision elements of writing effective literature review papers: Empirical evidence from multiple stakeholders from POWER framework. In *Advancing methodologies for conducting literature reviews in management (Review of management literature)* (Vol. 2, pp. 1–26). https://doi.org/10.1108/S2754-586520230000002001

Rasheed, R., & Siddiqui, S. H. (2022). Impact of demand side factors on adoption of Islamic finance by SMEs: A way forward for sustainable financial markets. *International Journal of Business and Globalisation*, *31*(1), 113–130. https://doi.org/10.1504/IJBG.2022.124526

Rehman, A., Ullah, I., Afridi, F. e. A., Ullah, Z., Zeeshan, M., Hussain, A., & Rahman, H. U. (2021). Adoption of green banking practices and environmental performance in Pakistan: A demonstration of structural equation modelling. *Environment, Development and Sustainability*, *23*(9), 13200–13220. https://doi.org/10.1007/s10668-020-01206-x

Rifat, A., Nisha, N., Iqbal, M., & Suviitawat, A. (2016). The role of commercial banks in green banking adoption: A Bangladesh perspective. *International Journal of Green Economics*, *10*(3/4), 226. https://doi.org/10.1504/ijge.2016.10002862

Rosado-Serrano, A., Paul, J., & Dikova, D. (2018). International franchising: A literature review and research agenda. *Journal of Business Research*, *85*(January), 238–257. https://doi.org/10.1016/j.jbusres.2017.12.049

Rubel, M. R. B., Kee, D. M. H., & Rimi, N. N. (2020). The influence of green HRM practices on green service behaviors: The mediating effect of green knowledge sharing. *Employee Relations*, *43*(5), 996–1015. https://doi.org/10.1108/ER-04-2020-0163

Ryszko, A. (2016). Proactive environmental strategy, technological eco-innovation and firm performance-case of Poland. *Sustainability*, *8*(2). https://doi.org/10.3390/su8020156

Saif-Alyousfi, A. Y. H., Saha, A., & Alshammari, T. R. (2023). Bank diversification and ESG activities: A global perspective. *Economic Systems*, *47*(3). https://doi.org/10.1016/j.ecosys.2023.101094

Sardana, V., Mohapatra, A. K., Singhania, S., & Chakrabarti, D. (2014). Changing dynamics of banking landscape: What do we know and what lies ahead? *Prabandhan: Indian Journal of Management*, *17*(1), 8–23. https://doi.org/10.17010/pijom%2F2024%2Fv17i1%2F173288

Sarker, N. I., & Rashid, H. O. (2015). An impact of banking activities of private commercial Islamic bank to economic development in Bangladesh: A case study on First Security Islami Bank Limited (FSIBL). *Journal of Investment and Management*, *4*(5), 264. https://doi.org/10.11648/j.jim.20150405.28

Sharma, M., & Choubey, A. (2022). Green banking initiatives: A qualitative study on Indian banking sector. *Environment, Development and Sustainability*, *24*(1), 293–319. https://doi.org/10.1007/s10668-021-01426-9

Sirmon, D. G., Hitt, M. A., Ireland, R. D., & Gilbert, B. A. (2011). Resource orchestration to create competitive advantage: Breadth, depth, and life cycle effects. *Journal of Management*, *37*(5), 1390–1412. https://doi.org/10.1177/0149206310385695

Strauß, N., Krakow, J., & Chesney, M. (2023). It's the news, stupid! The relationship between news attention, literacy, trust, greenwashing perceptions, and sustainable finance investment in Switzerland. *Journal of Sustainable Finance and Investment*, *13*(4), 1480–1505. https://doi.org/10.1080/20430795.2023.2226792

Suchman, M. C. (1995, July). Managing legitimacy: Strategic and institutional approaches. *Academy of Management Review*, *20*(3), 571–610. https://www.jstor.org

Taneja, S., & Ali, L. (2021). Determinants of customers' intentions towards environmentally sustainable banking: Testing the structural model. *Journal of Retailing and Consumer Services, 59*. https://doi.org/10.1016/j.jretconser.2020.102418

Tara, K., Singh, S., Kumar, R., & Sundararajan, M. (2019). Geographical locations of banks as an influencer for green banking adoption. *Prabandhan: Indian Journal of Management, 12*(1), 21–35. https://doi.org/10.17010/pijom/2019/v12i1/141425

Thistlethwaite, J. (2014). Private governance and sustainable finance. *Journal of Sustainable Finance and Investment, 4*(1), 61–75. https://doi.org/10.1080/20430795.2014.887348

Venkatesh, V., Morris, M. G., Davis, G. B., & Davis, F. D. (2003). User acceptance of information technology: Toward a unified view. *MIS Quarterly, 27*(3), 425–478. https://doi.org/10.2307/30036540

Venkatesh, V., Thong, J. Y. L., & Xu, X. (2012). Consumer acceptance and use of information technology: Extending the unified theory of acceptance and use of technology. *MIS Quarterly: Management Information Systems, 36*(1), 157–178. https://doi.org/10.2307/41410412

Wasan, P., Kumar, A., & Luthra, S. (2021). Green finance barriers and solution strategies for emerging economies: The case of India. *IEEE Transactions on Engineering Management*, 1–12. https://doi.org/10.1109/TEM.2021.3123185

Xiliang, Q., Kuo, Y. K., Abourehab, M. A. S., Mabrouk, F., Ramirez-Asis, E., Abdul-Samad, Z., & Makes, N. (2023). The impact of ICT, green finance, and CSR on sustainable financial performance: Moderating role of perceived organizational support. *Economic Research-Ekonomska Istrazivanja, 36*(3). https://doi.org/10.1080/1331677X.2022.2151489

Zhang, D. (2022). Green financial system regulation shock and greenwashing behaviors: Evidence from Chinese firms. *Energy Economics, 111*. https://doi.org/10.1016/j.eneco.2022.106064

Zhao, D., McCoy, A. P., Agee, P., Mo, Y., Reichard, G., & Paige, F. (2018). Time effects of green buildings on energy use for low-income households: A longitudinal study in the United States. *Sustainable Cities and Society, 40*(May), 559–568. https://doi.org/10.1016/j.scs.2018.05.011

Zhu, Y., Zhang, J., & Duan, C. (2023). How does green finance affect the low-carbon economy? Capital allocation, green technology innovation and industry structure perspectives. *Economic Research-Ekonomska Istrazivanja, 36*(1), 3519–3541. https://doi.org/10.1080/1331677X.2022.2110138

Save Today, Secure Tomorrow: A Systematic Review of Literature on Retirement Planning Behaviour Using the TCM-ADO Framework

Amit Kumar Singh and Devyani Negi

University of Delhi, India

ABSTRACT

As the world is ageing, many of the global economies are on the verge of silver tsunami/grey tsunami. Given the scenario, the need for retirement planning cannot be overlooked. This study presents a systematic literature review on retirement planning behaviour. A total of 142 documents extracted from the Scopus database were reviewed, and the analysis is presented using Theory, Context and Methodology (TCM), Planning, Operationalizing, Writing, Embedding and Reflecting (POWER) and Antecedents, Decisions and Outcomes (ADO) frameworks. The study offers valuable insights with respect to the theoretical foundation, geographical concentration of research, research methods and techniques applied. The study also highlights the diverse retirement planning decisions an individual makes, their antecedents and the outcomes of such decisions. The study shall aid policymakers and industry practitioners in fostering retirement planning habits among people and thereby facilitate their overall welfare.

Keywords: Systematic literature review; retirement planning behaviour; POWER framework; TCM framework; ADO framework

1. INTRODUCTION

Maintaining a healthy financial status and fulfilling future financial goals depends on a crucial skill, i.e. personal financial planning (Mahapatra et al., 2019). Kapoor et al. (2014) defined personal financial planning as a process of handling

Reviewing the Latest Trends in Management Literature
Review of Management Literature, Volume 4B, 125–149

Published under exclusive licence by Emerald Publishing Limited
ISSN: 2754-5865/doi:10.1108/S2754-58652025000004B005

personal wealth with the ultimate aim of attaining economic satisfaction. In essence, it entails six broad areas related to financial planning, namely cash flow management, investment planning, tax planning, estate planning, risk management and retirement planning (Altfest, 2004). Preferably, an ideal financial plan should encompass all the areas of financial planning; however, the life stage and the circumstances surrounding an individual distract him/her from focusing more on some specific area (Yeo et al., 2023). For example, a person who got laid off might not be involved in investment planning. Similarly, a pre-retiree might be more conscious of retirement planning.

While each element of financial planning is crucial for a financially peaceful life, this paper specifically focuses on the financial preparation for life after retirement. Retirement planning plays a vital role for the economies and individuals all around the world (Vieira et al., 2023). As the world is ageing, many of the global economies are on the verge of silver tsunami/grey tsunami. It is a metaphor used to describe the demographic shift due to the rapid increase in the number of people entering their retirement phase, resulting in increasing dependence on the already scarce resources. According to the WHO (Ageing and Health, 2022), by 2030, one of every six people will be of age above 60 years. Also, by 2050 the number of older people (60 years and above) is expected to reach 2.1 billion (double of 2020 records). While a high-income country like Japan is already experiencing the heat of the Silver Tsunami (30% older population), it is expected that 80% of the older population will reside in middle- and low-income countries. This calls for serious efforts in the area of strong healthcare and social security systems across the world.

The shift from defined benefit to defined contribution pension has strengthened the social security system (Mata, 2021), thereby reducing the unreasonable burden on the government. Greater responsibility now lies on individuals to safeguard their post-retirement lives. However, the reality is unsettling, i.e. majority of the population is struggling with their retirement. They lack even a basic retirement plan in their life (González-Núñez & Mariné-Osorio, 2023). Another disturbing reality is the inadequacy of the existing retirement pension plans to fulfil retirement needs (Gritten, 2011). This accelerated demographic shift coupled with an incompetent social security system has resulted in various international organizations, like the United Nations and the International Social Security Association constantly promoting the significant role of private pension plans for a secured retirement life (UN, Department of Economic and Social Affairs, Population Division, 2020; WEF, 2019).

Before diving deeper into the main objective of the study, firstly there is a need to understand the concept of retirement planning. The is no single definition of retirement planning in the literature. The most comprehensive definition of retirement planning was given by Sinha and Irala (2024), who defined retirement planning as 'a process that requires conscious efforts in ascertaining the sufficiency of savings, collecting information, estimating the needs, and making a plan for accumulating assets for the future.' They also proposed a 'Tripple A framework' of retirement planning where the whole process is classified into three steps, i.e. Awareness (about the current situation from a retirement perspective), Assessment (involving gathering information on different means of saving for retirement and creating the elaborate plan) and Accumulation (the actual act of wealth accumulation for retirement).

1.1 Gap and Contribution of the Study

Many existing literature reviews have been thoroughly examined to understand the current situation. The literature review by Ingale and Paluri (2023) shed light on the determinants of retirement planning and their measurement scale. Another study by Sinha and Irala (2024) identified the lack of conceptual clarity on the definition of retirement planning and proposed a comprehensive definition via the Triple-A framework. Kerry (2018) also aimed to offer conceptual clarity on the focal construct, i.e. retirement planning. Kumar et al. (2019) focused only on financial planning for the retirement of women. Other reviews linked retirement planning with some key constructs like financial literacy (Gallego-Losada et al., 2021), life expectancy (Jantan, 2020), etc.

By reviewing the existing review papers, it was found that while many authors shed light on the determinants of retirement planning, very few discussed the types of decisions being made regarding retirement planning. Also, there was no evidence regarding the outcome of retirement planning being assessed in the existing reviews. Thus, the current study aims to address this gap. The current study also intends to use the latest review frameworks for in-depth analysis and better results.

2. REVIEW METHODOLOGY

2.1 Review Procedure: Planning, Operationalizing, Writing, Embedding and Reflecting (POWER) Framework

It is an integral part of research and offers a holistic overview of the domain (Farrukh & Sajjad, 2023) Therefore, a systematic review is the best way to present the current knowledge and forecast future avenues. It is not just a compilation of existing studies but requires intelligent and insightful synthesis (Dhiman et al., 2023). It not only provides knowledge about the research field but also offers new perspectives and opportunities for theoretical formation (Rammal, 2023). The present study aims to conduct an SLR and draw valuable insights in the area of retirement planning. It aims to answer research questions like 'What are the determinants of retirement planning, the types of decisions encompassing retirement planning, and the outcomes of such decisions?'

A few protocols exist for conducting SLR. Among them all, the POWER framework has become quite popular among researchers (Quttainah et al., 2023; Sardana et al., 2024). As proposed by Rana et al. (2022, 2023), the framework is a scientific and holistic approach that ensures a meaningful and insightful review of the literature. The POWER framework will enhance understanding of the state of the art and thereby stimulate knowledge creation in the review domain. Fig. 1 elucidates the applied review procedure.

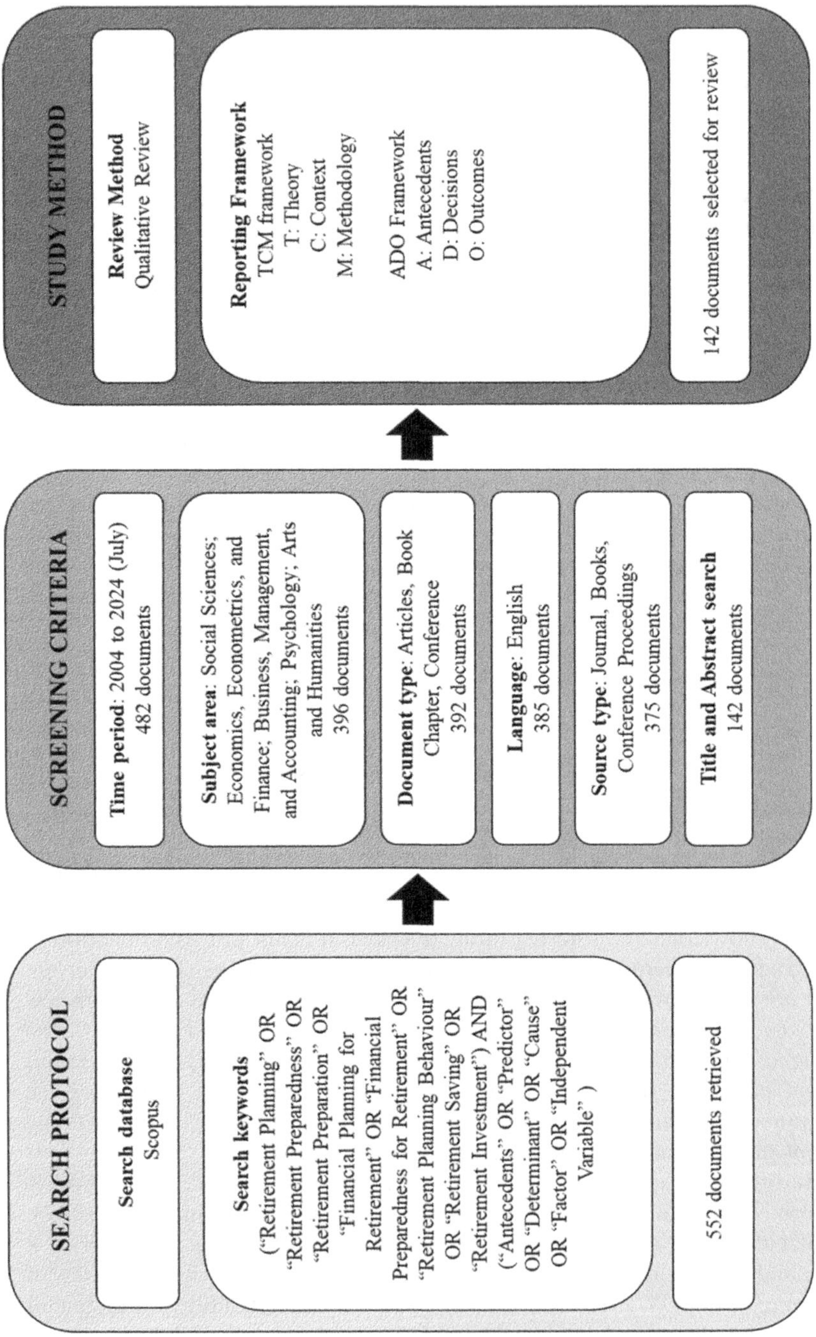

Fig. 1. Review Procedure. *Source:* Author's compilation.

The review procedure entails three stages i.e. search protocol, screening criteria and study method. The first stage entails the selection of a database and search keywords. The documents were sourced from the SCOPUS database. The purpose of using the SCOPUS for document search is its connection with myriads of reputed publishers and the elimination of predatory journals. The keyword search under the title, abstract and keywords search function. The second stage involves establishing inclusion and exclusion criteria. The documents were filtered based on the time period, subject area, document type, language and source type. Next, all the documents with out-of-context focus (like driver retirement, athletes' retirement, bridge employment, retirement adjustment, etc.) were removed via title and abstract read. The last stage involves decisions regarding the study method. The qualitative review is conducted, and the findings are reported using the TCM framework (Paul et al., 2017) and the ADO framework (Paul & Benito, 2017). Both the frameworks are quite popular among researchers (Singh et al., 2022).

3. REVIEW FINDINGS

3.1 TCM Analysis

3.1.1 Theory

Retirement planning is multidisciplinary in nature, i.e. it takes inferences from disciplines like economics, sociology, psychology, finance, family studies, etc. (Schuchardt et al., 2007). Hence, the literature entails different theories from different domains that have contributed to the conceptualization of the phenomenon of retirement planning. The most popular theories are the *Theory of Planned Behaviour* and the *Theory of Reasoned Action* by Ajzen (1991). From a retirement perspective, the theory explains the influence of retirement attitude, subjective norms and perceived behavioural control on retirement planning intention and actual planning behaviour (Harahap et al., 2022; Kimiyagahlam et al., 2019; Mata, 2021; Nga & Yeoh, 2018; She et al., 2024; Yeung et al., 2023). Another theory that explains the role of personality on retirement preparedness is the *3M Theory of Personality* by Mowen (2000) and *Image Theory* by Beach (1998). Image theory proposes that decision-makers represent information as images, and each is linked with the other in hierarchical order till the decision is made. The 3M theory of personality classifies personalities into three categories, i.e. cardinal traits, central traits and surface traits, and proposes that these traits influence behaviour in a hierarchical order. Tomar et al. (2021), França and Hershey (2018) and Hershey et al. (2010) explored the hierarchical relationship between psychological factors and retirement planning.

Modigliani and Brumberg's (1954) *Life-Cycle Theory* also served as the basis for retirement planning literature. The authors proposed that spending and saving is a lifelong process and people tend to deviate from optimal saving patterns because of circumstances. Based on this theory, Rasiah et al. (2020) found that the conflict of interest negatively impacts retirement preparedness. Griffin et al. (2012) drawing on the tenets of *Socioemotional Selective Theory* proposed that subjective life expectancy can significantly affect retirement planning decisions, i.e. post-retirement work decisions in this case. Chung and Park (2019) revealed the significance of financial knowledge and financial network building for better retirement planning using *Social Cognitive Theory* and *Social Network Theory*. *Life Course, Ecological Theory* established the relationship between environmental factors, i.e. work environment and retirement planning (Jais & Asokumar, 2020). Harahap et al. (2022) proposed the impact of herding behaviour on retirement planning using *Prospect Theory*. Tomar et al. (2021) established the relationship between social influence and retirement planning behaviour using *Social Influence Theory*.

Capacity, Willingness, Opportunity (CWO) model given by Hershey et al. (2012) is the most widely referred model in the literature. The model categorizes factors affecting financial planning for retirement into three dimensions. Capacity means the ability to plan for retirement and includes cognitive factors. Willingness entails the factors that motivate an individual to plan for retirement and includes personality and motivation factors. Lastly, opportunity includes the external factors that facilitate retirement planning like social support, financial advice, retirement saving programs, etc. The extended version of the CWO model was proposed by Topa et al. (2018), by taking inspiration from the *Intentional Change Theory* (Boyatzis, 2006), with additional psychosocial moderator variables like procrastination, emotional intelligence, fear of death, etc. More determinants are added under each dimension of the CWO model. Another model namely, the *Retirement Engagement model* was proposed by Eberhardt et al. (2022), explaining the relationship between cognitive factors, emotional engagement and socio-demographic factors with engagement in retirement planning.

3.1.2 Context

On analyzing the existing literature, it was found that the research primarily belongs to the American, European and Asian regions. Evidence emerged from both developed and developing nations. In North America, the United States (50 studies), Mexico (3 studies) and Canada (2 studies) are the main research centres, and in South America, the research belonged to Brazil (5 studies) and Chile (1 study). In Asia, Malaysia leads the research (19 studies) followed by China (12 studies), India (8 studies), Thailand (5 studies), Vietnam (4 studies), etc. Only a handful of studies were found from the Middle East region, i.e. UAE (2 studies), Turkey (2 studies), Israel and Saudi Arabia (1 study each). The European region too has contributed substantially with contributions coming from the United Kingdom (10 studies), Spain (5 studies), Germany (3 studies), Portugal (3 studies), Switzerland (3 studies), Ireland, Poland (2 studies), etc. Australia (10 studies) and New Zealand (6 studies) are the contributors from the Oceania region. From the African region, the studies primarily belonged to Nigeria (2 studies), Namibia and Uganda (1 study each).

Upon closer inspection, it was found that the studies are majorly standalone, i.e. studies based on one country (Huang et al., 2023; Jais & Asokumar, 2020; Ketkaew et al., 2022; Larisa et al., 2020; Qian et al., 2024; Saini et al., 2024; She et al., 2024).

Only a handful of studies were comparative in nature, i.e. with two or more countries. The multi-country studies mainly belonged to the European region (Fernández-López et al., 2010; Garcia & Marques, 2017; Rey et al., 2015; Rey-Ares et al., 2018).

3.1.3 Methodology

The deeper analysis of the methodologies of the existing literature revealed that the majority of the studies are primary in nature (78%) followed by secondary (20%) and hybrid studies (2%). Secondary studies included survey data from various professional agencies and government bodies (Chen, Chang, et al., 2024, Chen, Fan, et al., 2024; Garcia & Marques, 2017; Lim & Lee, 2021; Magwegwe & Lim, 2021; Mata, 2021; Zhou et al., 2022). With respect to data collection methods, under the quantitative method, cross-sectional and longitudinal surveys were the prime choice (88%). The survey data were either primary or secondary (pre existing survey data) in nature. The experiment (4%) was another quantitative method used in the literature (Cardella et al., 2023; Chaiwat et al., 2024; Fenton et al., 2023). Among the qualitative methods, interviews (6%) (Bednarczyk et al., 2021; Ketkaew et al., 2022) and focus groups (2%) (Blanco et al., 2017; Lee et al., 2016) are the preferred methods of data collection. Further, the methodological synthesis revealed that structural equation modelling (SEM) and regression were the top choices for data analysis. Various regression techniques, like probit regression (Chen, Fan, et al., 2024; Kanime et al., 2021; Yorgason et al., 2020), OLS regression (Detthamrong et al., 2023; Tomar et al., 2021; Zhou et al., 2022) and logit regression (Chua & Chin, 2022; Pospíšil et al., 2023; Syihab & Nurhakim, 2022), were applied. Among other techniques used in the literature are confirmatory factor analysis (CFA), confirmatory tetrad analysis (CTD-PLS), correlation and ANOVA.

3.2 ADO Analysis

Fig. 2 presents the antecedents, decisions and outcomes concerning retirement planning in the existing literature.

3.2.1 Antecedents

Numerous factors affect the retirement planning decisions of an individual. The antecedents are classified into internal and external antecedents. Internal antecedents are the ones directly associated with the individual. External antecedents are the ones where the influence is coming from outside. The internal antecedents are further classified into psychological and non-psychological determinants. Psychological determinants include the ones associated with mind and mental processes. The non-psychological factors also influence an individual's behaviour but have no relation to mind and mental processes (Table 1).

Knowledge Factors: Financial literacy and financial knowledge/financial planning knowledge are the most widely studied determinants of retirement planning. The studies attributed financial literacy to positively impact the

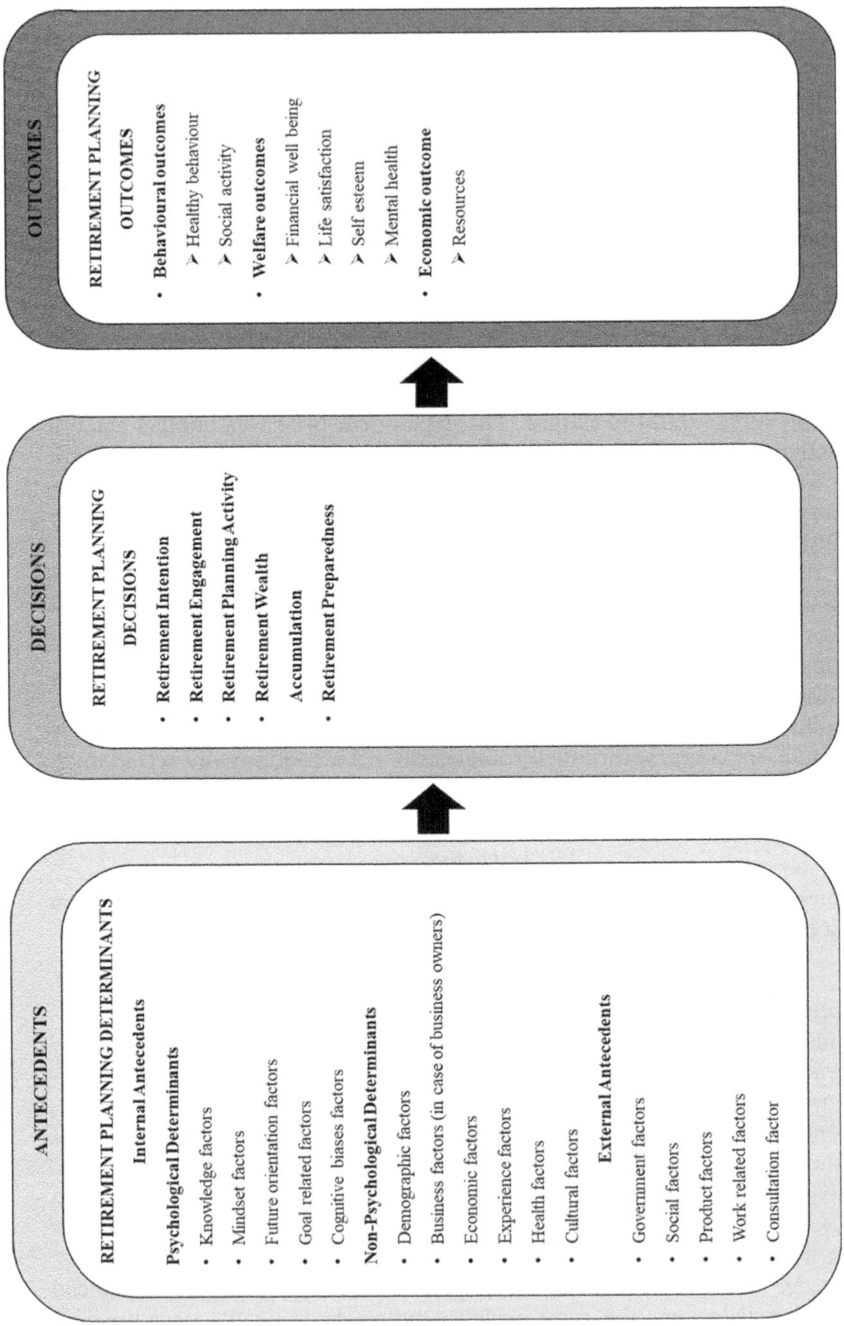

Fig. 2. Antecedents, Decisions and Outcomes of Retirement Planning. *Source:* Author's compilation.

Table 1. Retirement Planning Antecedents.

Internal Antecedents			
Psychological Determinants			
Knowledge Factors	Financial Literacy	Knowledge of financial concepts like interest, tax, investment, etc.	Qian et al. (2024), Yeung et al. (2023), Ketkaew et al. (2022), Nguyen et al. (2022), Larisa et al. (2020), Jais and Asokumar (2020), and Lusardi and Mitchelli (2007)
	Financial Knowledge/Financial Planning Knowledge	Individuals' knowledge about saving, pension and investment	Saini et al. (2024), Chen, Chang, et al. (2024), Detthamrong et al. (2023), Mata (2021), Janposri (2021), Bongini and Cucinelli (2019), Clark et al. (2017), Lee et al. (2013) and Hershey et al. (2010)
Mindset Factors	Financial Attitude	An individual's values and beliefs towards financial matters	Indapurkar et al. (2024), Mustafa et al. (2023) and Afthanorhan et al. (2020)
	Retirement Attitude/Perception	Overall outlook towards post-retirement life	She et al. (2024), Pospíšil et al. (2023), Noone et al. (2010, 2022), and Magwegwe and Lim (2021)
	Financial Self-Efficacy	Individual's beliefs on their ability to manage finance	Ghadwan et al. (2023) and Eberhardt et al. (2022)
	Locus of Control/Perceived Behavioural Control	The belief of an individual about his/her control over circumstances	She et al. (2024), Magwegwe and Lim (2021), Bongini and Cucinelli (2019), and Piotrowska (2019)
Future Orientation Factors	Future Time Perspective	Orientation towards life in the future	Voleti et al. (2024), Alkhawaja and Albaity (2022), Larisa et al. (2020), Piotrowska (2019), França and Hershey (2018), and Earl et al. (2015)
	Subjective Life Expectancy	Individual's beliefs about the maximum attainable age	Zhou et al. (2022), Thakur et al. (2020), and Griffin et al. (2012)
Goal Related Factors	Retirement Goal Clarity	Individual's clarity regarding their post-retirement aspirations and purpose	Ghadwan et al. (2023), Detthamrong et al. (2023), Tomar et al. (2021), Rasiah et al. (2020), and Hershey et al. (2010)
	Flexible Goal Adjustment	Modification of goals in the presence of changing circumstances	Liu et al. (2024)
Cognitive Biases factors	Cognitive Reflection	Individual's ability to resist intuitions or impulsive behaviour and consider issues thoughtfully	Chaiwat et al. (2024)
	Behavioural Biases	Includes present bias, herding, intervention, procrastination	Bajtelsmit and Coats (2023), Harahap et al. (2022), Blanco et al. (2020), and Piotrowska (2019)
Non-psychological Determinants			
	Demographics		

(Continued)

Table 1. *(Continued)*

Demographic Factors		Includes income, gender, background, education level, marital status, employment status, etc.	González-Núñez and Mariné-Osorio (2023), Qi et al. (2022), Chan and Au-Yeung (2021), Ali and Frank (2019), Rey-Ares et al. (2018), and Garcia and Marques (2017)
Business Factors	Business Characteristics (in the case of business owners)	Includes age, net worth, etc. of business	Kim et al. (2019)
Economic Factors	Financial Status/Economic Resources/ Risky Indebtedness Behaviour	Overall financial position i.e. income, savings and debt	Detthamrong et al. (2023), Vieira et al. (2023), Bednarczyk et al. (2021), and Lim and Lee (2021)
Experience Factors	Financial Experiences/Challenges/Strain	Past experiences like the inability to save for 12 months or a recessionary situation	Innocenti et al. (2024), Mustafa et al. (2023), and Afthanorhan et al. (2020)
Health Factors	Physical and Mental Health	Individual's beliefs regarding their health (physical and mental)	Kung et al. (2023), Kim et al. (2021), Thakur et al. (2020), Nga and Yeoh (2018), and Rey et al. (2015)
Cultural Factors	Culture	Cultural beliefs and values	Ghadwan et al. (2022), Yorgason et al. (2020), and Blanco et al. (2017)
	Religiosity	Belief in gods will	Blanco et al. (2017)
External Antecedents			
Government Factors	Government Policy/Pension System	Government regulations related to retirement planning activity/pension system	Ghadwan et al. (2023) and Hershey et al. (2010)
Social Factors	Social Norms/Social Influence/Social Interaction/Parental influence	Support and interaction with family and friends and their Influence on decision-making	Yeung et al. (2023), Tomar et al. (2021), Kanime et al. (2021), Lee et al. (2013), and Hershey et al. (2010)
Product Factors	Communication Message Strategy/ Interaction Online Planner/Financial Software	Includes message frame and message appeal/ financial software for information and tracking	Fenton et al. (2023), Hoffmann and Plotkina (2020), and Bi et al. (2017)
Environmental Factors	Work Environment/Work Pattern	Current working conditions and satisfaction	Jais and Asokumar (2020) and Noone et al. (2010)
	Family Environment	Relationship dynamics with family members	Jais and Asokumar (2020)
Consultation Factor	Financial Advice	Taking financial advice from experts for financial decision-making	Fang et al. (2022), Kanime et al. (2021), Nga and Yeoh (2018), and Lee et al. (2013)

Source: Author's compilation.

retirement planning (Chen, Chang, et al., 2024; Qian et al., 2024), intention to purchase saving products (Yeung et al., 2023), investments and expected returns (Bajtelsmit & Coats, 2023) and retirement readiness (Ketkaew et al., 2022). A similar relationship is found between financial knowledge/financial planning knowledge and retirement planning decisions (Alkhawaja & Albaity, 2022; Bongini & Cucinelli, 2019; Clark et al., 2017; Detthamrong et al., 2023; Hershey et al., 2010, 2007; Janposri, 2021; Lee et al., 2016; Mata, 2021; Nga & Yeoh, 2018; Saini et al., 2024; Thakur et al., 2020). However, Nguyen et al. (2022) objected to the viability of using subjective financial literacy as it exerts a negative influence on retirement saving intention and behaviour. Overall, the literature highlights the need for mandatory and effective financial literacy and education programs for retirement planning adoption.

Mindset Factors: The word mindset signifies both attitude (mental feeling) and perception (mental image). Thus, financial attitude, retirement attitude, financial self-efficacy and locus of control/perceived behavioural control form part of mindset factors. Mustafa et al. (2023) reported that a positive financial attitude is important for financial retirement planning as it makes people aware of their current position and plan accordingly. Hoffmann and Plotkina (2020) proposed that a positive retirement attitude can influence the financial outlook of an individual for the better, thus affecting their retirement saving intention. Ghadwan et al. (2023) document a positive relationship between financial self-efficacy and financial retirement planning among respondents as higher financial self-efficacy gave them confidence in their ability to plan and save for the future. Piotrowska (2019) registered a positive relationship between locus of control and retirement savings, thereby signifying the importance of self-control for achieving long-term financial goals.

Future Orientation Factors: Voleti et al. (2024) reported a positive relationship between future time perspective and financial preparedness for retirement indicating that those who are concerned about their future or believe that their end is near are better planned than the others. Similar results were reported by Alkhawaja and Albaity (2022) for financial planning for retirement. Also, Griffin et al. (2012) reported that subjective life expectancy significantly influences the intended retirement age and the amount needed for retirement preparation. Under or over-estimation of subjective life expectancy can severely affect retirement planning decisions thereby causing distress post-retirement.

Goal-Related Factors: Yeung et al. (2023) registered a positive relationship between retirement goal clarity and intention to purchase financial products for retirement because a clearer view of the retirement goals will help in identifying the suitable investment products needed to fulfil that goal. Ghadwan et al. (2023) also registered a significant relationship between retirement goal clarity and financial planning for retirement. Liu et al. (2024) studied the impact of goal-pursuit tendencies on retirement planning and found that flexible goal adjustment significantly influences retirement planning.

Cognitive Bias Factors: Chaiwat et al. (2024) present the role of cognitive reflections on the intention to indulge in complex tax incentive retirement saving options and reported a positive relationship between the two. This highlights the importance of cognitive abilities in making financial decisions. Harahap et al. (2022) reported that herding behaviour strengthens/moderates the relationship between financial literacy and retirement planning among medium entrepreneurs. Piotrowska (2019) reported the negative influence of procrastination on retirement saving intention. It means that people who procrastinate tend to lag when planning for the future.

Demographic Factors: Studies by González-Núñez and Mariné-Osorio (2023), Qi et al. (2022), Gornick and Sierminska (2021), Ali and Frank (2019) and many others have registered significant impact of demographic characteristics like age, education, marital status, employment type, etc. on various retirement planning decisions. In several studies, they have taken up the moderating role (Afthanorhan et al., 2020; Lim & Lee, 2021).

Business Factors: While studying the retirement planning behaviour of sole proprietary business owners, Kim et al. (2019) found that intermixing of personal and business assets, business age and net worth had a significant influence on establishing retirement as a saving goal and likelihood of choosing defined benefit or defined contribution retirement saving option.

Economic Factors: Detthamrong et al. (2023) reported a significant relationship between financial status and financial planning for retirement, thus showcasing the need for a thorough analysis of financial status from time to time. Vieira et al. (2023) documented a significant negative relationship between risky indebtedness behaviour and financial preparation for retirement, thereby affecting financial well-being. This calls out to policymakers to formulate policies that promote healthy financial behaviour and control reckless financial behaviour.

Experience Factors: Innocenti et al. (2024) registered that people who have not been able to save in the past 12 months lack the propensity to save for the future and are concerned about their retirement. They also lack savings in supplementary pension funds. Further, Payne et al. (2014) reported that couples who were finding it difficult to make their ends meet (financial strain) were facing difficulty in saving for retirement.

Health Factors: Kung et al. (2023) studied the desire for early retirement during the COVID-19 period and found that poor self-reported health negatively affected the intention to retire early. Isa and Daukin (2022) also reported that the unexpected arrival of the COVID-19 pandemic clubbed with current financial status significantly affects retirement planning. Noone et al. (2022) also reported strong predictive power of health towards retirement planning.

Cultural Factors: Ghadwan et al. (2022) documented a significant relationship between cultural forces and retirement planning. Culture further moderated the relationship between financial literacy, financial risk tolerance and retirement planning. They proposed that people who respect traditional values are associated with the ones with strong personal finance knowledge, thus they indulge in planning for retirement. Blanco et al. (2017) reported that people who had a belief that God would take care of everything significantly lacked retirement savings.

Government Factors: Ghadwan et al. (2023) studied the role of government policy on financial planning for retirement and found a positive relationship between them, i.e. positive perception of the government pension system will increase public participation and savings. Further, it moderates the relationship between retirement goal clarity and retirement planning. Hershey et al. (2010) while studying the saving adequacy of American and Dutch people found conflicting outcomes. The greater trust in government pensions disincentivized Dutch people to save. On the other hand, lack of trust among Americans motivated them to indulge in saving activity on their own.

Social Factors: Yeung et al. (2023) reported that both social norms and social support significantly influence the intention to purchase retirement-saving products via retirement goal clarity. Tomar et al. (2021) also reported a significant positive relationship between social support and retirement planning behaviour, indicating that social support from family, friends and peers influence future goals and offers motivation to achieve them.

Product Factors: Fenton et al. (2023) discovered that communication message strategy, i.e. message frame and message appeal significantly influence retirement saving intention. Hoffmann and Plotkina (2020) also highlighted the significant role of financial information messages on retirement planning intention and behaviour. Bi et al. (2017) reported that given the complexity of the financial decision-making process, the use of financial software for making retirement calculations fosters retirement savings.

Environment Factors: Jais and Asokumar (2020) and Noone et al. (2010) reported a significant relationship between work environment and retirement planning decisions, i.e. people who are disconnected from their workplace are more likely to indulge in retirement planning activity. Jais and Asokumar (2020) also reported a significant relationship between family environment and retirement planning, i.e. a close-knit family (prefers to spend time together) is likely to plan for retirement and indulge in retirement-related discussions.

Consultation Factor: Chen, Chang, et al. (2024) reported that trust in financial advisors can promote retirement planning activity among people. People with low financial literacy will indulge in retirement planning when they have trust in their financial advisor. Fang et al. (2022) also found that the decision to take financial advice and the quality of financial advice, both significantly affect retirement saving decisions.

3.2.2 Decisions

Retirement planning is a very crucial aspect of any individual's life. Ideally, the phrase 'the earlier the better' fits well with it. However, the reality is far from the ideal state. Many researchers in the past have attempted to understand the concept of retirement planning. Every research differed in the sense that different authors equated retirement planning with different aspects (Table 2). Terms like retirement planning behaviour (Alessie et al., 2011; Clark et al., 2017; Kimiyaghalam et al., 2017), perceived financial preparedness for retirement (Hershey & Mowen, 2000; Hershey et al., 2007), retirement saving behaviour (Alkhawaja & Albaity, 2022),

Table 2. Retirement Planning Decisions.

Intention	Retirement Intention	An individual's mindset regarding engagement in retirement planning activity	She et al. (2024), Pospíšil et al. (2023), Mata (2021) and Hoffmann and Plotkina (2020)
	Desires Retirement Age	The age at which an individual wants to retire	Shin and Lee (2019)
Engagement	Retirement Engagement	Information search for retirement planning	Eberhardt et al. (2022)
	Financial Planning for Retirement	Individuals making necessary calculations regarding retirement needs (subjective)	Ghadwan et al. (2023), Ghadwan et al. (2022), Thakur et al. (2020), Kimiyagahlam et al. (2019), Hershey et al. (2010) and Noone et al. (2010)
Planning Activity	Retirement Planning	A multidimensional construct including different aspects of retirement like finance, health, leisure and work/three-structure construct, i.e. public protection, self-protection and self-insurance	Qian et al. (2024), Chen, Chang, et al. (2024), Mustafa et al. (2023), Harahap et al. (2022) and Griffin et al. (2012)
Wealth Accumulation	Retirement Saving	Engagement in saving money for retirement and satisfaction/lack of retirement savings/retirement saving adequacy	Innocenti et al. (2024), Fang et al. (2022), Nguyen et al. (2022), Alkhawaja and Albaity (2022), Janposri (2021), Nga and Yeoh (2018), Clark et al. (2017) and Payne et al. (2014)
	Retirement Investment	The choice between employer and self-managed retirement investment plans/choice between typical and complex tax-deductible investment plans/ retirement pension insurance participation	Saini et al. (2024), Chen, Fan, et al. (2024), Yeung et al. (2023), Blanco et al. (2020) and Chung and Park (2019)
Preparedness	Perceived Retirement Preparedness	Individual's belief regarding their retirement readiness	Hutchinson and Ausman (2024), Voleti et al. (2024), Qi et al. (2022), Rasiah et al. (2020) and Lusardi and Mitchelli (2007)

Source: Author's compilation.

retirement saving adequacy (Lim & Lee, 2021), retirement preparation (Chua & Chin, 2022) and financial planning for retirement (Alkhawaja & Albaity, 2022; Topa et al., 2018) have been used in the past.

Based on the shreds of evidence found in the literature, retirement planning decisions are classified into five broad decision heads (Table 2). Some explained retirement planning by *intention,* i.e. either the intention to engage in retirement planning activity or the age at which they intend to retire. In terms of *engagement*, retirement planning is defined as individuals engaging in retirement-related information search or whether they have made necessary calculations regarding retirement. With respect to *retirement planning activity*, two multi-dimensional constructs are popular among researchers. First, where retirement planning is a combination of financial planning, health planning, work planning and leisure planning. Second, where retirement planning is defined as a three-structure construct, i.e. public protection, self-protection and self-insurance. Decisions related to *retirement savings and investments (wealth accumulation)* are extensively researched as well like retirement saving adequacy, lack of retirement saving account, choice between retirement saving accounts through employer or independent retirement saving accounts, choice between basic and complex tax-deductible retirement saving options, etc. A substantial number of researchers have studied retirement planning from the point of view of *retirement preparedness or readiness.*

3.2.3 Outcomes

The literature consists of a plethora of studies exploring various retirement planning decisions; however, only a handful of studies focused on the outcomes of such decisions (Table 3). Studying the outcomes of retirement planning behaviour is essential as it facilitates learning and improvement. Documentation of positive outcomes of retirement planning will help in improving public engagement towards such a crucial life decision. For analysis, the reported outcomes in the literature are divided into three categories, i.e. *behavioural outcome, welfare outcome* and *resource outcome.* Behaviour outcomes entail individuals' engagement in healthy lifestyles (Gubler & Pierce 2014; Huang et al., 2023; Liu et al., 2021) and social activities (Micheel, 2021; Wu & Chao, 2024) post-retirement. Welfare is a combination of physical, mental and emotional state. Thus, retirement planning results in post-retirement financial well-being (Chan et al., 2021; Vieira et al., 2023; Yeung & Zhou, 2017), gives a feeling of life satisfaction (Earl et al., 2015; Hutchinson & Ausman, 2024; Liu et al., 2021),

Table 3. Retirement Planning Outcomes (Post-retirement).

Behavioural Outcome	Healthy behaviour	Includes healthy living behaviour	Huang et al. (2023), Liu et al. (2021) and Gubler and Pierce (2014)
	Social activity	Engagement in social activities with friends and peers	Wu and Chao (2024) and Micheel (2021)
Welfare Outcomes	Financial well-being	The feeling of security, satisfaction and control regarding post-retirement finances	Vieira et al. (2023), Chan et al. (2021), Lim and Lee (2021), Yeung and Zhou (2017), Muratore and Earl (2015) and Earl et al. (2015)
	Life satisfaction	It means social connections and meaningful activities in retirement	Hutchinson and Ausman (2024), Amorim and de Freitas Pinho França (2022), Liu et al. (2021), Kim et al. (2021), Muratore and Earl (2015) and Earl et al. (2015)
	Self-esteem	Perception about oneself	Wu and Chao (2024)
	Mental health	The emotional and psychological well-being of an individual	Wu and Chao (2024)
Resource Outcome	Post-retirement resources	Includes health, financial and psychosocial resources	Noone et al. (2022)

Source: Author's compilation.

boosts self-esteem and improves mental health (Wu & Chao, 2024). Retirement planning is also found to have a significant impact on post-retirement resources (Noone et al., 2022), be it economic, health or psychosocial resources.

4. DISCUSSION AND FUTURE RESEARCH DIRECTIONS

It would be incorrect to say that the domain of retirement planning is an under-researched area. It has been thoroughly researched; however, there still exists scope for further research. This section offers insights into the opportunities for advancement of the retirement planning literature.

Theory: In the past, researchers have borrowed theories from the corresponding domains of psychology, economics, behavioural finance, etc. to lay the theoretical foundation for retirement planning behaviour. It is clear from the literature that most of the theories focus on the relationship between retirement planning behaviour and internal factors like knowledge, future orientation, mindset, demographics, etc. However, there is limited theoretical evidence on external factors like social (Social Cognitive Theory and Social Network Theory), environmental (Life Course; Ecological Theory), etc. Thus, there is a need for more research on theories associated with external antecedents. Also, multiple factors of varying natures affect retirement planning behaviour simultaneously. A single theory alone cannot justify the cause of behaviour, which is common in most of the extant literature. The domain calls for more research using a collective approach, i.e. combining two or more theories to develop a concrete model of retirement planning The same is done by a few authors (Chung & Park, 2019; Hoffmann & Plotkina, 2020; Tomar et al., 2021). It was in recent years that the amalgamation of theories was adopted. Moreover, the lack of specialisation is a common limitation among all the existing research because of the lack of a dedicated theory on the retirement planning phenomenon. All the existing literature is based on the theories adapted from corresponding domains. Thus, future researchers need to work on generating theories, specially dedicated to retirement planning behaviour.

Context: The contextual analysis revealed the research dominance of American and European nations in the domain of retirement planning. Although there has been some significant contribution from the Asian region as well, however, a lot more is needed from the region. Given the fact that two nations, i.e. Japan and South Korea, which are currently facing the heat of demographic shift are the part of Asia region signifies the need for more research from the given region. The negligible research from the African region also offers scope for future researchers. Moreover, cross-country research on retirement planning has a lot to offer than stand-alone research. It helps in identifying the behavioural differences between the nations, the differences in the social security systems and government regulations and ways for improvement. However, the literature is scarce concerning cross-country studies, which offers the opportunity for future researchers.

Methodology: The methodological analysis of the literature uncovered the dominance of quantitative methods like surveys and experiments as the choice of data collection method among researchers in the past. The limited research using qualitative research methods, like interviews and focus group techniques, acts as a research gap that future research can fill. Perhaps they might offer a deeper understanding of the concept of retirement planning. Researchers can also opt for combined research, i.e. qualitative and quantitative approaches in the future. Moreover, most of the studies rely on conventional data analysis techniques like SEM, regression, CFA, correlation, etc. There is a need to explore modern data analysis techniques, like machine learning, which facilitate higher predictability and accuracy.

Antecedents: Past researchers have identified numerous factors affecting different dimensions of retirement planning. The classification of the factors into internal and external antecedents and further classification of the internal antecedents into psychological and non-psychological determinants have offered clarity concerning the factors that need more attention. Certain internal psychological factors have been thoroughly explored in the past like financial literacy, financial knowledge, retirement goal clarity and future time perspective. More research is needed in other aspects like cognitive biases, flexible goal adjustment, financial self-efficacy and locus of control. Also, the literature calls for more research on some internal non-psychological determinants like business (in the case of business owners), culture, and experience factors. In countries like Saudi Arabia, India, Indonesia, Sri Lanka, etc. where cultural faith and beliefs have a strong hold on human behaviour, analyzing such beliefs from the retirement planning perspective becomes crucial (Ghadwan et al., 2022). Culture also influences the social support mechanism that underlines retirement planning activity (Hershey et al., 2010). Given that the COVID-19 pandemic has caused worldwide financial distress, examining its impact on retirement planning activity is a must.

The external factors like environment, government and product factors too need significant attention. The literature has reported a positive link between work environment and wealth accumulation specifically among women (Gornick & Sierminska, 2021). On the other hand, a poor work environment is associated with active retirement planning activity as well (Jais & Asokumar, 2020). The social security system and regulations surrounding it shape the retirement planning scenario within the country. Some nations are more retirement-ready than others because of the favourable government regulations. Thus, understanding the role of such regulations becomes important. As the world is getting digitalized, information management and its dissemination and user interface are important aspects of digital products. Product factors mainly include the role of communication style and financial software usage on retirement planning behaviour (Bi et al., 2017; Fenton et al., 2023). Such research studies are experimental in nature, which was not a popular choice among researchers in the past. Hence, such factors need immediate attention. The limited empirical evidence on non-psychological and external antecedents results in a lack of generalization. Thus, future researchers need to focus on the less explored antecedents.

Decisions: Based on the shreds of evidence found in the existing literature, there is inconsistency in the definition of retirement planning. In the study, it has been classified into intention, engagement, planning activity, wealth accumulation (saving and investment) and preparedness. Among them all, intention and preparedness decisions need more attention. Also, each aspect of retirement planning has been explored as a stand-alone. However, all these decisional aspects are interconnected. Thus, there is a need for research where all these decisions are explored simultaneously. This will also help in identifying how one decision affects the other. The same is proposed by Sinha and Irala (2024) when defining the concept of retirement planning using the triple A framework. They proposed that retirement planning is a hierarchical process consisting of three stages, i.e. awareness, assessment and accumulation, and the whole process must be studied collectively for a holistic understanding.

Outcomes: Examining the outcomes of any decision/behaviour is equally important as exploring the actual decision/behaviour. It will help in identifying the problems and ways for improvement in the future. It is easier to influence people to behave in a certain manner if they are aware of its positive outcomes. Thus, exploring the outcomes of retirement planning is necessary as it will facilitate the development of retirement planning habits among people. While some existing studies have studied the post-retirement behavioural, welfare and resource outcomes of retirement planning decisions, the scanty literature calls for more research. It will help in further validation of outcomes of retirement planning behaviour.

5. CONCLUSION AND LIMITATIONS

Given the looming threat of the silver tsunami, the significance of retirement planning at an individual as well as global level is paramount. Despite the existence of some insightful reviews on the given domain, gaps were identified concerning decisions and outcomes of retirement planning. The study fills these gaps by performing review synthesis using the POWER and TCM-ADO framework. The review resulted in the identification of various types of decisions associated with retirement planning, the antecedents of such decisions and the outcomes of these decisions post-retirement. The study also uncovered the greater reliance on corresponding domains like psychology, economics, etc. for establishing the theoretical foundation, perhaps because of a lack of conceptualization of the construct. Also, there is a need for more studies from the developing regions and the countries experiencing the heat of demographic shift. The domain also calls for a shift towards qualitative research and modern and advanced statistical techniques for data analysis. All the factors, decisions and outcomes identified have implications for people, industry practitioners and policymakers. All the existing and future knowledge can help in fostering retirement planning habits among people and thereby facilitate their overall welfare.

Though the study offers some valuable insights, it still has some limitations. First, the use of only the Scopus database might have led to some articles going unnoticed. Second, the language barrier (only English language studies) might have resulted in limited contributions from certain classes of countries in the review.

Third, the study includes literature from the past two decades only. Lastly, some corresponding constructs like bridge employment, retirement adjustment, retirement transition and retirement security were excluded from the study, which can be explored in the future.

REFERENCES

Afthanorhan, A., Mamun, A. A., Zainol, N. R., Foziah, H., & Awang, Z. (2020). Framing the retirement planning behavior model towards sustainable wellbeing among youth: The moderating effect of public profiles. *Sustainability*, *12*(21), 8879. https://doi.org/10.3390/su12218879

Ajzen, I. (1991). The theory of planned behavior. *Organizational Behavior and Human Decision Processes*, *50*(2), 179–211.

Alessie, R. J., Van Rooij, M., & Lusardi, A. (2011). *Financial literacy, retirement preparation and pension expectations in The Netherlands* (No. w17109). National Bureau of Economic Research. https://doi.org/10.3386/w17109

Ali, S. B., & Frank, H. A. (2019). Retirement planning decisions: Choices between defined benefit and defined contribution plans. *The American Review of Public Administration*, *49*(2), 218–235. https://doi.org/10.1177/0275074018765809

Alkhawaja, S. O., & Albaity, M. (2022). Retirement saving behavior: Evidence from UAE. *Journal of Islamic Marketing*, *13*(2), 265–286. https://doi.org/10.1108/JIMA-03-2020-0072

Altfest, L. (2004). Personal financial planning: Origins, developments and a plan for future direction. *The American Economist*, *48*(2), 53–60. https://doi.org/10.1177/056943450404800204

Amorim, S. M., & de Freitas Pinho França, L. H. (2022). Health, financial and social resources as mediators to the relationship between planning and satisfaction in retirement. *Current Psychology*, *41*(6), 3510–3524. https://doi.org/10.1007/s12144-020-00836-8

Bajtelsmit, V., & Coats, J. (2023). Designing behavioral prompts to improve saving decisions: Implications for retirement plans. *Financial Planning Review*, *6*(2), e1163. https://doi.org/10.1002/cfp2.1163

Beach, L. R. (Ed.). (1998). *Image theory: Theoretical and empirical foundations*. Lawrence Erlbaum Associates Publishers.

Bednarczyk, T. H., Skibińska-Fabrowska, I., & Szymańska, A. (2021). An empirical study on the financial preparation for retirement of the independent workers for profit in Poland. *Risks*, *9*(9), 160. https://doi.org/10.3390/risks9090160

Bi, Q., Finke, M., & Huston, S. J. (2017). Financial software use and retirement savings. *Journal of Financial Counseling and Planning*, *28*(1), 107–128.

Blanco, L. R., Aguila, E., Gongora, A., & Duru, O. K. (2017). Retirement planning among Hispanics: In God's hands? *Journal of Aging & Social Policy*, *29*(4), 311–331. https://doi.org/10.1080/08959420.2016.1272161

Blanco, L. R., Duru, O. K., & Mangione, C. M. (2020). A community-based randomized controlled trial of an educational intervention to promote retirement saving among Hispanics. *Journal of Family and Economic Issues*, *41*, 300–315. https://doi.org/10.1007/s10834-019-09657-9

Bongini, P., & Cucinelli, D. (2019). University students and retirement planning: Never too early. *International Journal of Bank Marketing*, *37*(3), 775–797. https://doi.org/10.1108/IJBM-03-2018-0066

Boyatzis, R. E. (2006). An overview of intentional change from a complexity perspective. *The Journal of Management Development*, *25*(7), 607–623. https://doi.org/10.1108/02621710610678445

Cardella, E., Kalenkoski, C. M., & Parent, M. (2023). Less is not more: 401 (k) plan information and retirement planning choices. *Journal of Pension Economics and Finance*, *22*(3), 331–351. https://doi.org/10.1017/S1474747221000445

Chaiwat, T., Muthitacharoen, A., & Chaisrilak, C. (2024). Cognitive reflection and social proof: Navigating complex tax incentives for retirement savings. *Journal of Aging & Social Policy*, 1–23. https://doi.org/10.1080/08959420.2024.2347808

Chan, K. K., & Au-Yeung, T. C. (2021). Impact of precarious employment on retirement planning for young workers and their parents: The case of Hong Kong. *International Journal of Sociology & Social Policy*, *41*(11/12), 1278–1289. https://doi.org/10.1108/IJSSP-07-2020-0265

Chan, M. C., Chung, E. K., & Yeung, D. Y. (2021). Attitudes toward retirement drive the effects of retirement preparation on psychological and physical well-being of Hong Kong Chinese retirees over time. *The International Journal of Aging and Human Development*, *93*(1), 584–600. https://doi.org/10.1177/0091415020926843

Chen, C. Y., Chang, C. C., Hsiao, Y. J., Chen, H. T., & Lin, T. M. (2024). Trust in and demand for financial advice. *Journal of Management and Business Research (2521–4306)*, *41*(1). https://doi.org/10.6504/JMBR.202403_41(1).0005

Chen, F., Fan, Y., Jiang, G., & Chen, J. (2024). How overconfident financial knowledge hinders retirement planning? Mediating analysis and heterogeneity of retirement funding sources. *Sage Open*, *14*(2). https://doi.org/10.1177/21582440241242615

Chua, S. M., & Chin, P. N. (2022). What drives working adults to be better prepared for their retirements? *Managerial Finance*, *48*(9/10), 1317–1333. https://doi.org/10.1108/MF-07-2021-0327

Chung, Y., & Park, Y. (2019). What I know, what I think I know, and whom I know. *Journal of Consumer Affairs*, *53*(3), 1312–1349. https://doi.org/10.1111/joca.12231

Clark, R., Lusardi, A., & Mitchell, O. S. (2017). Employee financial literacy and retirement plan behavior: A case study. *Economic Inquiry*, *55*(1), 248–259. https://doi.org/10.1111/ecin.12389

Detthamrong, U., Nguyen, L. T., & Wirapong, C. (2023). An empirical study on predicting financial planning for retirement. *Journal of System and Management Sciences*, *13*(6), 144–158. https://doi.org/10.33168/JSMS.2023.0609

Dhiman, R., Srivastava, V., Srivastava, A., Rajni, & Uppal, A. (2023). How to plan and write for systematic literature review papers in management domain. In S. Rana, J. Singh, & S. Kathuria (Eds.), *Advancing methodologies of conducting literature review in management domain (Review of management literature)* (Vol. 2, pp. 37–55). Emerald Publishing Limited. https://doi.org/10.1108/S2754-586520230000002003

Earl, J. K., Bednall, T. C., & Muratore, A. M. (2015). A matter of time: Why some people plan for retirement and others do not. *Work, Aging and Retirement*, *1*(2), 181–189. https://doi.org/10.1093/workar/wau005

Eberhardt, W., Post, T., Hoet, C., & Brüggen, E. (2022). Exploring the first steps of retirement engagement: A conceptual model and field evidence. *Journal of Service Management*, *33*(6), 1–26. https://doi.org/10.1108/JOSM-11-2020-0402

Fang, J., Hao, W., & Reyers, M. (2022). Financial advice, financial literacy and social interaction: What matters to retirement saving decisions? *Applied Economics*, *54*(50), 5827–5850. https://doi.org/10.1080/00036846.2022.2053654

Farrukh, A., & Sajjad, A. (2023). A critical review of literature review methodologies. In S. Rana, J. Singh, & S. Kathuria (Eds.), *Advancing methodologies of conducting literature review in management domain (Review of management literature)* (Vol. 2, pp. 103–123). Emerald Publishing Limited. https://doi.org/10.1108/S2754-586520230000002006

Fenton, A. G., Sands, S., Ferraro, C., Pallant, J. I., & Ghafoori, E. (2023). Preparing for retirement: The influence of message frame, message appeal and life stage. *Journal of Social Marketing*, *13*(4), 572–592. https://doi.org/10.1108/JSOCM-04-2023-0081

Fernández-López, S., Otero, L., Vivel, M., & Rodeiro, D. (2010). What are the driving forces of individuals' retirement savings? *Finance a Uver: Czech Journal of Economics & Finance*, *60*(3).

França, L. H., & Hershey, D. A. (2018). Financial preparation for retirement in Brazil: A cross-cultural test of the interdisciplinary financial planning model. *Journal of Cross-Cultural Gerontology*, *33*, 43–64. https://doi.org/10.1007/s10823-018-9343-y

Gallego-Losada, R., Montero-Navarro, A., Rodríguez-Sánchez, J., & González-Torres, T. (2021). Retirement planning and financial literacy, at the crossroads. A bibliometric analysis. *Finance Research Letters*, *44*, 102109. https://doi.org/10.1016/j.frl.2021.102109

Garcia, M. T. M., & Marques, P. D. C. V. (2017). Ownership of individual retirement accounts–an empirical analysis based on SHARE. *International Review of Applied Economics*, *31*(1), 69–82. https://doi.org/10.1080/02692171.2016.1221389

Ghadwan, A., Wan Ahmad, W. M., & Hanifa, M. H. (2022). Financial planning for retirement: The mediating role of culture. *Risks*, *10*(5), 104. https://doi.org/10.3390/risks10050104

Ghadwan, A. S., Wan Ahmad, W. M., & Hisham Hanifa, M. (2023). Financial planning for retirement: The moderating role of government policy. *Sage Open*, *13*(2). https://doi.org/10.1177/21582440231181300

González-Núñez, J. C., & Mariné-Osorio, F. J. (2023). Lack of retirement saving accounts: Empirical evidence in Mexico. *The Journal of Retirement*, *11*(4), 87–104. https://doi.org/10.3905/jor.2023.1.129

Gornick, J. C., & Sierminska, E. (2021). Wealth accumulation and retirement preparedness in cross-national perspective: A gendered analysis of outcomes among single adults. *Journal of European Social Policy*, *31*(5), 549–564. https://doi.org/10.1177/09589287211056174

Griffin, B., Hesketh, B., & Loh, V. (2012). The influence of subjective life expectancy on retirement transition and planning: A longitudinal study. *Journal of Vocational Behavior*, *81*(2), 129–137. https://doi.org/10.1016/j.jvb.2012.05.005

Gritten, A. (2011). New insights into consumer confidence in financial services. *International Journal of Bank Marketing*, *29*(2), 90–106. https://doi.org/10.1108/02652321111107602

Gubler, T., & Pierce, L. (2014). Healthy, wealthy, and wise: Retirement planning predicts employee health improvements. *Psychological Science*, *25*(9), 1822–1830. https://doi.org/10.1177/0956797614540467

Harahap, S., Thoyib, A., Sumiati, S., & Djazuli, A. (2022). The impact of financial literacy on retirement planning with serial mediation of financial risk tolerance and saving behavior: Evidence of medium entrepreneurs in Indonesia. *International Journal of Financial Studies*, *10*(3), 66. https://doi.org/10.3390/ijfs10030066

Hershey, D. A., Henkens, K., & Van Dalen, H. P. (2010). Aging and financial planning for retirement: Interdisciplinary influences viewed through a cross-cultural lens. *The International Journal of Aging and Human Development*, *70*(1), 1–38. https://doi.org/10.2190/AG.70.1.a

Hershey, D. A., Jacobs-Lawson, J. M., & Austin, J. T. (2012). Effective financial planning for retirement. In M. Wang (Ed.), *The Oxford handbook of retirement* (pp. 402–430). Oxford University Press.

Hershey, D. A., Jacobs-Lawson, J. M., McArdle, J. J., & Hamagami, F. (2007). Psychological foundations of financial planning for retirement. *Journal of Adult Development*, *14*, 26–36. https://doi.org/10.1007/s10804-007-9028-1

Hershey, D. A., & Mowen, J. C. (2000). Psychological determinants of financial preparedness for retirement. *The Gerontologist*, *40*(6), 687–697. https://doi.org/10.1093/geront/40.6.687

Hoffmann, A. O., & Plotkina, D. (2020). Why and when does financial information affect retirement planning intentions and which consumers are more likely to act on them? *Journal of Business Research*, *117*, 411–431. https://doi.org/10.1016/j.jbusres.2020.06.023

Huang, N. C., Kuo, P. H., Hsu, W. C., & Hu, S. C. (2023). Retirement planning and types of healthy lifestyle after retirement: A Nationwide Survey in Taiwan. *Health Promotion International*, *38*(3). https://doi.org/10.1093/heapro/daad044

Hutchinson, S. L., & Ausman, C. (2024). Not just one long vacation: Revisiting the importance of lifestyle planning in the transition to retirement. *Canadian Journal on Aging/La Revue canadienne du vieillissement*, 1–13. https://doi.org/10.1017/S0714980823000788

Indapurkar, K., Pal, A., Tiwari, C. K., & Mavuri, S. (2024). Exploring financial well-being's impact on retirement planning: The mediating role of financial attitude. *FIIB Business Review*. https://doi.org/10.1177/23197145241244620

Ingale, K. K., & Paluri, R. A. (2023). Retirement planning – A systematic review of literature and future research directions. *Management Review Quarterly*. https://doi.org/10.1007/s11301-023-00377-x

Innocenti, S., Clark, G. L., & McGill, S. (2024). Experience of financial challenges, retirement concerns, and planning: Evidence from representative samples of workers in 16 countries. *Journal of Pension Economics and Finance*, *23*(2), 183–201. https://doi.org/10.1017/S1474747223000082

Isa, M. Y. B. M., & Daukin, M. (2022). The influence of present health status (post Covid-19) on retirement planning in Malaysia. *Global Business & Finance Review*, *27*(6), 81–88. https://doi.org/10.17549/gbfr.2022.27.6.81

Jais, J. B., & Asokumar, A. (2020). Psychological process, social and environmental influence on retirement planning: Malaysian energy industry perspective. *Management & Marketing*, *15*(2), 134–153. https://doi.org/10.2478/mmcks-2020-0009

Janposri, P. (2021). The role of financial literacy in retirement planning and wealth accumulation among self-employed Thai workers. *Journal of Population & Social Studies*, *29*(1), 177–194. http://doi.org/10.25133/JPSSv292021.011

Jantan, M. S. (2020). The improvement in life expectancy: Systematic literature review of retirement saving. *SSRN Electronic Journal*. https://doi.org/10.2139/ssrn.3582234

Kanime, M. M., Mukong, A. K., & Kaulihowa, T. (2021). The determinants of retirement planning behaviour: Evidence from the Ministry of Home Affairs and Immigration in Namibia. *African Journal of Business and Economic Research*, *16*(4), 31. https://doi.org/10.31920/1750-4562/2021/v16n4a2

Kapoor, J. R., Dlabay, L. R., & Hughes, R. J. (2014). *Personal finance* (11th ed.). McGraw Hill Education.

Kerry, M. J. (2018). Psychological antecedents of retirement planning: A systematic review. *Frontiers in Psychology*, *9*. https://doi.org/10.3389/fpsyg.2018.01870

Ketkaew, C., Van Wouwe, M., Jorissen, A., Cassimon, D., Vichitthamaros, P., & Wongsaichia, S. (2022). Towards sustainable retirement planning of wageworkers in Thailand: A qualitative approach in behavioral segmentation and financial pain point identification. *Risks*, *10*(1), 8. https://doi.org/10.3390/risks10010008

Kim, K. T., Lee, J. M., & Anderson, S. G. (2019). Retirement savings habits of business-owning families in the United States. *Family and Consumer Sciences Research Journal*, *48*(1), 65–84. https://doi.org/10.1111/fcsr.12333

Kim, M. L., Lee, Y. H., & Hong, S. Y. (2021). Examining the factors that affect the preparation of life after retirement and quality of life of South Korean adults across different age groups. *Sustainability*, *13*(10), 5351. https://doi.org/10.3390/su13105351

Kimiyagahlam, F., Safari, M., & Mansori, S. (2019). Influential behavioral factors on retirement planning behavior: The case of Malaysia. *Journal of Financial Counseling and Planning*, *30*(2), 244–261. https://doi.org/10.1891/1052-3073.30.2.244

Kimiyaghalam, F., Mansori, S., Safari, M., & Yap, S. (2017). Parents' influence on retirement planning in Malaysia. *Family and Consumer Sciences Research Journal*, *45*(3), 315–325. https://doi.org/10.1111/fcsr.12203

Kumar, S., Shukla, G. P., & Sharma, R. (2019). Analysis of key barriers in retirement planning. *Journal of Modelling in Management*, *14*(4), 972–986. https://doi.org/10.1108/jm2-09-2018-0134

Kung, C. S., Zhu, J., Zaninotto, P., & Steptoe, A. (2023). Changes in retirement plans in the English older population during the COVID-19 pandemic: The roles of health factors and financial insecurity. *European Journal of Ageing*, *20*(1), 22. https://doi.org/10.1007/s10433-023-00770-1

Larisa, L. E., Njo, A., & Wijaya, S. (2020). Female workers' readiness for retirement planning: An evidence from Indonesia. *Review of Behavioral Finance*, *13*(5), 566–583. https://doi.org/10.1108/RBF-04-2020-0079

Lee, A., Xu, Y., & Hyde, K. F. (2013). Factors influencing investor choice of retirement funds. *Journal of Financial Services Marketing*, *18*(2), 137–151. https://doi.org/10.1057/fsm.2013.8

Lee, A., Xu, Y., & Hyde, K. F. (2016). Factors influencing investor choice of retirement funds. In T. Harrison (Ed.), *Financial literacy and the limits of financial decision-making* (pp. 224–245). Palgrave Macmillan. https://doi.org/10.1007/978-3-319-30886-9_11

Lim, H., & Lee, J. M. (2021). Retirement income sources and subjective financial well-being: A comparison of retirees and non-retirees. *Journal of Financial Counseling & Planning*, *32*(3), 517. https://doi.org/10.1891/JFCP-19-00101

Liu, C., Bai, X., & Knapp, M. (2021). Multidimensional retirement planning behaviors, retirement confidence, and post-retirement health and well-being among Chinese older adults in Hong Kong. *Applied Research in Quality of Life*, 1–17. https://doi.org/10.1007/s11482-020-09901-7

Liu, P., Thrasher, G. R., Ye, Y., & Shi, J. (2024). Goal-pursuit tendencies and retirement planning: A time-lagged and multi-dimensional investigation. *Work, Aging and Retirement*, *10*(3), 300–307. https://doi.org/10.1093/workar/waad002

Lusardi, A., & Mitchelli, O. S. (2007). Financial literacy and retirement preparedness: Evidence and implications for financial education: The problems are serious, and remedies are not simple. *Business Economics*, *42*, 35–44. https://doi.org/10.2145/20070104

Magwegwe, F. M., & Lim, H. (2021). Factors associated with the ownership of individual retirement accounts (IRAs): Applying the theory of planned behavior. *Journal of Financial Counseling and Planning*, *32*(1), 116–130. https://doi.org/10.1891/JFCP-19-00023

Mahapatra, M. S., Raveendran, J., & De, A. (2019). Building a model on influence of behavioural and cognitive factors on personal financial planning: A study among Indian households. *Global Business Review*, *20*(4), 996–1009. https://doi.org/10.1177/0972150919844897

Mata, O. G. (2021). The effect of financial literacy and gender on retirement planning among young adults. *International Journal of Bank Marketing*, *39*(7), 1068–1090. https://doi.org/10.1108/ijbm-10-2020-0518

Micheel, F. (2021). The intention to paid and/or unpaid activities in retirement. A study of older workers in Germany. *Journal of Aging & Social Policy*, *33*(2), 101–119. https://doi.org/10.1080/08959420.2019.1685354

Mowen, J. C. (2000). *The 3M model of motivation and personality: Theory and empirical applications to consumer behavior*. Springer. https://doi.org/10.1007/978-1-4757-6708-7

Muratore, A. M., & Earl, J. K. (2015). Improving retirement outcomes: The role of resources, pre retirement planning and transition characteristics. *Ageing and Society*, *35*(10), 2100–2140. https://doi.org/10.1017/S0144686X14000841

Mustafa, W. M. W., Islam, M. A., Asyraf, M., Hassan, M. S., Royhan, P., & Rahman, S. (2023). The effects of financial attitudes, financial literacy and health literacy on sustainable financial retirement planning: The moderating role of the financial advisor. *Sustainability*, *15*(3), 2677. https://doi.org/10.3390/su15032677

Nga, K. H., & Yeoh, K. K. (2018). An exploratory model on retirement savings behaviour: A Malaysian study. *International Journal of Business and Society*, *19*(3), 637–659.

Nguyen, L. T. M., Nguyen, P. T., Tran, Q. N. N., & Trinh, T. T. G. (2022). Why does subjective financial literacy hinder retirement saving? The mediating roles of risk tolerance and risk perception. *Review of Behavioral Finance*, *14*(5), 627–645. https://doi.org/10.1108/RBF-03-2021-0036

Noone, J., Alpass, F., & Stephens, C. (2010). Do men and women differ in their retirement planning? Testing a theoretical model of gendered pathways to retirement preparation. *Research on Aging*, *32*(6), 715–738. https://doi.org/10.1177/0164027510383531

Noone, J., Earl, J., Stephens, C., Rafalski, J., Allen, J., Alpass, F., & Topa, G. (2022). An application of the resource-based dynamic process model in the context of retirement planning. *Work, Aging and Retirement*, *8*(3), 225–240. https://doi.org/10.1093/workar/waab006

Paul, J., & Benito, G. R. G. (2017). A review of research on outward foreign direct investment from emerging countries, including China: What do we know, how do we know and where should we be heading? *Asia Pacific Business Review*, *24*(1), 90–115. https://doi.org/10.1080/13602381.2017.1357316

Paul, J., Parthasarathy, S., & Gupta, P. (2017). Exporting challenges of SMEs: A review and future research agenda. *Journal of World Business*, *52*(3), 327–342. https://doi.org/10.1016/j.jwb.2017.01.003

Payne, S. H., Yorgason, J. B., & Dew, J. P. (2014). Spending today or saving for tomorrow: The influence of family financial socialization on financial preparation for retirement. *Journal of Family and Economic Issues*, *35*, 106–118. https://doi.org/10.1007/s10834-013-9363-2

Piotrowska, M. (2019). The importance of personality characteristics and behavioral constraints for retirement saving. *Economic Analysis and Policy*, *64*, 194–220. https://doi.org/10.1016/j.eap.2019.09.001

Pospíšil, R., Kročil, O., & Sadílek, T. (2023). Determinants of young generation retirement planning behaviour-the case of Czechia. *International Journal of Economic Policy in Emerging Economies*, *18*(2), 219–234. https://doi.org/10.1504/IJEPEE.2023.135524

Qi, J., Chatterjee, S., & Liu, Y. (2022). Retirement preparedness of generation X compared to other cohorts in the United States. *International Journal of Financial Studies*, *10*(2), 45. https://doi.org/10.3390/ijfs10020045

Qian, Y., Tan, W., & Wu, J. (2024). Household financial literacy and retirement planning in rural China. *International Review of Financial Analysis, 93*, 103130. https://doi.org/10.1016/j.irfa.2024.103130

Quttainah, M., Singhania, S., & Rana, S. (2023). Gender diversity and financial performance: A quantified review based on bibliometric and cluster analysis. *International Studies of Management & Organization, 53*(4), 291–312. https://doi.org/10.1080/00208825.2023.2257537

Rammal, H. G. (2023). Systematic literature reviews: Steps and practical tips. In S. Rana, J. Singh, & S. Kathuria (Eds.), *Advancing methodologies of conducting literature review in management domain (Review of management literature)* (Vol. 2, pp. 27–35). Emerald Publishing Limited. https://doi.org/10.1108/S2754-586520230000002002

Rana, S., Sakshi, & Singh, J. (2022). Presenting the POWER framework of conducting literature review. In S. Rana, Sakshi, & J. Singh (Eds.), *Exploring the latest trends in management literature (Review of management literature)* (Vol. 1, pp. 1–13). Emerald Publishing Limited. https://doi.org/10.1108/S2754-586520220000001001

Rana, S., Singh, J., & Kathuria, S. (2023). Parameters and decision elements of writing effective literature review papers: Empirical evidence from multiple stakeholders on POWER framework. In S. Rana, J. Singh, & S. Kathuria (Eds.), *Advancing methodologies of conducting literature review in management domain (Review of management literature)* (Vol. 2, pp. 1–25). Emerald Publishing Limited. https://doi.org/10.1108/S2754-586520230000002001

Rasiah, R., Bilong, F., Turner, J., Waheed, H., Somasundram, S., Leng, K. & Tee. (2020). A structural equation modelling study of the determinants of retirement preparedness. *International Journal of Innovation, Creativity and Change, 11*(6).

Rey, L., Fernández, S., Vivel, M., & Lado, R. (2015). Private saving for retirement: How well-prepared are European peripheral countries? *Advances in Business and Management, 7*, 89–109.

Rey-Ares, L., Fernández-López, S., & Vivel-Búa, M. (2018). The influence of social models on retirement savings: Evidence for European countries. *Social Indicators Research, 136*, 247–268. https://doi.org/10.1007/s11205-016-1533-9

Saini, S., Sharma, T., & Parayitam, S. (2024). The relationship between financial knowledge, investment strategy and satisfaction from pension schemes: Evidence from India. *Asia-Pacific Financial Markets, 31*(1), 101–135. https://doi.org/10.1007/s10690-023-09408-9

Sardana, V., Singhania, S., Chavali, K., & Quttainah, M. (2024). Non-performing assets: Navigating the banking woes through an integrative review. *International Studies of Management & Organization*, 1–25. https://doi.org/10.1080/00208825.2024.2339773

Schuchardt, J., Durband, D., Bailey, W. C., DeVaney, S. A., Grable, J. E., Leech, I. E., Lown, J. M., Sharpe, D. L., & Xiao, J. J. (2007). Personal finance: An interdisciplinary profession. *Journal of Financial Counseling and Planning, 18*(1).

She, L., Rasiah, R., Weissmann, M. A., & Kaur, H. (2024). Using the theory of planned behaviour to explore predictors of financial behaviour among working adults in Malaysia. *FIIB Business Review, 13*(1), 118–135. https://doi.org/10.1177/23197145231169336

Shin, M. H., & Lee, Y. M. (2019). Analyses on the determinants of elderly workers' plans to retire and desired retirement age. *International Journal of Economic Policy in Emerging Economies, 12*(2), 158–165. https://doi.org/10.1504/IJEPEE.2019.099737

Singh, R., Aggarwal, S., & Sahni, S. (2022). A systematic literature review of work-life balance using ADO model. *FIIB Business Review, 12*(3), 243–258. https://doi.org/10.1177/23197145221115530

Sinha, P., & Irala, L. R. (2024). Prepared for retirement? Think again: A systematic review and future research agenda. *Management Review Quarterly*. https://doi.org/10.1007/s11301-024-00437-w

Syihab, F., & Nurhakim, M. L. (2022). Retirement financial planning: Gender, age-related, and expenditure differences among Indonesian households. *Advances in Business-Related Scientific Research Journal, 13*(2).

Thakur, R., Hale, D., & AlSaleh, D. (2020). Retirement planning: Its application to marketing practices. *Health Marketing Quarterly, 37*(2), 91–107. https://doi.org/10.1080/07359683.2020.1713574

Tomar, S., Baker, H. K., Kumar, S., & Hoffmann, A. O. (2021). Psychological determinants of retirement financial planning behavior. *Journal of Business Research, 133*, 432–449. https://doi.org/10.1016/j.jbusres.2021.05.007

Topa, G., Lunceford, G., & Boyatzis, R. E. (2018). Financial planning for retirement: A psychosocial perspective. *Frontiers in Psychology*, *8*, 2338. https://doi.org/10.3389/fpsyg.2017.02338

United Nations, Department of Economic and Social Affairs, Population Division. (2020). *World population ageing 2019*. United Nations.

Vieira, K. M., Matheis, T. K., & Maciel, A. M. H. (2023). Risky indebtedness behavior: Impacts on financial preparation for retirement and perceived financial well-being. *Journal of Risk and Financial Management*, *16*(12), 519. https://doi.org/10.3390/jrfm16120519

Voleti, K. K., Kumar, P., Nanda, S. S., & Debata, B. R. (2024). Perceived financial preparedness for retirement of technical teachers: An empirical study in Andhra Pradesh, India. *Prabandhan: Indian Journal of Management*, *17*(6), 8–26. https://doi.org/10.17010/pijom/2024/v17i6/173558

World Economic Forum. (2019, June). *Investing in (and for) our future*. World Economic Forum.

Wu, J., & Chao, Q. (2024). How older adults fulfill their retirement plans relates to positive mental health: A path model analysis of social activity and self-esteem. *Current Psychology*, *43*(7), 5963–5974. https://doi.org/10.1007/s12144-023-04735-6

Yeo, K. H. K., Lim, W. M., & Yii, K. (2023). Financial planning behaviour: A systematic literature review and new theory development. *Journal of Financial Services Marketing*, 1–23. https://doi.org/10.1057/s41264-023-00249-1

Yeung, D. Y., Ho, A. K., Lam, A. H., & Lam, A. C. (2023). An integrated model on purchase intentions of typical and tax-deductible saving products: The roles of retirement goal clarity and age. *Journal of Behavioral and Experimental Economics*, *104*, 101995. https://doi.org/10.1016/j.socec.2023.101995

Yeung, D. Y., & Zhou, X. (2017). Planning for retirement: Longitudinal effect on retirement resources and post-retirement well-being. *Frontiers in Psychology*, *8*, 1300. https://doi.org/10.3389/fpsyg.2017.01300

Yorgason, J. B., Segel-Karpas, D., Wheeler, B. E., Malig Canlas, J., & Smith, J. (2020). Change in retirement plans among midlife couples during an economic recession. *The Journals of Gerontology: Series B*, *75*(4), 827–836. https://doi.org/10.1093/geronb/gbz076

Zhou, M., Wang, Y., Liang, Y., Shi, R., & Zhao, S. (2022). The effect of subjective life expectancy on the participation in commercial pension insurance of Chinese elderly. *Frontiers in Psychology*, *13*, 969719. https://doi.org/10.3389/fpsyg.2022.969719

Mapping Digital Leadership and Creative Performance: A Review Using Text Analysis and TCCM Framework for Future Research*

Yasmeen Shamsi Rizvi and Aleena Ilyaz

Jamia Millia Islamia, India

ABSTRACT

In today's disruptive digital age, digital leadership plays a pivotal role in successfully transforming organizations by fostering a culture of creativity to ensure sustainable competitive advantage. This new realm of leadership is expanding, with very few studies focusing on the collective understanding of digital leadership and creative performance. The current study presents a systematic literature review and bibliometric analysis combined with text analysis using the Scopus database to draw an overarching picture of the extant literature and deploy the theory-context-characteristic-method (TCCM) framework to offer fresh insights into future research avenues. A review of 90 publications from 63 journals published between 2014 and 2024 underpins the current study. The newness and emerging nature of the topic are increasingly gaining attention across multiple fields, as indicated by publications from diverse journals and countries. The review presents the future research agenda across four themes pertinent to theory, context, characteristics and methodology, thus promising future research potential.

Keywords: Digital leadership; creative performance; systematic literature review; text analysis; TCCM framework

*This paper has been presented (and modified) at the ICSSR-sponsored first International Conference on Business Research and Innovation (BRAIN'24) held at Netaji Subhas University of Technology, Delhi, India.

Reviewing the Latest Trends in Management Literature
Review of Management Literature, Volume 4B, 151–174

Published under exclusive licence by Emerald Publishing Limited
ISSN: 2754-5865/doi:10.1108/S2754-586520250000004B006

1. INTRODUCTION

> A digital leader is not just one who helps a company find cutting-edge alternatives to legacy systems. They are also the ones who approach problems with an open mind and show great curiosity in their work, which leads them to make all efforts toward encouraging creativity among teams. (Katanic, 2021, para 12)

Both academia and organizations are witnessing a multifold interest in digital transformation that leverages the latest technologies and digital tools for driving business models, performance and productivity in the digital age (Markus & Rowe, 2023). For surviving in a continuously evolving and dynamic business environment, digital technology emphasizes the pivotal role of digital leaders in adapting innovative approaches that can offer competitive advantage and unique value creation (Türk, 2023). For this, digital leaders are expected to integrate digital technologies at every stage of business and cater to people's challenges by driving their efforts towards creativity. According to the World Economic Forum's report on the Future of Jobs, almost 73% of organizations voted creativity as the top-most priority for contemporary businesses to thrive (World Economic Forum, 2023). Additionally, Statista surveyed approximately 803 global organizations, of which 70% consider creativity and analytical skills to be the most crucial competencies between 2023 and 2027 (Sharif, 2023). As digital leaders navigate the transitions at work by adopting new technologies like Artificial Intelligence (AI), the Internet of Things (IoT), blockchain and big data, they also need to fuel the creativity coefficient for building a digital culture of collaboration and creation. Thus, the real challenge that contemporary organizations need to address is how the transforming role of digital leaders can help build and retain employees' creative performance while balancing digital disruptions. This is where the need for studying digital leadership and creativity in a digital workplace comes in, so that both can be understood and appreciated together.

Digital leadership is the leader's ability to effectively utilize, develop and manage digital technologies and tools for driving continuous growth and success (Brunner et al., 2023). It differs from traditional leadership as it demands trust-based leadership rather than competency-based leadership for fostering innovation and inspiring the workforce in a digital environment (Abbu et al., 2022). Along with managing and leading the employees, leaders with practical digital skills tend to focus on task orientation and relationship-building that positively influence employees' adaptability and creative thinking process (Ahuja et al., 2023). This paradigm shift in leadership style requires a mix of digital competence, skills and leadership abilities (Fenech et al., 2019). Leaders are pivotal in leveraging disruptive technologies like AI, IoT, blockchain, cloud computing and 5G technologies to build competitive advantage and innovative business models (Mishra & Singh Kaurav, 2024). Amid the turbulent and disruptive digital age, digital leaders are responsible for articulating a digital vision that promotes creativity, agility and longevity (AlNuaimi et al., 2022). In addition to strategic business skills, digital-age leaders need to possess a specific 'digital leadership skill set' comprising of digital communication skills, the ability to build a digital culture and competence to foster a digital mindset that motivates the workforce towards knowledge sharing, open collaboration, creative thinking and problem-solving. This evolving behaviour of digital leaders can be reflected within the scope of the resource-based view of the firm and dynamic capabilities theory for ensuring sustainable competitive advantage (Barney, 2001; Karakose et al., 2021; Sagbas et al., 2023; Teece et al., 1997).

Extant literature focuses on the primary role of leadership in driving employee outcomes like creative performance (Mihardjo & Rukmana, 2018; Korzynski et al., 2019). Creative performance is an amalgamation of individual creativity and individual innovative behaviour that circles the generation of new ideas and their implementation to deliver effective problem-solving (Mutonyi et al., 2020). According to Li et al. (2022), creative performance is the individual's cognitive process to gather, exchange and evaluate ideas and information to reach innovative solutions to a problem. Such a combination of ideas, actions and behaviours enables organizations to strengthen their competitive edge consistently (Xu et al., 2022). For this reason, the significantly positive relationship between digital leadership and creative performance has gained scholarly attention. Still, academic attempts are lacking to consolidate the extant literature on digital leadership and creative performance through a review methodology. For instance, studies including Aggarwal and Kumar (2022), Karakose et al. (2022), Sağbaş and Erdoğan (2022), Ratajczak (2022), Alawiah and Tukiran (2024) have reviewed the literature on digital leadership in isolation, without taking into consideration the nexus between digital leadership and creative performance. Such a cavity, thus, highlights the fragmented and incomprehensive state of scholarly knowledge and, therefore, calls for a holistic approach to comprehensively review the literature on digital leadership and creative performance using the latest review methodologies. Reviewing this nexus is critical to propose future research avenues that can be adopted by digital leaders in digital-age organizations to sustain their topmost capability, competitive advantage and creative performance.

To close this research gap in the literature, the current study aims to provide an overarching picture of the existing studies that examine digital leadership and creativity through a comprehensive literature review guided by the theory-context-characteristic-method (TCCM) framework for future research agendas. The novelty of the current review lies in its goal to advance the existing body of knowledge using the TCCM framework. It sheds light on how theoretical frameworks from different disciplines like social behaviour, strategic management, psychology, personal behaviour and technology adoption can be used to advance future research. Further, it proposes new research designs using mixed and non-linear methodologies to explore complex relationships. Also, it suggests a new lens for future researchers to conduct studies on digital leadership and creative performance in different contextual settings using other organizational, team and individual level factors. Specifically, the current review addresses the following three research questions:

RQ1. What is the current state of research on digital leadership and creative performance based on the distribution of articles, citation patterns and bibliographic coupling?
RQ2. What are the major themes and trends studied in the existing literature on digital leadership and creative performance?
RQ3. How can the extant literature on digital leadership and creative performance be advanced using the TCCM framework?

The paper follows this structure to answer the above research questions: Section 2 discusses the review methodology adopted for the study and the descriptive analysis of the final studies included in the review. Further, Section 3 presents the review results, including bibliographic coupling and citation analysis. Section 4 focuses on text analysis, including clustering and thematic evaluation of each cluster. Lastly, Section 5 discusses the future research agenda using the TCCM framework.

2. REVIEW METHODOLOGY

Systematic literature review and bibliometric analysis are robust methods for comprehensively summarizing a topic by recognizing its boundaries and recommending avenues for future research with minimum subjective bias (Caviggioli & Ughetto, 2019; Fahimnia et al., 2015). Past studies have demonstrated the use of these methods for identifying the intellectual structure of research topics across numerous domains like the IoT (Zaid & Farooqi, 2024), leadership (Jiang et al., 2024; Vedula & Agrawal, 2024), corporate social responsibility (Dzage & Szabados, 2024), tourism (Kumar et al., 2022), big data analytics (Khanra et al., 2020), manufacturing (Caviggioli & Ughetto, 2019), finance (Xu et al., 2018), emerging technologies (Li et al., 2018), innovation (Van Oorschot et al., 2018) and sustainability (Fahimnia et al., 2015), and among others. Prior studies show the prevalence of literature reviews in the managerial domain for determining the research front and intellectual structures of the research topic as well as elucidating future research directions (Caviggioli & Ughetto, 2019; Fahimnia et al., 2015; Khanra et al., 2020). The current study follows the bibliometric protocol proposed by Khanra et al. (2020), who developed the protocol based on commonly used techniques in previous studies. Fig. 1 outlines the three sequential phases: scanning, curating and analyzing the document profile.

The Scopus database, through its robust bibliographic base, is a crucial resource for the comprehensive coverage of research topics across several domains in the academic community (Khanra et al., 2020; Martínez-López et al., 2018; Tandon et al., 2020). Furthermore, it is the largest repository for peer-reviewed interdisciplinary literature in the social science domain (Ansari & Kant, 2017; Bartol et al., 2014; Fahimnia et al., 2015; Donthu et al., 2020). As

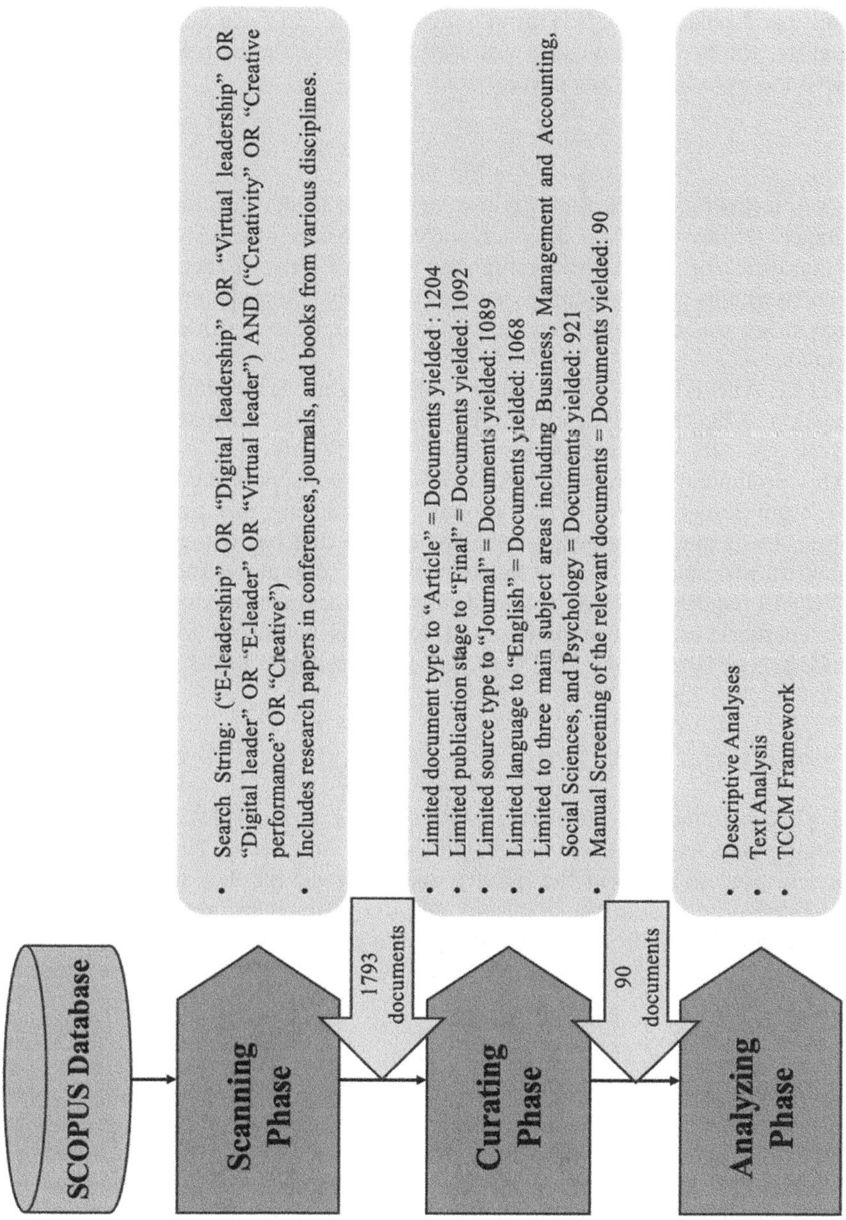

Fig. 1. Three Phases for Reviewing the Literature. *Source:* Authors' creation.

compared to the Web of Science, which contains information only about the first authors of cited publications, the Scopus database is more suitable as it includes bibliographic data for all the authors in cited references, thus rendering more accurate and reliable results (Durán-Sánchez et al., 2019; Zupic & Čater, 2015). Therefore, the Scopus database was used to retrieve the pertinent resources to achieve the objectives of the current study.

2.1 Scanning Phase

The key terms for the current study were 'digital leadership' and 'creative performance'. However, it was also necessary to consider alternative terms used in the literature for digital leadership and creative performance that conveyed similar meanings in the present context of the study. Consequently, the following search string was employed for the current research on the title, keywords and abstracts.

TITLE-ABS-KEY ("E-leadership" OR "Digital leadership" OR "Virtual leadership" OR "Digital leader" OR "E-leader" OR "Virtual leader") AND ("Creativity" OR "Creative performance" OR "Creative").

This preliminary search yielded 1,793 documents published before 4 June 2024, from January 2014. The rationale for choosing this timeframe was to analyze the extant literature over the last decade that has witnessed accelerated digital transformation due to the adoption of digital technologies and the COVID-19 pandemic. These included different document types such as articles, book chapters, conference papers and editorials belonging to other sources, including journals, books and conference proceedings across various subject areas.

2.2 Curating Phase

In this phase, numerous filters were used to refine the results determined from the scanning phase, as depicted in Fig. 1 (Pahlevan & Sharif et al., 2019). The manual screening process involved the quality assessment of the 921 articles based on pre-defined criteria like the focus of the study, its relevance, study context, methodological soundness, research design and generalizability of findings. Based on these criteria, articles beyond the scope of the current review were excluded.

2.3 Analyzing Stage: Descriptive Analysis for Document Profiling

Descriptive analysis aimed to profile 90 documents in the final bibliographic database. Such analysis will help access the formal state of literature and significant dimensions to understand the distribution of articles over time and to get an overview of leading authors, journals and countries. Similar to studies by Seuring and Gold (2012) and Orioli and Veríssimo (2023), the descriptive analysis includes the following literature classification.

2.3.1 Year-Wise Distribution of Articles

Fig. 2 shows the distribution of the final 90 articles in the bibliographic database across the years. The line graph shows an increasing trend in articles published on digital leadership and creative performance. One of the earliest studies exploring this relationship is traced back to 2014, which studies the role of emergent virtual leadership competencies necessary for ensuring performance effectiveness (Ziek & Smulowitz, 2014). The bar graph shows a significant increase in the number of publications from 2020 due to accelerated digital transformation triggered by COVID-19, rapid adoption of disruptive technologies, increased focus on creativity to manage digital changes and transition to alternate work arrangements like remote/hybrid work, freelancing and work from home.

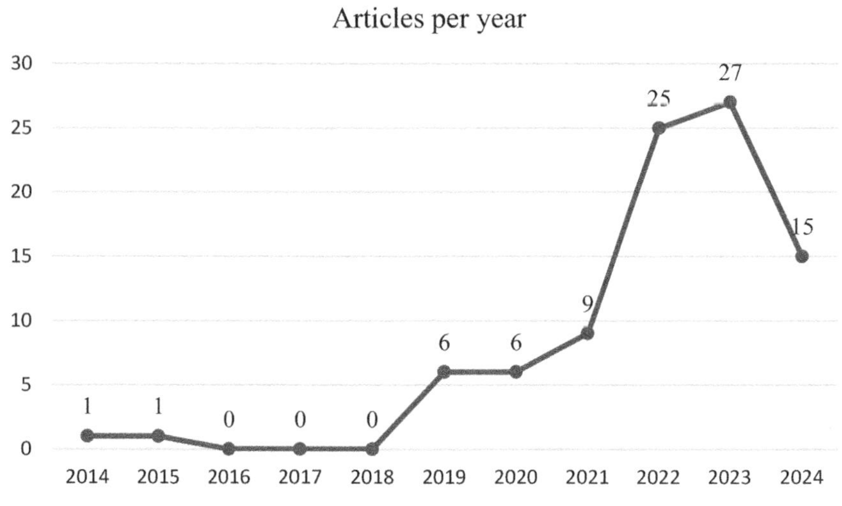

Fig. 2. Year-Wise Distribution of Articles. *Source:* Authors' creation.

2.3.2 Journal-Wise Distribution of Articles

The selected articles for this review have been published across 63 reputed journals. As depicted in Table 1, the top three journals within this group include *Frontiers in Psychology* (9), followed by *Journal of Business Research* (4) and *Sustainability* (4). Moreover, many journals have contributed to this research field with one publication, thus highlighting the prominent dispersion of research across numerous journals. This verifies the interdisciplinary and dynamic aspect of the research domain, resulting in studies from various established fields. Furthermore, it also highlights the emerging nature of the research field with the need for a well-established set of core journals.

Table 1. Top Authors, Countries and Journals Based on Number of Contributions, Bibliographic Coupling and Citation Analysis.

Top 10 Authors					
Number of Contributions		Bibliographic Coupling		Citation Analysis	
Authors	Articles	Authors	Total Link Strength	Authors	Total Link Strength
Elidjen D.	4	Ardi	1,509	Büttgen M.	5
Mihardjo L.W.W.	4	Bernarto I.	1,509	Lehmann C.	5
Sasmoko S.	3	Djati S.P.	1,509	Schuster T.	5
Alamsjah F.	3	Nanda H.A.	1,509	Curado C.	2
Tigre F. B.	2	Nanda K.A.	1,509	Santarsiero F.	2
Henriques P. L.	2	Sudibjo N.	1,509	Schettini E.	2
Curado C.	2	Yulianeu A.	1,509	Schiuma G.	2
Kanbach D. K.	2	Lehmann C.	559	Tigre F.B.	2
Brunner T. J. J.	2	Schuster T.	559	Kanbach D.K.	1
Schuster T.	2	Santarsiero F.	445	Ardi	0

Top 10 Countries					
Number of Contributions		Bibliographic Coupling		Citation Analysis	
Countries	Articles	Countries	Total Link Strength	Countries	Total Link Strength
China	16	United States	1,073	Germany	11
Germany	9	India	1,012	China	10
Indonesia	7	Germany	951	Turkey	5
India	6	China	911	Italy	4
Turkey	5	Italy	769	United Arab Emirates	4
Italy	4	United Kingdom	665	India	3
United Arab Emirates	3	United Arab Emirates	485	United Kingdom	3
Portugal	3	Indonesia	456	United States	2
Malaysia	3	Turkey	427	Indonesia	0
South Korea	3	Malaysia	302	Malaysia	0

Top 5 Journals					
Number of Contributions		Bibliographic Coupling		Citation Analysis	
Journals	Articles	Journals	Total Link Strength	Journals	Total Link Strength
Frontiers in Psychology	9	*Frontiers in Psychology*	300	*Journal of Business Research*	3
Journal of Business Research	4	*Behavioural Sciences*	171	*International Journal of Innovation Management*	2
Sustainability	4	*Journal of Business Research*	150	*Behavioural Sciences*	1
Behavioural Sciences	3	*Sustainability*	130	*Frontiers in Psychology*	1

Table 1. *(Continued)*

Top 5 Journals					
Number of Contributions		Bibliographic Coupling		Citation Analysis	
Journals	Articles	Journals	Total Link Strength	Journals	Total Link Strength
International Journal of Innovation Management	3	*International Journal of Innovation Management*	90	*German Journal of Human Resource Management*	1

Source: Authors' creation.

2.3.3 Country-Wise Distribution of Articles

Thirty-two developing and developed countries contributed to the studies exploring digital leadership and creativity. Regarding the significant contributing countries, Table 1 shows that China contributed the highest number of publications (16), followed by Germany (9) and Indonesia (7). China has emerged as the top-most contributing country due to its significant investments in disruptive technologies across diverse industries, resulting in a surge in research on digital leadership. Additionally, Germany's significant position can be attributed to its focus on industry 4.0 initiatives and innovative practices, while Indonesia's emerging tech sector has resulted in its growth of research. India is still in the budding stage, with contributions equal to six, emphasizing the need for scholarly attention in this domain, which has promising potential for future growth as India witnesses technological advancements in every field (Economic Times, 2024).

2.3.4 Major Authors Within the Research Domain

The selected 90 articles were a result of effective collaboration among a total number of 268 authors. Table 1 presents the significant authors contributing to the research field. Elidjen D. and Mihardjo L.W.W. are the most representative authors within the group, as they contributed to four articles each. This is followed by Sasmoko S. and Alamsjah F., each contributing three studies that examine the topic of interest for this literature review. Interestingly, these top four authors are affiliated with Bina Nusantara University in Jakarta, Indonesia, which makes it a significant knowledge centre for this research domain.

2.3.5 Major Research Methodologies Used Within the Research Domain

Research methodologies adopted in the 90 articles were categorized into numerous qualitative and quantitative research methods, including survey, literature review, conceptual, mixed, interview, experimental study, secondary research, case study and diary study. As depicted in Fig. 3, approximately 60% of the publications used the survey method, indicating the scholarly attention

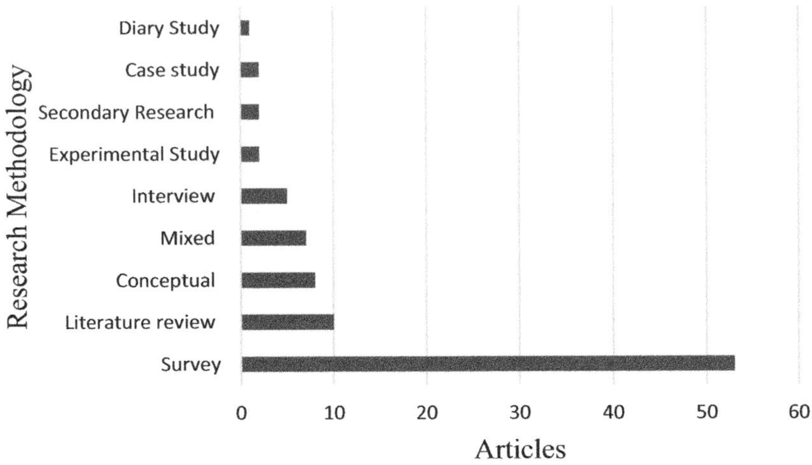

Fig. 3. Major Research Methodologies Used Within the Research Domain. *Source:* Authors' creation.

centred on empirical testing and validation of the existing theories and models in the research domain. It also signifies the increasing interest in gauging real-world applications through these empirical studies' findings, interventions and recommendations.

3. REVIEW RESULTS

To analyze the bibliometric data, VOS (visualization of similarities) viewer software was deemed to be pertinent as it offers a range of sophisticated options for visualizing and mapping the scientific literature (Fahimnia et al., 2015; Khanra et al., 2020; Zupic & Čater, 2015). To answer the first research question pertinent to the knowledge base and intellectual structure of the extant literature, the current study utilized bibliographic coupling and citation analysis through the full counting method of bibliometric links among the items (Khanra et al., 2020).

3.1 Bibliographic Coupling

Bibliographic coupling uses the 'backward citation chaining' technique for assessing the influence of publications in the bibliographic dataset using different units of analysis (Khanra et al., 2020). Bibliographic coupling is a phenomenal technique for capturing the intellectual structure of a research field as it pairs two documents that cite a third common document, resulting in the shared intellectual capital represented by a higher linkage occurrence of common references (Khanra et al., 2020; Vedula & Agrawal, 2024; Xu et al., 2018). Table 1 showcases the top authors, journals and countries significantly contributing to digital leadership and creative performance literature. The present study identified Ardi,

Bernarto I. and Djati S.P. as the top three authors. Among the most influential countries, the United States, India and Germany were identified as the most prominent countries advancing the research field under study. Finally, Frontiers in Psychology, with the most articles and a strong total link strength, indicates its centrality and significance in developing this research area.

3.2 Citation Analysis

Past studies have often suggested complementing the findings from bibliographic coupling with citation analysis, which is a 'forward citation chaining' technique to grasp the knowledge base of a research domain (Fahimnia et al., 2015; Khanra et al., 2020; Vedula & Agrawal, 2024). Citation analysis helps in effectively gauging the scholarly reception of a publication based on the number of citations it has accrued over the period (Khanra et al., 2020). Table 1 reveals the most influential authors, countries and journals based on citation analysis. Büttgen M., Lehmann C. and Schuster T. were the top three authors. Further, Germany, China and Turkey were the leading countries. *Journal of Business Research*, *International Journal of Innovation Management*, and *Behavioral Sciences* were acknowledged as the most popular journals within the digital leadership and creative performance literature.

4. TEXT ANALYSIS

Text analysis is a robust technique for generating network maps based on text data extracted from the bibliographic database (Xu et al., 2021). VOSviewer uses text-mining functionality to build and visualize co-occurrence network maps of key terms appearing in the final database. Such co-occurrence analysis of the key terms helps identify prominent relationships and interconnectedness among units of analysis for identifying related themes under the research domain (Bukar et al., 2023). Our study is among the few studies that have used VOSviewer for text analysis complemented with bibliometric analysis (Bukar et al., 2023; Gandasari et al., 2024). As Bukar et al. (2023) suggested, Table 2 demonstrates the text analysis protocol used for the current study.

4.1 Clustering Based on Text Analysis

Text networks built through co-occurrences of terms help construct text clusters, also called communities of terms. A community of terms can be understood as 'a group of terms that cluster collectively in the text network' (Bukar et al., 2023). Multiple communities of terms can suggest broad research areas pertinent to each community. The current study used VOSviewer's textual clustering method to determine the relevant clusters for the study. Fig. 4 represents the four clusters (Cluster 1: Diamond, Cluster 2: Triangle, Cluster 3: Star, Cluster 4: Circle) obtained from text analysis, with each cluster representing a unique topic related to digital leadership and creative performance. Additionally, Table 3 lists the relevant terms of each cluster and the significant themes studied in each cluster.

Table 2. Text Analysis Protocol.

Protocol	Description
Type of data	A map based on text data
Data source	Bibliographic database file: Scopus
Fields from which terms are extracted	Title and abstract fields • Excluding structured abstract labels • Excluding copyright statements
Stop words like 'was', 'the', 'also'	Stop words were removed
Counting method	Full counting
Minimum number of occurrences of a term	15
Total terms extracted	2,317
Total terms meeting the threshold	43
Number of terms selected based on relevant scores	26

Source: Authors' creation.

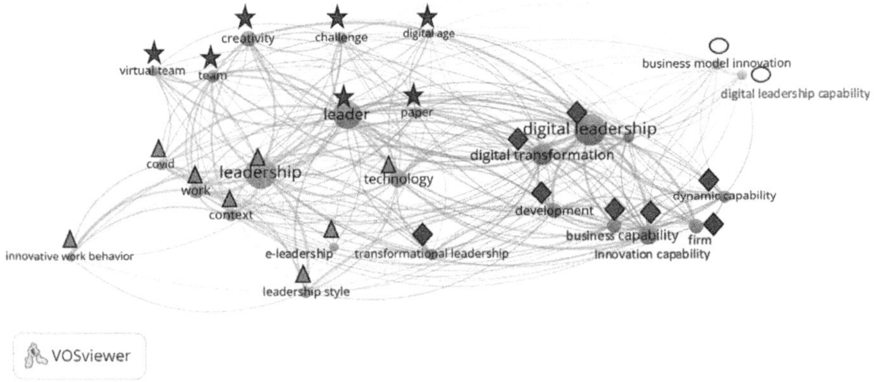

Fig. 4 Clusters Obtained From Text Data. *Source:* Authors' creation.

4.2 Thematic Assessment of Clusters

The following section aims to understand the research front of digital leadership and creative performance literature through a thematic assessment of each cluster.

4.2.1 Digital Leadership and Organizational Capabilities for Digital Transformation (Cluster 1)

The theme in cluster one points to the necessity of digital leadership and other organizational capabilities in driving digital transformation. Digital transformation is characterized by an organizational shift to digital technologies, platforms and processes integrating big data, AI, cloud, IoT and social media platforms to revolutionize the value created for different stakeholders. However, digital transformation is futile when dealing with technological changes without holistic digital

Table 3. Major Themes Identified From Clustering Based on Text Analysis.

Cluster	Term	Occurrences	Relevance	Major Theme
Cluster 1 (Diamond: nine items)	Business	23	0.62	Digital leadership and organizational capabilities for digital transformation
	Capability	55	1.10	
	Development	38	0.50	
	Digital leadership	127	0.76	
	Digital transformation	67	0.41	
	Dynamic capability	28	1.75	
	Firm	35	0.86	
	Innovation capability	33	1.62	
	Transformational leadership	22	0.33	
Cluster 2 (Triangle: eight items)	Context	32	0.82	E-leadership and technology in the challenging context of COVID-19
	COVID	23	1.03	
	E-leadership	18	0.48	
	Innovative work behaviour	18	2.14	
	Leadership	126	0.58	
	Leadership style	26	0.53	
	Technology	51	0.13	
	Work	39	1.11	
Cluster 3 (Star: seven items)	Challenge	25	0.31	Role of virtual team leadership in driving creative performance
	Creativity	41	0.43	
	Digital age	15	0.19	
	Leader	108	0.20	
	Paper	25	0.13	
	Team	29	0.69	
	Virtual team	21	1.24	
Cluster 4 (Circle: two items)	Business model innovation	24	3.70	Digital leadership capabilities for business innovation
	Digital leadership capability	21	4.33	

Source: Authors' creation.

strategies at every level. AlNuaimi et al. (2022) emphasized the role of organizational agility, digital strategy and digital transformational leadership in driving digital transformation. Bansal et al. (2023) further expanded the dynamic capabilities perspective to innovation capabilities empowered by digital infrastructure, creativity and tech-savvy architecture to keep up with the turbulent times. Further, innovation management capabilities such as radical innovation, ambidexterity, strategic flexibility and green process innovation (Elidjena & Rukmanac, 2019; Mihardjo et al., 2019; Sarfraz et al., 2022; Sasmoko et al., 2019), digital capabilities including digital knowledge and platform digitization (Hoang et al., 2024; Park et al., 2021; Wang, 2022) and managerial capabilities including cognition, social capital and entrepreneurial skills (Heubeck, 2023; Amoako et al., 2022) play a critical role in accelerating businesses performance.

4.2.2 E-Leadership and Technology in the Challenging Context of COVID-19 (Cluster 2)

The central theme in cluster two discussed the emerging role of digital technologies and e-leadership amid uncertain circumstances such as COVID-19 that necessitated new leadership roles for managing new ways of work, like remote/hybrid work. More specifically, Krehl and Büttgen (2022) and Kashive et al. (2022) explored e-leadership practices critical for navigating crisis-induced complexities, which included collaboration, team building, trust building and feedback. Coun et al. (2021) studied the association between digital leadership styles and innovative work behaviour for empowering and motivating employees to develop novel solutions. The publication by Li and Xiao (2023) focused on the interplay between leadership behaviour and the use of technology and how it can be leveraged to promote innovative behaviour among employees by adding psychological capital and affective commitment to e-leadership. Similarly, Doghri et al. (2021) also discussed the linkage between e-leadership, organizational collaboration and innovation for exploring new ideas.

4.2.3 Role of Virtual Team Leadership in Driving Creative Performance (Cluster 3)

Cluster three sheds light on the significance of virtual leadership in promoting creative performance that acts as a critical competitive advantage in the Volatility, Uncertainty, Complexity, and Ambiguity (VUCA) world. Wang et al. (2024) emphasized the leaders' role in facilitating virtual communication to induce team-level creativity for mitigating the negative impact of working digitally. The publication by Tigre et al. (2024) discussed five leadership elements, including digital savvy, result-oriented, collaborative teamwork, business skills and team resourcefulness, which are pivotal for enabling creative problem solutions to reach organizational goals. Yang et al. (2024) further examined the positive impact of digital platform leadership in driving organizational creativity from an entrepreneur's perspective. Research by Öngel et al. (2023) and Zhu et al. (2022) dwelt on the significant effect of digital leadership on employee performance outcomes, which further results in high-performance work systems leveraging digital tools and fostering employee creativity.

4.2.4 Digital Leadership Capabilities for Business Innovation (Cluster 4)

In cluster four, the running theme centred on digital leadership capabilities for building and developing business model innovation in the digital workplace to successfully transform and stay competitive in the digital age. In their study, Pandey et al. (2023) investigated the significance of digital leadership capabilities in facilitating IT adoption and innovation for business success that is strengthened by digital agility. In Chatterjee et al. (2023), the authors used a dynamic capabilities perspective to validate the role of digital leadership in driving organizational innovation by accelerating the digital transformation process. Furthermore, Benitez et al. (2022) discussed the leading role of platform digitization capability and digital leadership in promoting creative business performance that can effectively result in successful IS (information systems) integration.

5. FUTURE RESEARCH AGENDA

The present study deploys the TCCM framework (Paul et al., 2023; Paul & Rosado-Serrano, 2019) to answer the third research question entailing future research avenues that scholars can explore to advance their understanding of digital leadership and creative performance. TCCM has been widely used across multiple disciplines, including brand hate (Yadav & Chakrabarti, 2022), spiritual leadership (Vedula & Agarwal, 2024) and merchandising (Basu et al., 2022), showing its widespread acceptability.

5.1 Theory

The review enabled us to identify multiple theories and frameworks contributing to the digital leadership and creative performance nexus. Scholarly attention has been drawn towards the knowledge-based and dynamic capabilities view theory in understanding the role of digital leadership for creativity and business model innovation in complex business environments (Eng et al., 2023; Faiz et al., 2024; Heubeck, 2023; Muneeb et al., 2023). The work of AlNuaimi et al. (2022) and Ahmad et al. (2022) incorporated institutional theory for testing digital transformational leadership in driving digital transformation and digital strategy that helps businesses come up with creative solutions. Moreover, studies by Wang et al. (2022) and Borah et al. (2022) used a resource-based view of the firm to study the role of organizational factors like digital organizational culture, entrepreneurial orientation and digital platform capability to study digital leadership's impact in cultivating creative performance. Future studies can explore other strategic management theories like the job demands and resources (JD-R) model and flexible firm theory (FFT) to understand organizational mechanisms, strategies and policy implications that will support or hinder digital leadership for creative performance. Furthermore, future research can investigate the relationship between digital leadership and creative performance through the lens of social behaviour theories such as social capital theory, social exchange theory and social cognitive theory. These theories will help understand how employees exchange information and build relationships within their social networks to boost their creative performance as they embrace new work arrangements like remote/hybrid work. Furthermore, an in-depth analysis pointed out the absence of cultural dimensions in assessing the relationship between digital leadership and creative performance. For future research, Hofstede's cultural framework can be integrated into digital leadership and creative performance literature (Hofstede,

2011). It will help gain a more profound understanding of the influence of multifaceted cultural dimensions on communication, leadership styles, creativity and decision-making processes. Furthermore, the framework will offer an insightful lens to evaluate cultural differences for developing a more inclusive work environment and culturally sensitive digital leadership practices that foster creative performance. Additionally, other groups of theories like personal behaviour theories, such as psychological contract theory, self-determination theory; motivation theories, including intrinsic motivation theory, motivation, ability, opportunity (MOA) framework; technology adoption theories like unified theory of acceptance and use of technology (UTAUT), technology acceptance model (TAM) can be studied to contribute towards multidisciplinary research. Using these theories from different disciplines will help academicians extend the extant literature from an interdisciplinary lens.

5.2 Context

Concerning the context of the research domain under review, past studies have examined digital leadership and creative performance across various industries and sectors. More specifically, Sarfraz et al. (2022) and Rodrigues et al. (2022) examined the role of creative skills and digital leadership in promoting sustainable performance in manufacturing firms. Publications by Carvalho et al. (2023), Muneeb et al. (2023), and Park et al. (2021) studied digital competence, innovative work behaviour and other organizational capabilities in the context of higher education institutions (HEIs), while Xu and Pan (2022) explored leadership challenges in a virtual workplace pertinent to the publishing industry. Further, certain significant publications, including Fatima and Masood (2024), Sagbas et al. (2023), and Pandey et al. (2023), contributed interesting empirical insights into the IT/ITeS sector by emphasizing the significance of digital leadership and digital agility in enhancing creative performance on the job. Authors extended the research avenues for digital leadership and creative performance by including context-specific empirical studies like banking (Adekanmbi & Ukpere, 2023; Al Issa & Omar, 2024; Kör et al., 2021), oil (Abdulmuhsin & Tarhini, 2021), textile (Erhan et al., 2022) and apparel industry for supply chain management (Eng et al., 2023). In Ramadan et al. (2023) and Borah et al. (2022), the authors studied digital leadership and innovation as key players for business's digital transformation in small and medium enterprises (SMEs). There is an urge to draw scholarly attention to other sectors like healthcare, hospitality, tourism, agriculture, supply chain and retail, as digital leadership and creative performance can drive innovation, enhance customer experience and improve efficiency. For instance, in the healthcare sector, digital leadership roles can be leveraged to advance cross-country research and medical technologies and use creativity for personalized treatment plans. Also, studying digital leadership and creative performance in the retail sector can help lead innovative market strategies and design engaging and real-time customer experiences. Moreover, boundary conditions like the organization's nature, mission and vision, and power structures should also be considered to determine well-suited digital leadership capabilities for enhancing the creative competencies of employees. We did not find any comparative analysis that can examine how the variables under study unfold in new work settings like WFH, hybrid or gig work. Embracing these new research directions can act as a starting point for future researchers to deepen the literature on digital leadership and creative performance.

5.3 Characteristics

The current review revealed that the extant literature had only a few studies that have examined the antecedents of digital leadership and outcomes other than creativity and innovation. For example, research by Benitez et al. (2022) examined the role of platform digitization capability, while Amoako et al. (2022) investigated employee technological capability as an antecedent for inducing creative performance. Future studies can work on unearthing other possible outcomes of digital leadership at organizational, team and individual levels. For example, scholars are encouraged to explore how creative performance facilitated through digital leadership can lead to organizational-level outcomes, including improved productivity, innovative capability, competitive advantage, stronger employer brand, flexibility, digital agility and financial stability. Team-level variables are equally significant in today's dynamic and digital age as collective efforts, skills and capabilities of teams are crucial in fostering team diversity, team creativity, cohesion, group engagement and effective performance. Furthermore, a potential future avenue of research can extend the current literature by investigating the influence of digital leadership and creative performance on individual-level outcomes like work-life balance, mental health, happiness, mindfulness and organizational citizenship behaviour. A paucity of research shows a greater concern towards green practices and sustainable approaches for organizations embracing digital leadership. For example, only a few studies, including Sarfraz et al. (2022), Borah et al. (2022), and Park et al. (2021), examined the influence of digital leadership and creative performance on the sustainable performance of organizations. This gap emphasizes the critical role of digital leaders in utilizing disruptive technologies to build sustainable organizations through green initiatives, a triple-bottom-line framework and improved environmental, social and governance (ESG) scores. In this regard, effective digital leadership can play a crucial role in enhancing the quality of life at personal and professional levels by thriving in new work arrangements like remote work to reduce carbon emissions, thus contributing towards Sustainable Development Goal (SDG) 13: Climate Action. Furthermore, leveraging digital leadership for creative performance will contribute to SDG 8: Decent Work and Economic Growth through skill development and new job opportunities focused on creatively using disruptive technologies to achieve sustainable goals. Lastly, we found no research that tried to explore the dark side of digital leadership and its potential negative ramifications due to complex virtual work settings that might impact creative performance. Consequently, research in the future can be conducted on similar lines to explore the challenges digital leaders face in building a culture of creativity and innovation.

5.4 Method

Rigorous use of research methodology and a combination of review protocols are pivotal in guiding future researchers to undertake in-depth literature reviews. In this regard, the research community can focus on the planning, operationalizing, writing, embedding and reflecting (POWER) framework while conducting literature reviews to enhance the robustness and quality of their research significantly (Rana et al., 2022, 2023). Further, the current review of the extant literature highlighted that most of the studies used the quantitative survey method as their research methodology (Faiz et al., 2024; Farhan et al., 2024; Gao & Gao, 2024). For future studies, it is recommended that digital leadership and creative performance literature be approached from other methodological paradigms like qualitative or mixed methods. Specifically, various qualitative research methodologies such as semi-structured interviews, case studies, content analysis and phenomenological approaches can be used by researchers to unravel deeper insights into leaders' and employees' experiences. Also, there is a need to encourage the adoption of an in-depth interview methodology for capturing, examining, consolidating and comparing the underlying antecedents, motivations, challenges and outcomes that digital leaders encounter in facilitating creative performance in organizations. Only two studies have used experimental research design (Philip & Gavrilova Aguilar, 2022; Weber et al., 2022). The extant literature can be enriched in the future through experimental designs that employ pretest and posttest control groups to reflect an accurate picture of the organizations in the VUCA world. Furthermore, future longitudinal studies can be undertaken through research methods like diary studies and reflection journals to map the digital transformation journey and comprehend the changes in leaders' styles, abilities and competencies needed to develop employees' creative skills. Additionally, quantitative studies employing surveys can be extended by collecting multi-source data to gauge the perspectives of leaders, employees and all other stakeholders to increase the generalizability and validity of the findings. As a potential future research recommendation, a mixed method approach can be used for undertaking a more comprehensive study by combining structural equation modelling (SEM) with newer methods like Importance-Performance Map Analysis (IPMA), Necessary Condition Analysis (NCA), combined IPMA (cIPMA). These will help understand necessary conditions and prioritize different digital leadership and creative performance factors based on importance, performance and necessity. Other non-linear methods like fuzzy-set qualitative comparative analysis (fsQCA) and artificial neural networks (ANNs) can uncover hidden patterns, perform predictive modelling and understand non-linear relationships. fsQCA, based on sufficiency logic, will help identify sufficient configurations of digital leadership roles for creative performance in hybrid work arrangements (Rihoux & Ragin, 2009). Undertaking future research using these new methodologies will offer advanced insights and fresh perspectives on digital leadership and creative performance literature.

6. CONCLUSION

The present review addresses the gap in literature about the current status of digital leadership and creative performance in today's digital era. However, no research is free of limitations and our study is also subjected to certain limitations pertinent to the sample drawn from the bibliographic database. The present study used only Scopus database for retrieving the articles in the research domain of digital leadership and creative performance. Future research may address this limitation by using other databases, including different sources such as books, conference proceedings, book chapters and reports. Nevertheless, our study organizes the fragmented literature by presenting one of the earliest reviews that uses text analysis for understanding the current state of the literature on digital leadership and creative performance. Using text analysis protocol, it assessed the major thematic areas in digital leadership and creative performance to offer an in-depth understanding of the research front. Furthermore, the use of TCCM framework for proposing actionable and structured future research avenues introduces a novel approach to systematic advancement of the extant literature. This review contributes both theoretically and practically to advance the existing literature and foster new pathways for industry practice. For academicians, the current review maps out the key underexplored areas for further exploration. For practitioners, this study sheds light on emerging knowledge areas to shape strategic decision-making in the current dynamic and digital environment.

REFERENCES

Abbu, H., Mugge, P., & Gudergan, G. (2022). Successful digital leadership requires building trust. *Research-Technology Management*, *65*, 29–33. https://doi.org/10.1080/08956308.2022.2095168

Abdulmuhsin, A. A., & Tarhini, A. (2021). Impact of knowledge leadership on virtual teams' challenges and innovative performance: An empirical examination in oil sector companies. *International Journal of Knowledge Management Studies*, *12*(1), 1–33.

Adekanmbi, F. P., & Ukpere, W. (2023). The impact of innovative work behavior, perceived Leadership 4.0, and corporate social responsibility on sustaining banking industry performance in Nigeria within the 4IR Era. *Banks and Bank Systems*, *18*(4), 1–11.

Aggarwal, S., & Kumar, A. (2022). Dealing with a new normal 'e-leadership': A study using bibliometric analysis and content analysis. *Vision*. https://doi.org/10.1177/09722629221130592

Ahmad, N. H., Teoh, M. F., Ramayah, T., & Halim, H. A. (2022). Digital business model innovation in SMEs: The roles of entrepreneurial leadership and government support. *Journal of Applied Structural Equation Modeling*, *6*(1), 1–25.

Ahuja, J., Puppala, H., Sergio, R., & Hoffman, E. (2023). E-leadership is un(usual): Multi-criteria analysis of critical success factors for the transition from leadership to e-leadership. *Sustainability*. https://doi.org/10.3390/su15086506

Al Issa, H. E., & Omar, M. M. S. (2024). Digital innovation drivers in retail banking: The role of leadership, culture, and technostress inhibitors. *International Journal of Organizational Analysis*, *32*(11), 19–43.

Alawiah, E. T., & Tukiran, M. (2024). Digital leadership and digital transformation: Systematic literature review. *International Journal of Social and Management Studies*, *5*(3), 27–34.

AlNuaimi, B. K., Singh, S. K., Ren, S., Budhwar, P., & Vorobyev, D. (2022). Mastering digital transformation: The nexus between leadership, agility, and digital strategy. *Journal of Business Research*, *145*, 636–648.

Amoako, R., Jiang, Y., Frempong, M. F., Tetteh, S., & Adu-Yeboah, S. S. (2022). Examining the effect of organizational leadership, organizational structure, and employee technological capability on the success of electronic human resource management. *Sage Open*, *12*(2). https://doi.org/10.1177/21582440221088852

Ansari, Z. N., & Kant, R. (2017). A state-of-art literature review reflecting 15 years of focus on sustainable supply chain management. *Journal of Cleaner Production*, *142*, 2524–2543. https://doi.org/10.1016/j.jclepro.2016.11.023

Bansal, A., Panchal, T., Jabeen, F., Mangla, S. K., & Singh, G. (2023). A study of human resource digital transformation (HRDT): A phenomenon of innovation capability led by digital and individual factors. *Journal of Business Research*, *157*, 113611.

Barney, J. B. (2001). Resource-based theories of competitive advantage: A ten-year retrospective on the resource-based view. *Journal of Management*, *27*(6), 643–650.

Bartol, T., Budimir, G., Dekleva-Smrekar, D., Pusnik, M., & Juznic, P. (2014). Assessment of research fields in Scopus and Web of Science in the view of national research evaluation in Slovenia. *Scientometrics*, *98*(2), 1491–1504. https://doi.org/10.1007/s11192-013-1148-8

Basu, R., Paul, J., & Singh, K. (2022). Visual merchandising and store atmospherics: An integrated review and future research directions. *Journal of Business Research*, *151*, 397–408.

Benitez, J., Arenas, A., Castillo, A., & Esteves, J. (2022). Impact of digital leadership capability on innovation performance: The role of platform digitization capability. *Information & Management*, *59*(2), 103590.

Borah, P. S., Iqbal, S., & Akhtar, S. (2022). Linking social media usage and SME's sustainable performance: The role of digital leadership and innovation capabilities. *Technology in Society*, *68*, 101900.

Brunner, T. J., Schuster, T., & Lehmann, C. (2023). Leadership's long arm: The positive influence of digital leadership on managing technology-driven change over a strengthened service innovation capacity. *Frontiers in Psychology*, *14*, 988808.

Bukar, U. A., Sayeed, M. S., Razak, S. F. A., Yogarayan, S., Amodu, O. A., & Mahmood, R. A. R. (2023). A method for analyzing text using VOSviewer. *MethodsX*, *11*, 102339.

Carvalho, L. P. D., Poleto, T., Ramos, C. C., Rodrigues, F. D. A., de Carvalho, V. D. H., & Nepomuceno, T. C. C. (2023). Predictors of digital competence of public university employees and the impact on innovative work behavior. *Administrative Sciences*, *13*(5), 131.

Caviggioli, F., & Ughetto, E. (2019). A bibliometric analysis of the research dealing with the impact of additive manufacturing on industry, business and society. *International Journal of Production Economics*, *208*, 254–268.

Chatterjee, S., Chaudhuri, R., Vrontis, D., & Giovando, G. (2023). Digital workplace and organization performance: Moderating role of digital leadership capability. *Journal of Innovation & Knowledge*, *8*(1), 100334.

Coun, M. J., Edelbroek, R., Peters, P., & Blomme, R. J. (2021). Leading innovative work-behavior in times of COVID-19: Relationship between leadership style, innovative work-behavior, work-related flow, and IT-enabled presence awareness during the first and second wave of the COVID-19 pandemic. *Frontiers in Psychology*, *12*, 717345.

Doghri, S. B. S., Horchani, S. C., & Mouelhi, M. (2021). The e-leadership linking inter-organisational collaboration and ambidextrous innovation. *International Journal of Innovation Management*, *25*(04), 2150043.

Donthu, N., Kumar, S., & Pattnaik, D. (2020). Forty-five years of Journal of Business Research: A bibliometric analysis. *Journal of Business Research*, *109*, 1–14. https://doi.org/10.1016/j.jbusres.2019.10.039

Durán-Sánchez, A., Del Río-Rama, M. D. L. C., Álvarez-García, J., & García-Vélez, D. F. (2019). Mapping of scientific coverage on education for entrepreneurship in higher education. *Journal of Enterprising Communities: People and Places in the Global Economy*, *13*(1/2), 84–104.

Dzage, E. J., & Szabados, G. N. (2024). The relationship of corporate social responsibility with business performance—A bibliometric literature review. *Sustainability*, *16*(7), 2637.

Economic Times. (2024, March 4). *India's digital landscape: World Bank report spotlights progress amid challenges*. https://bfsi.economictimes.indiatimes.com/news/industry/indias-digital-landscape-world-bank-report-spotlights-progress-amid-challenges/108224833

Elidjena, L. W., & Rukmanac, R. A. (2019). Intervening role of innovation management on relationship between digital leadership and dynamic capability accelerated by collaboration. *Focus*, *6*(1), 249–264.

Eng, T. Y., Mohsen, K., & Wu, L. C. (2023). Wireless information technology competency and transformational leadership in supply chain management: Implications for innovative capability. *Information Technology & People*, *36*(3), 969–995.

Erhan, T., Uzunbacak, H. H., & Aydin, E. (2022). From conventional to digital leadership: Exploring digitalization of leadership and innovative work behavior. *Management Research Review*, *45*(11), 1524–1543.

Fahimnia, B., Sarkis, J., & Davarzani, H. (2015). Green supply chain management: A review and bibliometric analysis. *International Journal of Production Economics*, *162*, 101–114.

Faiz, M., Sarwar, N., Tariq, A., & Memon, M. A. (2024). Mastering digital leadership capabilities for business model innovation: The role of managerial decision-making and grants. *Journal of Small Business and Enterprise Development*, *31*(3), 574–597.

Farhan, W., Chaudhry, I. S., Razmak, J., & El Refae, G. A. (2024). Leaders' behavioral approach in the digital era: Task vs relationship. *Journal of Organizational Effectiveness: People and Performance*, *11*(1), 135–161.

Fatima, T., & Masood, A. (2024). Impact of digital leadership on open innovation: A moderating serial mediation model. *Journal of Knowledge Management*, *28*(1), 161–180.

Fenech, R., Baguant, P., & Ivanov, D. (2019). The changing role of human resource management in an era of digital transformation. *International Journal of Entrepreneurship*, *22*(2), 166–175.

Gandasari, D., Tjahjana, D., Dwidienawati, D., & Sugiarto, M. (2024). Bibliometric and visualized analysis of social network analysis research on Scopus databases and VOSviewer. *Cogent Business & Management*, *11*(1), 2376899.

Gao, P., & Gao, Y. (2024). How does digital leadership foster employee innovative behavior: A cognitive–affective processing system perspective. *Behavioral Sciences*, *14*(5), 362.

Heubeck, T. (2023). Managerial capabilities as facilitators of digital transformation? Dynamic managerial capabilities as antecedents to digital business model transformation and firm performance. *Digital Business*, *3*(1), 100053.

Hoang, D., Minh, T., Toan, N., & Mai, V. (2024). Digital capabilities and innovation capabilities in Vietnamese SMEs. *International Journal of Data and Network Science*, *8*(2), 1073–1084.

Hofstede, G. (2011). Dimensionalizing cultures: The Hofstede model in context. *Online Readings in Psychology and Culture*, *2*(1), 2307–2919. https://doi.org/10.9707/2307-0919.1014

Jiang, Z., Zhao, X., Wang, Z., & Herbert, K. (2024). Safety leadership: A bibliometric literature review and future research directions. *Journal of Business Research*, *172*, 114437.

Karakose, T., Polat, H., & Papadakis, S. (2021). Examining teachers' perspectives on school principals' digital leadership roles and technology capabilities during the COVID-19 pandemic. *Sustainability*, *13*(23), 13448.

Karakose, T., Kocabas, I., Yirci, R., Papadakis, S., Ozdemir, T. Y., & Demirkol, M. (2022). The development and evolution of digital leadership: A bibliometric mapping approach-based study. *Sustainability*, *14*(23), 16171.

Kashive, N., Khanna, V. T., & Powale, L. (2022). Virtual team performance: E-leadership roles in the era of COVID-19. *The Journal of Management Development*, *41*(5), 277–300.

Katanic, S. (2021, July 21). *Effective digital leadership is key to digital transformation*. https://www.forbes.com/sites/forbesagencycouncil/2021/07/21/effective-digital-leadership-is-key-to-digital-transformation/#

Khanra, S., Dhir, A., & Mäntymäki, M. (2020). Big data analytics and enterprises: A bibliometric synthesis of the literature. *Enterprise Information Systems*, *14*(6), 737–768.

Kör, B., Wakkee, I., & van der Sijde, P. (2021). How to promote managers' innovative behavior at work: Individual factors and perceptions. *Technovation*, *99*, 102127.

Korzynski, P., Paniagua, J., & Rodriguez-Montemayor, E. (2019). Employee creativity in a digital era: The mediating role of social media. *Management Decision*, *58*(6), 1100–1117.

Krehl, E. H., & Büttgen, M. (2022). Uncovering the complexities of remote leadership and the usage of digital tools during the COVID-19 pandemic: A qualitative diary study. *German Journal of Human Resource Management*, *36*(3), 325–352.

Kumar, S., Goyal, P., Kumar, V., & Vandana. (2022). Cultural diversity in tourism: A bibliometric analysis of 33 years (1988–2021). In S. Rana, Sakshi, & J. Singh (Eds.), *Exploring the latest trends in management literature* (pp. 147–168). Emerald Publishing Limited.

Li, G., Lu, Y., & Eliason, R. G. (2022). How does ethical leadership enhance employee creativity during the COVID-19 Pandemic in China? *Ethics & Behavior*, *32*(6), 532–548.

Li, M., Porter, A. L., & Suominen, A. (2018). Insights into relationships between disruptive technology/innovation and emerging technology: A bibliometric perspective. *Technological Forecasting and Social Change*, *129*, 285–296.

Li, M., & Xiao, W. (2023). Research on the effect of e-leadership on employee innovation behavior in the context of "self" and "relationship". *Journal of Organizational and End User Computing*, *35*(1).

Markus, M. L., & Rowe, F. (2023). The digital transformation conundrum: Labels, definitions, phenomena, and theories. *Journal of the Association for Information Systems*, *24*(2), 328–335.

Martínez-López, F. J., Merigó, J. M., Valenzuela-Fernández, L., & Nicolás, C. (2018). Fifty years of the European Journal of Marketing: A bibliometric analysis. *European Journal of Marketing*, *52*(1/2), 439–468.

Mihardjo, L. W. W., & Rukmana, R. A. (2018). Does digital leadership impact directly or indirectly on dynamic capability: Case on Indonesia telecommunication industry in digital transformation? *The Journal of Social Sciences Research*, 832–841.

Mihardjo, L., Sasmoko, S., Alamsyah, F., & Elidjen, E. J. M. S. L. (2019). The influence of digital leadership on innovation management based on dynamic capability: Market orientation as a moderator. *Management Science Letters*, *9*(7), 1059–1070.

Mishra, V., & Singh Kaurav, R. P. (2024). Leveraging disruptive technologies and strategies for competitive advantage. In *Review of technologies and disruptive business strategies* (pp. 1–16). Emerald Publishing Limited.

Muneeb, D., Khattak, A., Wahba, K., Abdalla, S., & Ahmad, S. Z. (2023). Dynamic capabilities as a strategic flexibility enabler: Organizational responsiveness to COVID-19. *Journal of Asia Business Studies*, *17*(4), 824–849.

Mutonyi, B. R., Slåtten, T., & Lien, G. (2020). Organizational climate and creative performance in the public sector. *European Business Review*, *32*(4), 615–631.

Öngel, V., Günsel, A., Gençer Çelik, G., Altındağ, E., & Tatlı, H. S. (2023). Digital leadership's influence on individual creativity and employee performance: A view through the generational lens. *Behavioral Sciences*, *14*(1), 3.

Orioli, F. P., & Veríssimo, J. M. C. (2023). Organizational capabilities and SSCM: A bibliographic review and cluster analysis. *Benchmarking: An International Journal*, *31*(6), 1895–1921.

Pahlevan-Sharif, S., Mura, P., & Wijesinghe, S. N. (2019). A systematic review of systematic reviews in tourism. *Journal of Hospitality and Tourism Management*, *39*, 158–165.

Pandey, J., Majumdarr, S., Hassan, Y., & Benuyenah, V. (2023). Role of digital leadership capability in shaping IT innovation: A digital agility perspective. *Journal of Global Information Management*, *31*(8), 1–20.

Park, H., Kim, S., Choi, M., & Choi, J. (2021). Human, technical, and organizational drivers affecting sustainability of content firms through management and innovation capability during COVID-19. *Sustainability*, *13*(12), 6661.

Paul, J., Khatri, P., & Kaur Duggal, H. (2023). Frameworks for developing impactful systematic literature reviews and theory building: What, why and how? *Journal of Decision Systems*, 1–14.

Paul, J., & Rosado-Serrano, A. (2019). Gradual internationalization vs born-global/international new venture models: A review and research agenda. *International Marketing Review*, *36*(6), 830–858.

Philip, J., & Gavrilova Aguilar, M. (2022). Student perceptions of leadership skills necessary for digital transformation. *The Journal of Education for Business*, *97*(2), 86–98.

Ramadan, M., Bou Zakhem, N., Baydoun, H., Daouk, A., Youssef, S., El Fawal, A., Elia, J., & Ashaal, A. (2023). Toward digital transformation and business model innovation: The nexus between leadership, organizational agility, and knowledge transfer. *Administrative Sciences*, *13*(8), 185.

Rana, S., Sakshi, & Singh, J. (2022). Presenting the POWER framework of conducting literature review. In S. Rana, Sakshi, & J. Singh (Eds.), *Exploring the latest trends in management literature (Review of management literature)* (Vol. 1, pp. 1–13). Emerald Publishing Limited.

Rana, S., Singh, J., & Kathuria, S. (2023). Parameters and decision elements of writing effective literature review papers: Empirical evidence from multiple stakeholders on POWER framework. In S. Rana, J. Singh, & S. Kathuria (Eds.), *Advancing methodologies of conducting literature review in management domain (Review of management literature)* (Vol. 2, pp. 1–25). Emerald Publishing Limited.

Ratajczak, S. (2022). Digital leadership at universities–a systematic literature review. *Forum Scientiae Oeconomia, 10*(4), 133–150. Wydawnictwo Naukowe Akademii WSB.

Rihoux, B., & Ragin, C. C. (2009). *Configurational comparative methods: Qualitative comparative analysis (QCA) and related techniques*. Sage Publications.

Rodrigues, M., FRANCO, M., & Silva, R. (2022). Digitalisation and innovation in SMEs: Influences on the advantages of digital entrepreneurship. *International Journal of Innovation Management, 26*(08), 2250066.

Sağbaş, M., & Erdoğan, F. A. (2022). Digital leadership: A systematic conceptual literature review. *İstanbul Kent Üniversitesi İnsan ve Toplum Bilimleri Dergisi, 3*(1), 17–35.

Sagbas, M., Oktaysoy, O., Topcuoglu, E., Kaygin, E., & Erdogan, F. A. (2023). The mediating role of innovative behavior on the effect of digital leadership on intrapreneurship intention and job performance. *Behavioral Sciences, 13*(10), 874.

Sarfraz, M., Ivascu, L., Abdullah, M. I., Ozturk, I., & Tariq, J. (2022). Exploring a pathway to sustainable performance in manufacturing firms: The interplay between innovation capabilities, green process, product innovations and digital leadership. *Sustainability, 14*(10), 5945.

Sasmoko, S., Mihardjo, L., Alamsjah, F., & Elidjen, E. (2019). Dynamic capability: The effect of digital leadership on fostering innovation capability based on market orientation. *Management Science Letters, 9*(10), 1633–1644.

Seuring, S., & Gold, S. (2012). Conducting content-analysis based literature reviews in supply chain management. *Supply Chain Management: International Journal, 17*(5), 544–555.

Sharif, A. (2023, September 4). *Skills expected to rise in importance from 2023 to 2027*. https://www.statista.com/statistics/1383183/skills-on-the-rise/

Tandon, A., Dhir, A., Islam, A. N., & Mäntymäki, M. (2020). Blockchain in healthcare: A systematic literature review, synthesizing framework and future research agenda. *Computers in Industry, 122*, 103290.

Teece, D. J., Pisano, G., & Shuen, A. (1997). Dynamic capabilities and strategic management. *Strategic Management Journal, 18*(7), 509–533.

Tigre, F. B., Lopes Henriques, P., & Curado, C. (2024). Creativity for problem solving in the digital era: Configurations of leadership profiles. *Journal of Leadership Studies, 18*(1), 17–32.

Türk, A. (2023). Digital leadership role in developing business strategy suitable for digital transformation. *Frontiers in Psychology, 13*, 1066180.

Van Oorschot, J. A., Hofman, E., & Halman, J. I. (2018). A bibliometric review of the innovation adoption literature. *Technological Forecasting and Social Change, 134*, 1–21.

Vedula, S. B., & Agrawal, R. K. (2024). Mapping spiritual leadership: A bibliometric analysis and synthesis of past milestones and future research agenda. *Journal of Business Ethics, 189*(2), 301–328.

Wang, Y. (2022). Analyzing the mechanism of strategic orientation towards digitization and organizational performance settings enduring employee resistance to innovation and performance capabilities. *Frontiers in Psychology, 13*, 1006310.

Wang, L., Chen, X. P., & Yin, J. (2024). Leading via virtual communication: A longitudinal field experiment on work team creativity in an extreme context. *Asia Pacific Journal of Management, 41*(1), 195–231.

Wang, T., Lin, X., & Sheng, F. (2022). Digital leadership and exploratory innovation: From the dual perspectives of strategic orientation and organizational culture. *Frontiers in Psychology, 13*, 902693.

Weber, E., Büttgen, M., & Bartsch, S. (2022). How to take employees on the digital transformation journey: An experimental study on complementary leadership behaviors in managing organizational change. *Journal of Business Research*, *143*, 225–238.

World Economic Forum. (2023). *Future of Jobs Report*. World Economic Forum.

Xu, X., Chen, X., Jia, F., Brown, S., Gong, Y., & Xu, Y. (2018). Supply chain finance: A systematic literature review and bibliometric analysis. *International Journal of Production Economics*, *204*, 160–173. https://doi.org/10.1016/j.ijpe.2018.08.003

Xu, Z., Ge, Z., Wang, X., & Skare, M. (2021). Bibliometric analysis of technology adoption literature published from 1997 to 2020. *Technological Forecasting and Social Change*, *170*, 120896.

Xu, Z., Li, X., Sun, X., Cheng, M., & Xu, J. (2022). The relationship between self-sacrificial leadership and employee creativity: Multilevel mediating and moderating role of shared vision. *Management Decision*, *60*(8), 2256–2271.

Xu, W., & Pan, H. (2022). Leadership challenges in the context of "flexible working" and its implication to a virtual workplace: Case study of a China's publishing house. *Journal of Chinese Human Resources Management*, *13*(2), 12–25.

Yadav, A., & Chakrabarti, S. (2022). Brand hate: A systematic literature review and future research agenda. *International Journal of Consumer Studies*, *46*(5), 1992–2019.

Yang, X., Zhang, M., Meng, Z., Shen, Y., & Du, X. (2024). Cross-level transformation of creativity from entrepreneurs to organizations. *Frontiers in Psychology*, *15*, 1278996.

Zaid, M., & Farooqi, R. (2024). Exploring the Internet of Things-marketing connection: A bibliometric review and directions for future research. *Review of Technologies and Disruptive Business Strategies*, *3*, 275–292.

Zhu, J., Zhang, B., Xie, M., & Cao, Q. (2022). Digital leadership and employee creativity: The role of employee job crafting and person-organization fit. *Frontiers in Psychology*, *13*, 827057.

Ziek, P., & Smulowitz, S. (2014). The impact of emergent virtual leadership competencies on team effectiveness. *The Leadership & Organization Development Journal*, *35*(2), 106–120.

Zupic, I., & Čater, T. (2015). Bibliometric methods in management and organization. *Organizational Research Methods*, *18*(3), 429–472.

Mapping the Intersection of Artificial Intelligence and Supply Chain Resilience: A Literature Review and Future Research Agenda

Mohammad A.K. Alsmairat[a], Luay Jum'a[b], Mohammad Khaled Al-Nawayseh[a,c] and Ekta Singhal[d]

[a]*American University in the Emirates, UAE*
[b]*German Jordanian University, Jordan*
[c]*The University of Jordan, Jordan*
[d]*Lal Bahadur Shastri Institute of Management, India*

ABSTRACT

Artificial intelligence (AI) and supply chain resilience (SCR) are deeply interconnected. This study reviews the ways in which AI enhances SCR. The review is performed on 52 documents published between 2018 and 2023 and indexed in the Clarivate (Web of Science) and Scopus databases. This study underscores the comprehensive evolution of the literature on the role of AI in augmenting SCR. As a result, it identified six research themes at the intersection of AI and SCR. The results suggest that AI possesses considerable potential to enhance SCR by improving decision-making, increasing efficiency and fostering sustainable practices. This investigation offers key insights for policymakers and managers to leverage AI's benefits, challenges and capabilities of AI in SC. The study addresses gaps in various AI functions related to enhancing SCR and highlights several unresolved areas, including the intersection of AI and sustainable supply chains.

Keywords: AI; supply chain; supply chain resilience; bibliometric; developing and developed economies

---

Reviewing the Latest Trends in Management Literature
Review of Management Literature, Volume 4B, 175–199

Published under exclusive licence by Emerald Publishing Limited
ISSN: 2754-5865/doi:10.1108/S2754-58652025000004B007

1. INTRODUCTION

In the field of supply chain management (SCM), artificial intelligence (AI) and supply chain resilience (SCR) are key enablers but have not been well researched in recent years (Dey et al., 2023; Faggioni et al., 2024; Vishwakarma et al., 2023). SCR is fundamentally predicated on the premise that organizations can control the risk of SC interruptions and ensure that they offer goods and services to the market (Belhadi et al., 2022; Queiroz et al., 2023). Amidst the complexities of modern global commerce, AI integration into SCM has become imperative for firms seeking to thrive in an era characterized by profound interconnections and volatility (Cadden et al., 2022).

In unprecedented global challenges, firms are trying to achieve SCR by digitizing their supply chain (SC) processes and implementing innovative tools such as AI applications, especially in developing economies. While SCR allows firms to respond to disruptions, minimize risk and achieve a competitive advantage, AI is a set of intelligent engineering machines that support them in recording, maintaining and predicting future outcomes (Li et al., 2017), anticipating market demands and fluctuations (Jauhar et al., 2024), eliminating shocks, managing inventory efficiently and optimizing operations (Modgil, Singh, & Hannibal, 2022).

On the other hand, AI also increases transparency within the SC network (Sharma et al., 2022), bolsters sustainability (Damoah et al., 2021) and empowers firms to minimize environmental impact. Dauvergne (2022) observed that several leading global firms invest heavily in AI to enhance their SC performance and achieve a more resilient level. For instance, Oracle, Blue, Amazon, eBay, Philips, Microsoft, Google and BMW have benefited from adopting AI in their SC operations (Helo & Hao, 2022; Ivanov et al., 2022; Khalifa et al., 2021).

Although AI is widely recognized as a valuable tool for supporting SCR, there is a notable lack of thorough research examining the potential impact of AI technologies on SCR outcomes in the literature now in publication. Scholars such as Dey et al. (2023) and Jackson et al. (2024) have highlighted this gap, emphasizing the need for further investigation into how AI can contribute effectively to resilient supply chain networks. Themes connected to supply chain innovation, such as Industry 4.0, have been the subject of recent research, including Industry 4.0, technologies (Benitez et al., 2022; A. Kumar et al., 2024; Lu et al., 2024), big data capabilities (M. Kumar et al., 2024; Riggs et al., 2023) and lean innovations aimed at sustainability (Rahardjo et al., 2024; Singh & Maheswaran, 2024). However, the specific role of AI remains underexplored, particularly in the context of SCR. For instance, Wong et al. (2024) conducted an empirical investigation into AI's impact on supply chain risk management. Still, they did not adequately address the resilience aspects, indicating a critical gap in the literature. Furthermore, Naz et al. (2022) provided an extensive literature review on AI as an enabler of SCR; however, their focus was limited to research published until 2020, underscoring the need for updated analyses that reflect recent advancements in AI applications.

This study aims to fill the existing gaps by addressing the following research questions:

RQ1. How has the AI literature evolved over the years to achieve SCR?

Through the extensive review of existing literature, it has been observed that there is a lack of evidence for understanding the benefits of AI adoption in achieving SCR. Therefore, this study aims to offer crucial insights for policymakers on the key processes needed to overcome challenges and maximize benefits, while also helping to identify the capabilities necessary for successful AI adoption.

Despite the increasing adoption and widespread interest of scholars and managers, few studies have explored the application of AI technology in building SCR. Hence, the study aims to address the following second research question:

RQ2. What are the benefits and challenges of AI adoption in ensuring SCR?

The remainder of this paper is organized as follows. Section two briefly reviews the literature on AI, SCR, applications of AI and machine learning (ML) for SCR as well as the benefits and challenges in this context were reviewed. Section 3 presents the research methods, and Section 4 presents the limitations. Section 5 discusses future trends in AI and ML applications for enabling SC. Finally, Section 6 concludes the paper.

2. THEORETICAL BACKGROUND

2.1 AI Definition and Taxonomy

The concept of AI has evolved significantly since its introduction by John McCarthy in 1955 (Flasiński, 2016). McCarthy aimed to explore the potential of machines performing tasks associated with human intelligence, such as language processing and problem-solving (Flasiński, 2016). Despite over six decades of discussion, a universally accepted definition of AI remains elusive, underscoring its complex and dynamic nature. This section critically reviews various definitions of AI within theoretical frameworks, particularly in the context of SCR. Defining AI is challenging because of its wide range of interpretations across disciplines. Scholars such as Legg and Hutter (2007) and Nilsson (2011) have highlighted the difficulties in reaching a consensus on a standardized definition. Russel and Norvig (2012) proposed a dual-dimensional framework for evaluating AI systems. One dimension measures performance against human reasoning or ideal rationality, while the other assesses the system's ability to exhibit rational behaviour that meets or exceeds human capabilities. This framework illustrates the multifaceted nature of AI and emphasizes the importance of a nuanced understanding of its capabilities and limitations.

To provide clarity, this section introduces a three-layered taxonomy of AI that categorizes it into 'branch', 'application' and 'method'. The 'branch' identifies primary functional areas, the 'application' layer focuses on specific uses, and the 'method' layer details the technological foundations (see Fig. 1). This paper refrains

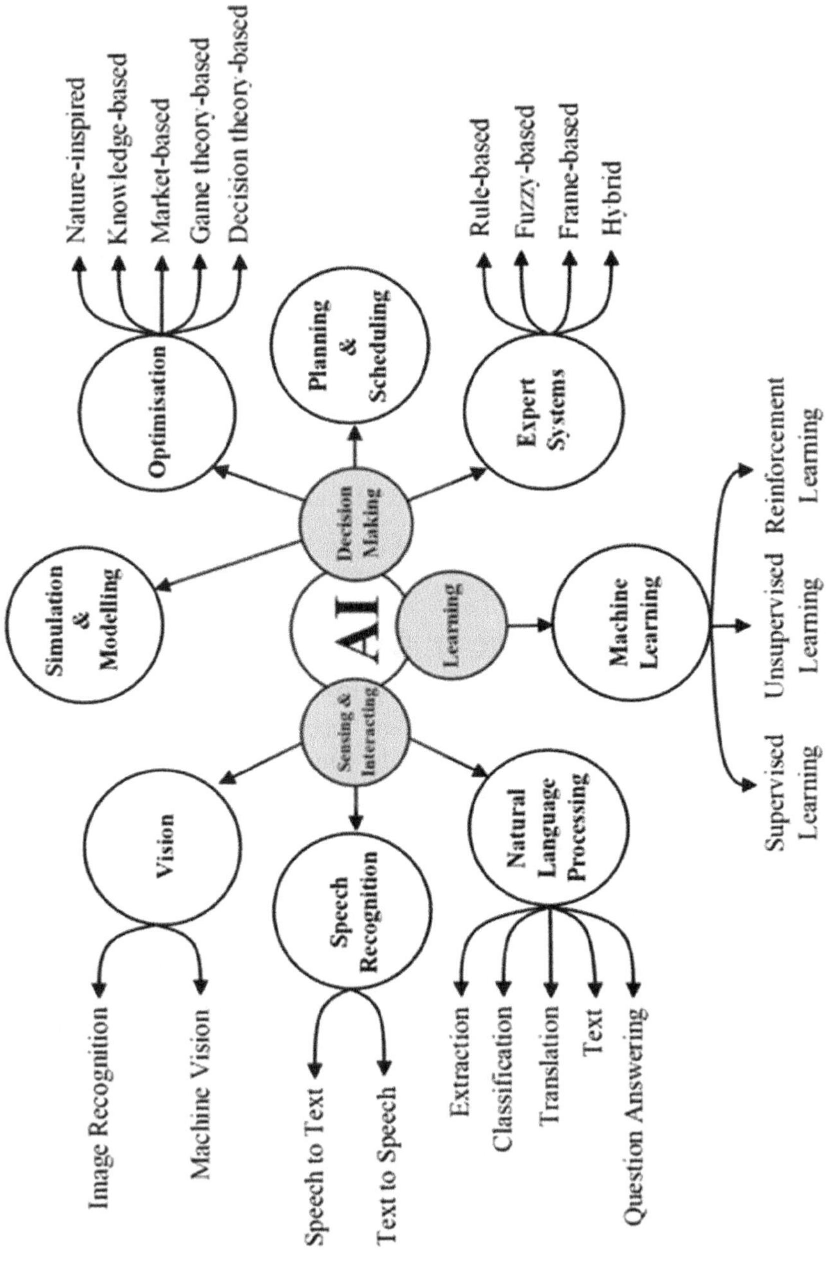

Fig. 1. AI Taxonomy. *Source:* Pourmader et al. (2021).

from delving into the details of individual algorithms, instead focusing on AI's broader implications within SCR. AI is divided into three branches based on its purpose within the system: media interaction (text, audio, video, speech, vision and natural language processing), data-driven learning (ML and deep learning) and decision-making tools (expert systems, planning, simulation, modelling, scheduling and optimization). This classification aligns with Pournader et al. (2021), who defined AI as a system's ability to interpret data, learn from it and leverage this knowledge to achieve specific tasks.

Grounding the discussion in relevant theoretical frameworks enhances our understanding of the role of AI in SCR. The technology acceptance model (TAM) and the diffusion of innovations (DOI) theory offer insights into the factors that influence AI adoption within organizations. TAM suggests that perceived ease of use and perceived usefulness significantly impact technology adoption (Davis, 1989), while DOI theory highlights the importance of social systems and communication channels in the spread of innovation (Rogers, 1995). These theoretical perspectives help explain the dynamics that facilitate or hinder AI adoption in supply chain, contributing to resilience.

AI's role in SCR is becoming increasingly vital in today's complex global environment, where organizations face challenges such as geopolitical tensions, natural disasters and pandemics (Zhou et al., 2022). AI technologies provide enhanced decision-making and predictive analytics, allowing organizations to process large amounts of data in real time (Wong et al., 2024). This capability helps anticipate disruptions and respond proactively, which is crucial for SCR principles that prioritize adaptability, flexibility and responsiveness under uncertainty (Zhao, 2023). However, integrating AI into supply chain presents several challenges. Issues such as data privacy, ethical considerations and organizational readiness must be addressed to ensure successful AI adoption. Moreover, the lack of standardized definitions and frameworks can hinder communication and collaboration among stakeholders, thus complicating AI implementation.

2.2 Supply Chain Resilience

The term 'supply chain resilience' pertains to the ability of companies to foresee and address unforeseen occurrences and disturbances in their supply chains (Zhou et al., 2022). This term, along with supply chain sustainability and agility, falls within the broader framework of 'supply chain viability' (Yin & Ran, 2021). Supply chain viability refers to the ability of supply chain networks to generate value through dynamic adaptability. This involves adjusting structures as needed, responding promptly to positive developments, recovering from adverse events and maintaining the ability to deliver products and services to society and markets over the long term (Yin & Ran, 2021). This resilience enables businesses to maintain operations during disruptions, proactively identify potential risks and establish early warning systems, leading to improved competitive advantages (Singh, Hamid, & Garza-Reyes, 2023; Singh, Modgil, & Shore, 2023).

In existing literature, scholars have defined supply chain resilience from two main perspectives: the supply chain system viewpoint and the organizational perspective (Hu et al., 2024). From a supply chain system perspective, Wieland and Durach (2021) introduce two resilience types: engineered resilience and social-ecological resilience. Engineered resilience, which treats the supply chain as a linear engineered system, aims to optimize its design for a rapid return to equilibrium. Key metrics for assessing performance here include time-to-recovery (how quickly the system returns to its optimal state) and time-to-survive (the system's ability to withstand disturbances). On the other hand, social-ecological resilience posits that these systems are nonlinear socio-ecological systems composed of multiple interconnected supply chain networks.

Supply chain resilience is classified into internal and external resilience from a company's point of view (Zhou et al., 2022). Internal resilience refers to a company's capacity to strategically prepare for recovery, stay informed about its surroundings and promptly adjust and respond to disruptions. This protects the firm's internal structure and operational effectiveness (Hundal et al., 2020). Conversely, external resilience guarantees the continuous exchange of products and services among a company, its suppliers and its customers, maintaining the supply and demand flow (Fosso Wamba et al., 2020). Achieving supply chain resilience necessitates elements of robustness and agility within an organization's supply chain, akin to the immunity of human beings. Appropriate resources support these attributes (Ivanov et al., 2021; Küffner et al., 2022). Robustness involves a supply chain's capacity to maintain functionality despite disruptions, achieved through preparedness and resilience within the supply chain system (Brandon-Jones et al., 2014). Conversely, agility enables supply chains to adapt operations and strategies in response to disruptions, swiftly adjusting to changing circumstances, customer needs and internal and external processes (Gligor et al., 2019).

In this context, Küffner et al., 2022 outlined three critical layers for supply chain resilience: organizational relationships and collaborations with supply chain partners, organizational structures and processes and the allocation of resources required for change implementation. Additionally, emerging Industry 4.0 technologies like Internet of Things (IoT), AI, ML and blockchain have been introduced to SCM, enhancing resilience and posing challenges (Ivanov et al., 2021). Utilizing digital tools like cloud computing, IoT, big data analytics, blockchain and AI can boost supply chain resilience through enhanced information gathering, processing and distribution. These advancements provide enhanced visibility, transparency and up-to-date data for supply chain stakeholders (Alvarenga et al., 2023).

3. REVIEW METHODOLOGY

This study uses a quantitative approach based on bibliometric analysis to assess, measure and illustrate the advancement of the topic under investigation. This analysis was conducted in four main stages: data retrieval and selection, systematic classification, citation network analysis and content analysis (Aparicio et al., 2021).

This analysis includes analyzing the published articles in terms of the journal title, themes of the article, publication year, author names, institutions, countries, author numbers, collaboration type and nature of the article (Rey-Martí et al., 2016; Z. Xu et al., 2021). Furthermore, bibliometric analysis was conducted using VOSviewer software. This software was developed by Van Eck and Waltman for establishing and visualizing scientific networks (Waltman et al., 2010). It allows researchers to represent data and build connections for scholars, journals, keywords and countries, based on co-citation, bibliometric coupling and co-authorship linkages. Fig. 2 depicts the methodology that led to the complete analysis procedure.

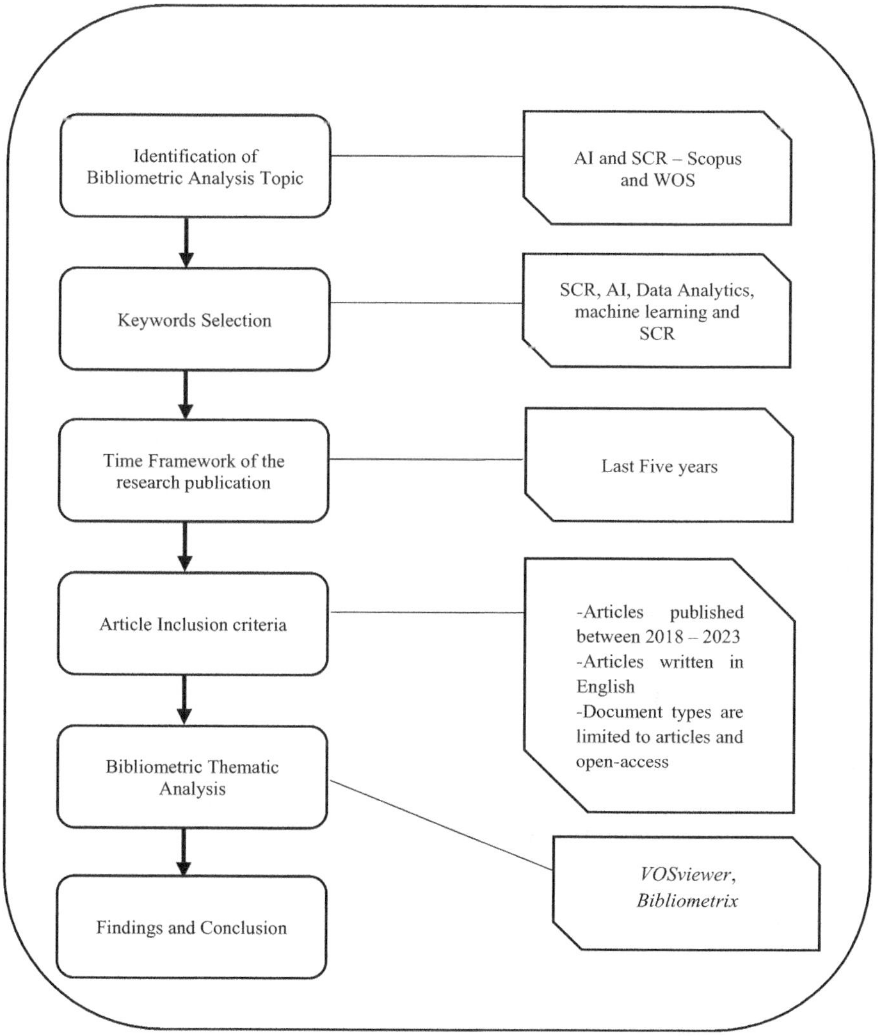

Fig. 2. Analysis Methodology. *Source:* Generated by authors.

3.1 Search and Selection Article Phase

All pertinent research articles regarding the use of AI and ML in highlighting supply chain resilience were collected from Scopus ('www.scopus.com') and Web of Science ('www.webofscience.com'). The study combines these two databases in R Studio to create one unified database. Keyword selection was performed using the following keywords: ("supply chain resilience" AND "Machine Learning" OR "artificial intelligence," OR "Data Analytics" OR "Data Mining"). Article selection according to the title, abstract and keyword searches resulted in 117 articles. After eliminating redundant articles, 52 were discovered, and the papers were subsequently screened to evaluate them based on the criteria for exclusion and inclusion. Table 1 displays the specific procedure for collecting articles from Scopus and Web of Science databases.

Table 1. 'Search and Select Articles'.

(A) Search and Select Articles		
Stage 1: Database query	Result: 69	Result: 48
Stage 2: Filter by Document Type and Language	Result: 35	Result: 17
Query Details	TITLE, ABSTRACT, KEYWORD: ("Supply Chain Resilience" AND "Artificial Intelligence") OR ("Supply Chain Resilience" AND "Machine Learning") OR ("Supply Chain Resilience" AND "Data Analytics") OR ("Supply Chain Resilience" AND "Data Mining") Limiting the database results from 2018–2023. Document Type: Article, Language: English	TITLE, ABSTRACT, KEYWORD: ("Supply Chain Resilience" AND "Artificial Intelligence") OR ("Supply Chain Resilience" AND "Machine Learning") OR ("Supply Chain Resilience" AND "Data Analytics") OR ("Supply Chain Resilience" AND "Data Mining") Limiting the database results last 5 Years. Document Type: Article, Language: English. Quick Filter: Open Access
Final Result	52 (after removing duplicates)	

Source: Generated by analysis of keywords in Scopus and WoS database.

4. RESULTS AND DISCUSSION

This study used a variety of bibliometric indicators to give a thorough overview and informative analysis. VOSviewer and R package software tools were employed for analyzing maps, bibliographic coupling, keyword co-occurrence analysis and evaluating coauthorship connections (Dhiaf et al., 2021). The study has significant potential for identifying published document kinds and investigating research prospects by applying various bibliometric analysis methodologies (Wang et al., 2020).

4.1 Annual Publication Trends

The peak in academic publications on supply chain resilience coincided with the emergence of the global COVID-19 pandemic. Beginning 2019, there was a significant rise in yearly publications per article, indicating increased research interest in supply chain resilience during the pandemic. These results align with expectations, as the pandemic's impact on supply chain was one of the most severe and unprecedented supply crises of the 21st century. It has also become one of the most extensively studied and well-documented crises in recent history (Donthu & Gustafsson, 2020). This research affirms the consistent increase in academic research on supply chain resilience, as shown by multiple studies (Golan et al., 2020; Harland et al., 2021), indicating a watershed moment in this field (Nikookar & Yanadori, 2022). Prior to the disruptions caused by pandemic, research was primarily focused on improving the efficiency of supply chains with more intricate structures designed to maximize benefits under normal conditions (Ribeiro & Barbosa-Povoa, 2018), in addition to managing the risks associated with supply chain disruptions that were markedly different from the effects of the pandemic. Fig. 3 depicts the current academic production trend on supply chain resilience.

4.1.1 Keyword Analysis

The word cloud shown in Fig. 4 shows the most frequently used keywords in the analyzed research papers. The top 10 keywords include 'supply chain resilience', 'supply chains', 'supply chain management', 'decision making', 'risk management', 'decision support systems', 'data analytics', 'global supply chain', 'artificial intelligence' and 'decision making'. A keyword co-occurrence analysis using author-assigned keywords from papers was conducted using the VOSviewer to

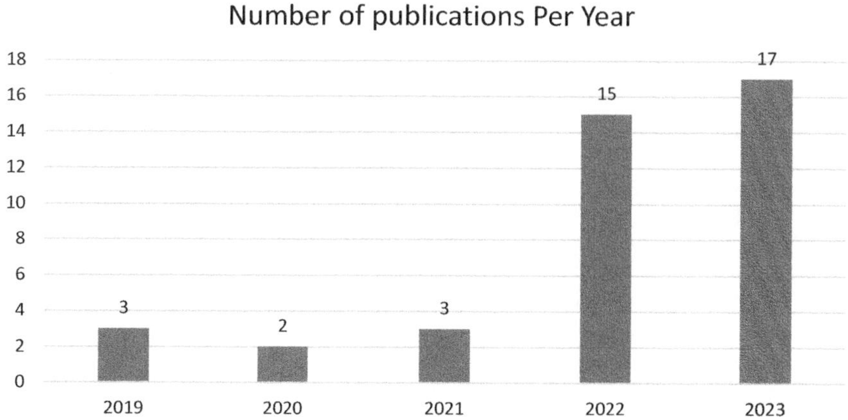

Fig. 3. Current Academic Production Trend on Supply Chain Resiliency.
Source: Analysis results.

Fig. 4. Word Cloud for Supply Chain Resilience. *Source:* Analysis results.

identify relevant themes within the domain of supply chain resilience research, as shown in Fig. 5. This study is based on the concept that author keywords are useful indicators for scholarly papers. The high co-occurrence of keywords is significant because it provides deeper insights into the intellectual structure of a specific area. When contextualized within the scope of a periodical, the knowledge created covers a wide range of issues within the intellectual framework of

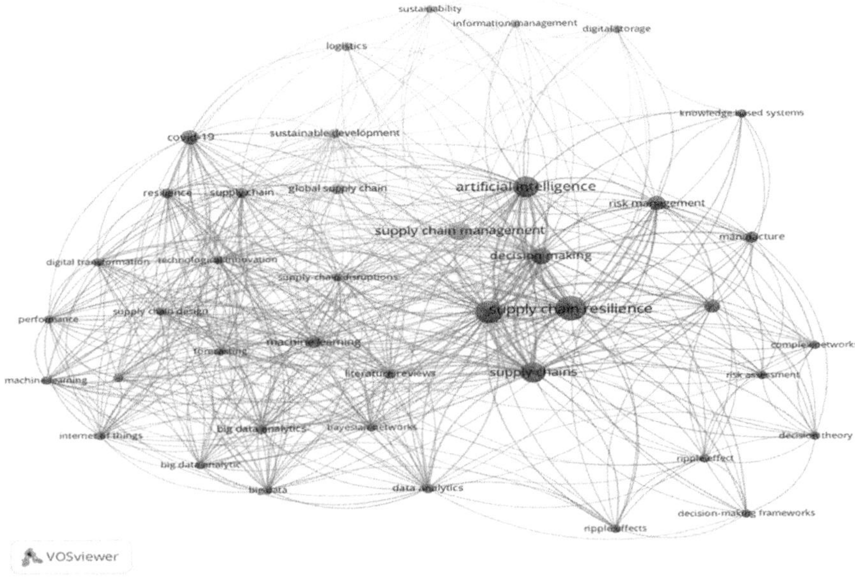

Fig. 5. Bibliometric Analysis of Keywords. *Source:* Analysis results.

Table 2. Top Keywords.

Keyword	Occurrences	Total Link Strength	Frequency
'Supply chain resilience'	15	120	23
'Supply chain resilience'	18	118	-
'Supply chains'	12	111	18
'Artificial intelligence'	13	94	14
'Supply chain management'	11	88	14
'Decision making'	8	80	10
'Machine learning'	5	49	4
'Risk management'	6	48	7
'Data analytics'	3	47	4
'Big data analytics'	3	40	2
'Covid-19'	19	23	4

Source: Analysis results.

supply chain resilience in developing nations. The co-occurrence network of terms reveals surprising patterns that provide useful information.

Table 2 details the prominence of the important phrases related to supply chain resilience and AI. The keyword 'supply chain resilience' appeared 33 times in papers related to the examined area. Following this, 'artificial intelligence' and 'supply chain' appeared 13 and 12 times, respectively. Table 2 contains a list of 20 keywords and their frequencies in the AI and supply chain resilience topics. Furthermore, Fig. 4 depicts a 'word cloud' containing keywords from the abstracts of publications, revealing the most frequently found terms in the databases. The magnitude of each word in the cloud corresponded to the frequency of occurrence in the selected articles. Fig. 4 shows that significant phrases in this study, such as 'supply chain resilience', 'supply chains', 'supply chain management' and 'AI', are centrally located on the map, indicating their recurring presence throughout the research.

Figs. 5 and 6 display the findings from a bibliometric study on the keyword network of supply chain resilience conducted using both WoS and Scopus.

Table 2 depicts the network of the most frequently occurring keywords in the domain of supply chain resilience, namely artificial intelligence, supply chain management, decision making, risk management, machine learning, decision support systems, COVID-19 and supply chains. The provided keyword analysis highlights the most frequently repeated and significant research subjects within a dataset, with particular emphasis on 'Supply Chain Resilience, Artificial Intelligence' and 'Supply Chain'. These keywords, 'Supply Chain Management' and 'Covid-19', collectively represent the research publications' main points of interest. Furthermore, themes such as 'Decision Making', 'Machine Learning', 'Risk Management', 'Data Analytics' and 'Big data analytics' contribute to a more in-depth examination of supply chain dynamics.

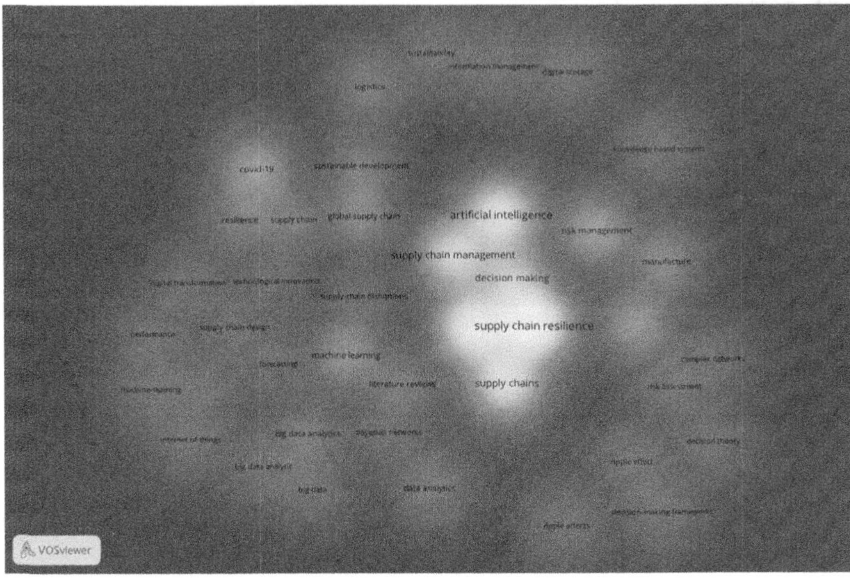

Fig. 6. Density Visualization for Most Using Keywords. *Source:* Analysis results.

4.1.2 Authors Analysis

Based on the amount of citations, the figure below depicts the most significant authors in the subject of supply chain resilience in AI and ML. Table 3 illustrates that many researchers in the WoS and Scopus have been interested in the topic of supply chain resilience in AI and ML, such as Belhadi A., Gupta, S., Ivanov, D., Kumar, A., Modgil. An examination of the collaborative network among authors reveals that the researcher 'Gupta, S' has the most contact with fellow researchers in terms of AI and ML in the context of supply chain resilience. The co-citation analysis in published publications does not differentiate between main and secondary authorship; consequently, it estimates the overall number of citations regardless of an author's name placement inside a citation. Notably, Shivam Gupta and Amine Belhadi, the

Table 3. Top Author.

Author	Documents	Total Link Strength
Gupta, S.	4	15
Belhadi A.	2	8
Kumar, A.	2	6
Modgil, S.	2	7
Blome, C.	1	6

Source: Analysis results.

group's most frequently mentioned authors, took the centre stage in this study. Mr Gupta, a prominent professor at France's NEOMA Business School, has published works in academic journals on supply chain resilience and AI. Mr Belhadi, Associate Professor at Rabat Business School in Morocco, has works focused on SCM and has many contributions with Mr Gupta.

Overall, this table provides a snapshot of these authors' publications and collaborative history within a specific research domain; however, more information is required to interpret the broader implications of these results or to comprehend the nature of the collaborations and the specific field of study involved.

4.1.3 Countries Analysis

Table 4 shows the nations with numbers of citations in WoS and Scopus on the subject of AI and ML in supply chain resilience. This bibliometric also examines leading national cooperation. Country co-authorship provides insight into the nature and degree of partnerships between distinct nations, indicating the formal international framework of research collaborations. This study sheds light on the nature and scope of international relationships (Donthu et al., 2021). Our analysis uncovered five major networks of collaboration, which we illustrated using the VOSviewer software (Fig. 4). France is the key node of the first important network, which is illustrated in cyan and represents international connections between India, the United Kingdom, the United States, Morocco and China. The United Kingdom is the primary node of the second main network, which is represented by the colour orange and includes overseas partners such as Turkey, Belgium and Hong Kong.

Morocco controls the third major network (red), which is shared by China, Belgium, Italy, Iran and Hong Kong, among others. The partnership network connects Germany and Bangladesh through the United States, which is illustrated in green and blue. It is a significant discovery that the connectivity of these critical networks may be encouraged to increase in terms of the breadth (more research studies in new countries) and depth (additional study among current countries) of international collaboration in the area. A cooperation network map exemplifies this dependence. The analysis of publication distribution across countries reveals that writers are actively involved in publishing articles on supply chain resilience, particularly in developing nations. France has emerged as the leading contributor to the debate on supply chain resilience in developing countries. As demonstrated in Table 4, the United States is the second-largest contributor, followed by India.

The results show related author nations with single-country and multi-country publications that provide significant insights into the collaborative dynamics and research significance in the subject of integrating AI and ML into supply chain resilience. The leading nations contributing to single-country publications are India, the United States and Bangladesh, which have separate research paths. Various single-country publications may reflect the individual contributions and skills of various nations in investigating this growing topic. However, the

Table 4. Top 10 Countries.

Country	Documents	Citations	Total Link Strength
France	11	371	17
India	14	270	15
UK/United Kingdom	9	178	14
USA/United States	11	269	13
Morocco	5	156	10
China	5	151	8
Belgium	22	55	4
Brazil	32	91	3
Germany	2	122	1
Bangladesh	3	3	1

Source: Analysis results.

inclusion of these nations, in the analysis of multiple-country publications, demonstrates their active participation in global research networks. The collaborative nature of multi-country publications hints at a joint effort to use varied knowledge and viewpoints in understanding the intricacies of AI-driven supply chain resilience. The presence of these nations in both single-country and multi-country publications demonstrates their importance in shaping the research landscape.

According to citations in the WoS and Scopus, France, Belgium, the USA, India and other nations are the most cited countries in the field of AI and ML in supply chain resilience as shown in Fig. 7. The order changes based on the number of publications, as shown in the table below. The nations displayed in Table 4 are among the top 10 in investigating the applications of AI and ML in supply chain resilience, according to the number of publications, citations and frequency.

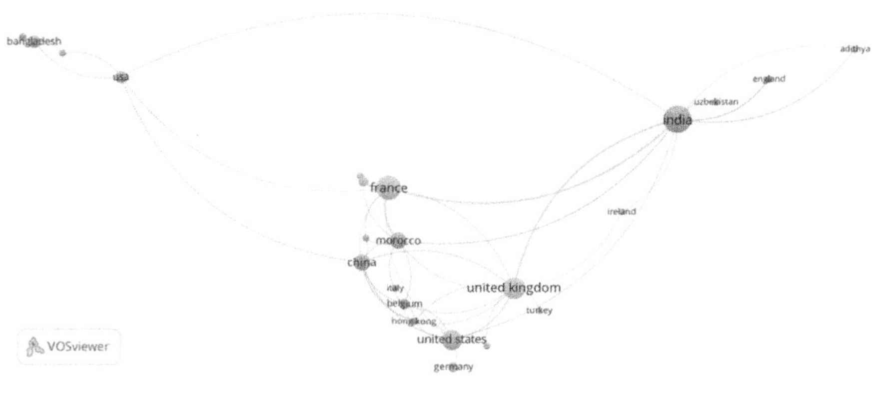

Fig. 7. Country Collaboration. *Source:* Analysis results.

The country analysis table provides information on research article production and international citations in various countries. France comes out with 11 research publications connected to a significant overall link strength of 17, showing high citation patterns. India comes in second with 14 articles and a total link strength of 15. The United States has 11 papers that show ongoing research production with a total link strength of 13. The United Kingdom, with nine articles, has a link strength of 14, indicating a substantial impact. Morocco and China, with five papers, respectively, demonstrate their research participation, with 156 and 151 citations. Brazil produces 32 publications and 91 citations, demonstrating its research presence despite Germany having fewer publications their scholarly contributions with 122.

The distribution of publications by country shows that authors from 36 different countries participated in and published articles on supply chain resilience in developing countries. According to data that breaks down contributions by country, India is the nation that contributes the most to supply chain resilience in developing nations (21%). France is the second greatest contributor (17%), followed by the United Kingdom (14%).

4.1.4 Organizations Analysis

The figure and table below reflect the world's most cited organizations on the issue of AI and ML in supply chain resilience. Table 5 shows the most relevant organizations in the topic of AI and ML in supply chain resilience based on the Web of Science database and Scopus. These are Bangladesh University, International Management Institute – Kolkata, University of California and Neoma

Table 5. Top Organizations.

Organization	Country	Articles
Bangladesh University	Bangladesh	3
International Management Institute – Kolkata	India	3
University of California	United States	3
NEOMA Business School	France	3
Aston University	United Kingdom	2
Berlin School of Economics and Law	Germany	2
Cadi Ayyad University	Morocco	2
College of Engineering and Technology	Various	2
EDHEC Business School	France	2
Indian Institute of Technology Kharagpur	India	2
Jinan University	China	2
Malaviya National Institute of Technology Jaipur	India	2
Michigan State University	United States	2
Paulista University (UNIP)	Brazil	2
School of Business Administration	Various	2

Source: Analysis results.

Business School. Table 5 ranks the top 15 organizations actively involved in the progress of AI in supply chain resilience research based on their prolific output. This includes both academic institutions and organizations. Notably, Bangladesh University, International Management Institute – Kolkata, the University of California and Neoma Business School have the greatest publication frequency in the Scopus database, with each contributing three publications. Table 5 reveals that two of these leading institutions are located in India, while the other two are in France and the United States.

5. RESEARCH THEMES

Research on AI and SCR has utilized a variety of methods, including structural equation modelling, interviews and surveys. These studies consistently explore the profound impacts of AI on SCR, focusing on themes such as effective decision-making, operational efficiency, optimization, sustainability and risk management. The hotspot analysis identified six key research themes at the intersection of AI and SCR, namely: (1) AI-driven predictive analytics for demand forecasting; (2) ML applications in SC optimization; (3) the role of AI in enhancing SC visibility; (4) AI-enabled risk management strategies; (5) the impact of AI on SC sustainability and (6) the integration of AI in SC decision-making processes.

As for the first theme, AI-driven predictive analytics is widely recognized for its capacity to enhance demand forecasting accuracy, enabling organizations to better anticipate market needs. Studies show that ML algorithms can effectively analyze historical data, uncover patterns and generate forecasts that improve inventory management and minimize stockouts (Abaku, 2024; Krishnan, 2024). For instance, in the agricultural sector, AI integration has yielded significant benefits by optimizing supply, improving demand forecasting and addressing the unique challenges of agricultural supply chains (Elufioye, 2024). Similarly, in sectors like IT and e-commerce, predictive analytics has bolstered decision-making processes by providing actionable insights aligned with market trends (Nzeako, 2024).

Another critical research theme is the application of ML in supply chain optimization. ML techniques have been applied to streamline operations, optimize distribution routes and improve inventory management (Odimarha, 2024; Polo-Triana, 2024). The adaptability of these algorithms allows organizations to respond swiftly to fluctuations in demand, which in turn boosts operational efficiency and competitive advantage (Muthaluri, 2024; Ghodake, 2024). Additionally, AI integration extends beyond operational efficiency, influencing marketing strategies and strategic decision-making processes, showcasing the multifaceted benefits of AI in SCM (Cadden et al., 2022).

Another important theme is that the role of AI in enhancing SC visibility is pivotal for fostering transparency and accountability throughout the supply chain. Emerging technologies such as the IoT enable real-time data collection and visibility across different stages of the SC process, improving risk identification and proactive decision-making (Adeusi, 2024). This improved visibility facilitates organizations' ability to mitigate potential disruptions effectively, particularly in complex and global supply chains (Bidin, 2024).

Another critical research theme is AI-enabled risk management strategies. Risk management has become even more critical in the post-pandemic world, where the need for resilient supply chains is paramount (Zhao, 2023). AI-driven risk management strategies provide companies with tools to anticipate and respond to potential disruptions in real time, thus enhancing overall resilience (Bidin, 2024). These technologies enable organizations to identify vulnerabilities, simulate potential risks and devise strategies to minimize the impact of disruptions (Modgil, Singh, & Hannibal, 2022). AI-enhanced resilience is not only essential for managing immediate crises but also for building long-term robustness in supply chains (Zhao, 2023).

The theme of AI's impact on supply chain sustainability is increasingly gaining attention from scholars. Sustainability has emerged as a growing concern for supply chains worldwide, and AI is playing an increasingly prominent role in fostering sustainable practices (Vishwakarma et al., 2023). AI-driven solutions optimize resource utilization, reduce waste and help firms minimize environmental impact (Gao, 2024; Eyo-Udo, 2024). Deep learning technologies further augment these efforts by enabling the development of closed-loop supply chains that prioritize both sustainability and operational efficiency (Gao, 2024). Moreover, AI integration enhances environmental process integration within the supply chain, utilizing both internal and external data in a synchronized manner, ultimately reducing emissions and promoting the use of eco-friendly resources (Rashid et al., 2024). This contributes to sustainability in product design and access to vital information, thus boosting sustainability performance, particularly in manufacturing (Rashid et al., 2024).

The final theme represents the integration of AI in SC decision-making processes, which significantly enhances the agility and responsiveness of supply chains (Wong et al., 2024). By leveraging AI data-driven insights, companies can make more informed decisions and respond more effectively to market changes (Singh, Hamid, & Garza-Reyes, 2023). This is especially crucial in an environment where agility is a competitive advantage for firms (Adenekan, 2024). However, AI implementation also raises ethical concerns, particularly around data privacy and algorithmic bias, which must be addressed to ensure the responsible deployment of AI technologies (Peng, 2024). These concerns are crucial as companies strive to balance the advantages of AI integration with the need for ethical and transparent decision-making.

6. RESEARCH SCHEMATA AND FUTURE RESEARCH AGENDA

The research schemata for AI and SCR are based on a comprehensive bibliometric and content analysis of the current literature. These schemata provide a detailed framework for researchers, delineating the knowledge base within the field and highlighting essential connections among various themes, especially regarding the application of AI to improve supply chain resilience. This approach enables researchers to identify gaps in the literature, particularly in domains where AI applications are insufficiently examined. AI is recognized as a significant factor in improving SCR. However, its integration with other emerging technologies, including blockchain, the IoT and big data analytics, reveals unexplored opportunities that require additional investigation.

A notable gap exists in comprehending the synergistic effects of AI in conjunction with these technologies in supply chain resilience, potentially transforming organizational preparedness and response to disruptions. Investigating these domains enhances theoretical knowledge and offers practical benefits, allowing industries to create more resilient, adaptive and flexible supply chains. Researchers may investigate the integration of AI across diverse industry contexts, including healthcare, manufacturing and retail, as each sector poses distinct challenges that AI-driven solutions can potentially mitigate. Contextual explorations will significantly enhance the customization of AI solutions to address specific resilience challenges in these sectors.

Longitudinal studies may yield significant insights regarding the long-term impacts of AI integration on sustainable supply chain practices. Analyzing the evolution of AI-driven strategies and their effects on SCR and sustainability can demonstrate their efficacy in sustaining resilience during extended disruptions or crises.

Ethical considerations, data governance and workforce dynamics are identified as essential domains for future investigation. The integration of AI into supply chains necessitates a critical examination of ethical issues related to data usage, privacy and algorithmic transparency to ensure responsible deployment of AI technologies. The role of data governance in managing large-scale AI implementations, particularly within decentralized supply chains, is essential for maintaining data integrity and ensuring efficient operations. The influence of AI on workforce dynamics, specifically regarding how automation and intelligent systems alter human roles, is insufficiently examined and requires additional investigation.

This study a systematic analysis derived from publications in the Web of Science and Scopus databases. The analysis identified several key themes and research questions that establish a basis for future research agendas.

- The role of AI in enhancing supply chain resilience: In what ways does the integration of AI technologies bolster the resilience of supply chains amid disruptions? Modgil, Gupta, et al. (2022) illustrated that AI's ability to foster SCR through dynamic capabilities was notably apparent during the COVID-19 pandemic. Naz et al. (2022) identified AI as a crucial factor in enhancing supply chain resiliency following the pandemic.
- The relationship between multi-dimensional supply chain flexibility and resilience: An examination of how AI can enhance this relationship. Research conducted by Piprani et al. (2022) and Singh, Modgil, and Shore (2023)

examines the influence of supply chain risk exposure, flexibility and resilience, emphasizing the significant impact of AI in improving this dynamic.
- AI adoption in supply chain management: What factors influence the adoption of AI technologies in SCM, and how do these factors impact overall supply chain resilience? Grover et al. (2020) examined AI adoption in operations management, whereas Olan et al. (2024) highlighted AI's contribution to sustainable supply chain finance and its association with enhanced resilience.
- Knowledge management and dynamic capabilities in supply chains: What is the interaction between knowledge management practices, dynamic capabilities and AI in enhancing supply chain resilience? Irfan et al. (2022) examined the essential function of knowledge management in developing resilient supply chains, whereas Zhao (2023) investigated innovation and flexibility as key factors influencing enterprise resilience within the supply chain framework.
- The role of AI in enhancing sustainability in resilient supply chains: How can the integration of AI be optimized to promote sustainability within these supply chains? Sarkis (2020) analyzed critical insights gained from the COVID-19 pandemic, highlighting the potential of AI in developing sustainable supply chains. Joshi et al. (2023) evaluated strategies for enhancing the resilience of food supply chains, focusing on sustainability in developing economies.

Themes and research questions highlight the complex relationship between AI and supply chain resilience. Investigating these areas allows researchers to deepen the understanding of how AI technologies can enhance supply chain resilience and sustainability within a complex global landscape. This study possesses certain limitations. The exclusion of papers from other databases or journals may limit the comprehensiveness of the findings. Furthermore, recent publications may be underrepresented in the citation network analysis due to the inherent lag in citation data relative to current trends and developments. The intellectual structure of this field is expected to evolve, requiring regular updates to the analysis. Future research should expand its scope by including articles from a diverse array of journals, especially those that utilize interdisciplinary methodologies in the fields of AI and SCM. Finally, researchers should investigate the influence of AI on supply chain resilience across various industrial sectors, including healthcare and manufacturing, to enhance the understanding of its implications for supply chain resilience. This would facilitate the creation of industry-specific frameworks for AI-driven resilience solutions.

7. IMPLICATIONS

This bibliometric research has substantial practical implications for firms seeking to improve their supply chain resilience using AI technology. The study offers practical insights that help guide strategic decision-making and enhance operational results. AI-driven predictive analytics improves demand forecasting accuracy by examining past data and recognizing trends that help predict future requirements. Organizations may deploy AI solutions to enhance customer demand forecasting, reduce stockouts and optimize inventory management. For instance, businesses might utilize AI to predict demand based on seasonal patterns, so assisting them in sustaining ideal inventory levels. Furthermore, ML may enhance several supply chain procedures using ML algorithms. Certain online businesses utilize ML to enhance delivery routes, facilitating quicker and more economical deliveries. Another pragmatic component is the utilization of AI technologies, like the IoT and blockchain, to facilitate real-time insight into supply chain processes, enabling enterprises to trace shipments and oversee inventories. Shipping businesses may utilize IoT and AI to monitor cargo movement in real time, therefore assuring timely delivery of products. Furthermore, AI improves risk management by offering predictive information regarding possible supply chain interruptions. Shipping businesses may utilize AI to evaluate risks in their supply chain by monitoring global events and evaluating data from meteorological predictions or political developments. This enables the firm to modify its logistical operations. Furthermore, AI may enhance sustainability by improving resource utilization and minimizing waste within supply chains. AI-driven technologies assist organizations in pinpointing inefficiencies and regions of excessive energy or material use. Ultimately, firms may effectively utilize AI systems to deliver data-driven insights that facilitate more informed decision-making in supply chains. Decision-makers can depend on AI to model various scenarios. Manufacturing businesses utilize AI within their supply chains to improve production decisions by predicting equipment failures and adjusting production schedules accordingly.

8. CONCLUSION

In conclusion, the bibliometric study of supply chain resilience, which included 52 published publications in the previous five years, offered a targeted and informative evaluation of the research environment and provided useful insights into the research landscape, trends and collaborative dynamics in this critical sector. The investigation highlighted major issues, authors, prolific institutions and active countries that are contributing to the supply chain resilience debate. The frequency of certain terms, such as ‘supply chain resilience’, ‘artificial intelligence’ and ‘supply chain management’, highlights the focus areas of academic discourse. Furthermore, the identification of widely referenced works and significant writers has offered a clear picture of the field’s seminal achievements. Despite the small number of publications examined, the research effectively discovered and highlighted critical trends, patterns and contributions in the subject of supply chain resilience. The limited dataset prompted a more detailed examination of each article, allowing for a full grasp of the important topics, significant authors and prevalent study paths.

This bibliometric analysis, in essence, serves as a foundation for understanding the evolving landscape of supply chain resilience research, providing valuable guidance for researchers, practitioners and policymakers to engage in further exploration, collaboration and strategic decision-making within this critical domain. The analysis of co-citation networks and author collaborations revealed the research's linked character, stressing the collaborative attempts within this specialized subject. Notably, while the dataset is small in size, the depth of insights gained from it is significant. The identification of key works often quoted authors and active institutions has shed light on the fundamental foundations around which the supply chain resilience discourse is built. This bibliometric analysis is an important beginning point for understanding the knowledge structure and trends, encouraging more research contributions and guiding strategic decisions in the subject of supply chain resilience. As the field evolves, our study demonstrates the importance of research even within a limited scope, highlighting the potential influence that a small number of studies may have in furthering understanding and practice in this crucial sector.

REFERENCES

Abaku, T. (2024). Theoretical approaches to AI in supply chain optimization: Pathways to efficiency and resilience. *International Journal of Science and Technology Research Archive*, *6*(1), 33–45. https://doi.org/10.53771/ijstra.2024.6.1.0033

Adenekan, O. (2024). Enhancing manufacturing productivity: A review of AI-driven supply chain management optimization and ERP systems integration. *International Journal of Management & Entrepreneurship Research*, *6*(5), 1126–1140. https://doi.org/10.51594/ijmer.v6i5.1126

Adeusi, A. (2024). The potential of IoT to transform supply chain management through enhanced connectivity and real-time data. *World Journal of Advanced Engineering Technology and Sciences*, *12*(1), 202–215. https://doi.org/10.30574/wjaets.2024.12.1.0202

Alvarenga, M. Z., Oliveira, M. P. V. D., & Oliveira, T. A. G. F. D. (2023). The impact of using digital technologies on supply chain resilience and robustness: The role of memory under the covid-19 outbreak. *Supply Chain Management: An International Journal*, *28*(5), 825–842.

Aparicio, G., Iturralde, T., & Rodríguez, A. V. (2021). Developments in the knowledge-based economy research field: A bibliometric literature review. *Management Review Quarterly*, 1–36.

Belhadi, A., Kamble, S., Fosso Wamba, S., & Queiroz, M. M. (2022). Building supply-chain resilience: An artificial intelligence-based technique and decision-making framework. *International Journal of Production Research*, *60*(14). https://doi.org/10.1080/00207543.2021.1950935

Benitez, G. B., Ferreira-Lima, M., Ayala, N. F., & Frank, A. G. (2022). Industry 4.0 technology provision: The moderating role of supply chain partners to support technology providers. *Supply Chain Management*, *27*(1). https://doi.org/10.1108/SCM-07-2020-0304

Bidin, N. (2024). Adaptive supply chain risk management using AI: Mitigating disruptions and enhancing resilience in the post-pandemic era. *Tjjpt*, *45*(2), 6294. https://doi.org/10.52783/tjjpt.v45.i02.6294

Brandon-Jones, E., Squire, B., Autry, C. W., & Petersen, K. J. (2014). A contingent resource-based perspective of supply chain resilience and robustness. *Journal of Supply Chain Management*, *50*(3). https://doi.org/10.1111/jscm.12050

Cadden, T., Dennehy, D., Mantymaki, M., & Treacy, R. (2022). Understanding the influential and mediating role of cultural enablers of AI integration to supply chain. *International Journal of Production Research*, *60*(14). https://doi.org/10.1080/00207543.2021.1946614

Damoah, I. S., Ayakwah, A., & Tingbani, I. (2021). Artificial intelligence (AI)-enhanced medical drones in the healthcare supply chain (HSC) for sustainability development: A case study. *Journal of Cleaner Production*, *328*. https://doi.org/10.1016/j.jclepro.2021.129598

Dauvergne, P. (2022). Is artificial intelligence greening global supply chains? Exposing the political economy of environmental costs. *Review of International Political Economy*, *29*(3). https://doi.org/10.1080/09692290.2020.1814381

Davis, F. D. (1989). Perceived usefulness, perceived ease of use, and user acceptance of information technology. *MIS Quarterly*, 319–340.

Dey, P. K., Chowdhury, S., Abadie, A., Vann Yaroson, E., & Sarkar, S. (2023). Artificial intelligence-driven supply chain resilience in Vietnamese manufacturing small- and medium-sized enterprises. *International Journal of Production Research*. https://doi.org/10.1080/00207543.2023.2179859

Dhiaf, M. M., Atayah, O. F., Nasrallah, N., & Frederico, G. F. (2021). Thirteen years of Operations Management Research (OMR) journal: A bibliometric analysis and future research directions. *Operations Management Research, 14*(3–4). https://doi.org/10.1007/s12063-021-00199-8

Donthu, N., & Gustafsson, A. (2020). Effects of COVID-19 on business and research. *Journal of Business Research, 117*. https://doi.org/10.1016/j.jbusres.2020.06.008

Donthu, N., Kumar, S., Mukherjee, D., Pandey, N., & Lim, W. M. (2021). How to conduct a bibliometric analysis: An overview and guidelines. *Journal of Business Research, 133*. https://doi.org/10.1016/j.jbusres.2021.04.070

Elufioye, T. (2024). AI-driven predictive analytics in agricultural supply chains: A review. *Computer Science & IT Research Journal, 5*(2), 817–830. https://doi.org/10.51594/csitrj.v5i2.817

Eyo-Udo, N. (2024). Leveraging artificial intelligence for enhanced supply chain optimization. *Open Access Research Journal of Multidisciplinary Studies, 7*(2), 001–015.

Faggioni, F., Rossi, M. V., & Sestino, A. (2024). Conceptualizing supply chain resilience in exogenous crisis times: Toward a holistic definition. *Journal of the Knowledge Economy*. https://doi.org/10.1007/s13132-024-01816-0

Flasiński, M. (2016). History of artificial intelligence. In *Introduction to artificial intelligence*. Springer. https://doi.org/10.1007/978-3-319-40022-8_1

Fosso Wamba, S., Queiroz, M. M., & Trinchera, L. (2020). Dynamics between blockchain adoption determinants and supply chain performance: An empirical investigation. *International Journal of Production Economics, 229*. https://doi.org/10.1016/j.ijpe.2020.107791

Gao, Y. (2024). Research on optimization strategies for closed-loop supply chain management based on deep learning technology. *International Journal of Information Systems and Supply Chain Management, 14*(4), 341–360. https://doi.org/10.4018/ijisscm.341802

Ghodake, S. (2024). Enhancing supply chain management efficiency: A data-driven approach using predictive analytics and machine learning algorithms. *International Journal of Advanced Computer Science and Applications, 15*(4), 469–480. https://doi.org/10.14569/ijacsa.2024.0150469

Gligor, D., Gligor, N., Holcomb, M., & Bozkurt, S. (2019). Distinguishing between the concepts of supply chain agility and resilience: A multidisciplinary literature review. *International Journal of Logistics Management, 30*(2). https://doi.org/10.1108/IJLM-10-2017-0259

Golan, M. S., Jernegan, L. H., & Linkov, I. (2020). Trends and applications of resilience analytics in supply chain modeling: Systematic literature review in the context of the COVID-19 pandemic. *Environment Systems and Decisions, 40*(2). https://doi.org/10.1007/s10669-020-09777-w

Grover, P., Kar, A. K., & Dwivedi, Y. K. (2020). Understanding artificial intelligence adoption in operations management: Insights from the review of academic literature and social media discussions. *Annals of Operations Research*. https://doi.org/10.1007/s10479-020-03683-9

Harland, C. M., Knight, L., Patrucco, A. S., Lynch, J., Telgen, J., Peters, E., Tátrai, T., & Ferk, P. (2021). Practitioners' learning about healthcare supply chain management in the COVID-19 pandemic: A public procurement perspective. *International Journal of Operations & Production Management, 41*(13). https://doi.org/10.1108/IJOPM-05-2021-0348

Helo, P., & Hao, Y. (2022). Artificial intelligence in operations management and supply chain management: An exploratory case study. *Production Planning & Control, 33*(16). https://doi.org/10.1080/09537287.2021.1882690

Hu, L., Zhou, J., Zhang, J. Z., & Behl, A. (2024). Blockchain technology adaptation and organizational inertia: Moderating role between knowledge management processes and supply chain resilience. *Kybernetes, 53*(2). https://doi.org/10.1108/K-12-2022-1661

Hundal, G. S., Thiyagarajan, S., Alduraibi, M., Laux, C. M., Furterer, S. L., Cudney, E. A., & Antony, J. (2020). Lean Six Sigma as an organizational resilience mechanism in health care during the era of COVID-19. *International Journal of Lean Six Sigma, 12*(4). https://doi.org/10.1108/IJLSS-11-2020-0204

Irfan, I., Sumbal, M. S. U. K., Khurshid, F., & Chan, F. T. S. (2022). Toward a resilient supply chain model: Critical role of knowledge management and dynamic capabilities. *Industrial Management & Data Systems*. https://doi.org/10.1108/imds-06-2021-0356

Ivanov, D., Blackhurst, J., & Das, A. (2021). Supply chain resilience and its interplay with digital technologies: Making innovations work in emergency situations. *International Journal of Physical Distribution & Logistics Management*, *51*(2). https://doi.org/10.1108/ijpdlm-03-2021-409

Ivanov, D., Dolgui, A., & Sokolov, B. (2022). Cloud supply chain: Integrating Industry 4.0 and digital platforms in the "Supply Chain-as-a-Service". *Transportation Research Part E: Logistics and Transportation Review*, *160*. https://doi.org/10.1016/j.tre.2022.102676

Jackson, I., Ivanov, D., Dolgui, A., & Namdar, J. (2024). Generative artificial intelligence in supply chain and operations management: A capability-based framework for analysis and implementation. *International Journal of Production Research*. https://doi.org/10.1080/00207543.2024.2309309

Jauhar, S. K., Jani, S. M., Kamble, S. S., Pratap, S., Belhadi, A., & Gupta, S. (2024). How to use no-code artificial intelligence to predict and minimize the inventory distortions for resilient supply chains. *International Journal of Production Research*, *62*(15). https://doi.org/10.1080/00207543.2023.2166139

Joshi, S., Sharma, M., Ekren, B. Y., Kazancoglu, Y., Luthra, S., & Prasad, M. (2023). Assessing supply chain innovations for building resilient food supply chains: An emerging economy perspective. *Sustainability*. https://doi.org/10.3390/su15064924

Küffner, C., Kopyto, M., Wohlleber, A. J., & Hartmann, E. (2022). The interplay between relationships, technologies and organizational structures in enhancing supply chain resilience: Empirical evidence from a Delphi study. *International Journal of Physical Distribution & Logistics Management*, *52*(8). https://doi.org/10.1108/IJPDLM-07-2021-0303

Khalifa, N., Abd Elghany, M., & Abd Elghany, M. (2021). Exploratory research on digitalization transformation practices within supply chain management context in developing countries specifically Egypt in the MENA region. *Cogent Business and Management*, *8*(1). https://doi.org/10.1080/23311975.2021.1965459

Krishnan, R. (2024). Enhancing supply chain efficiency to build next-gen AI/machine learning networks through AI-driven forecasting. *International Journal of Supply Chain Management*, *13*(3), 6244. https://doi.org/10.59160/ijscm.v13i3.6244

Kumar, A., Mangla, S. K., & Kumar, P. (2024). Barriers for adoption of Industry 4.0 in sustainable food supply chain: A circular economy perspective. *International Journal of Productivity and Performance Management*, *73*(2). https://doi.org/10.1108/IJPPM-12-2020-0695

Kumar, M., Raut, R. D., Mangla, S. K., Moizer, J., & Lean, J. (2024). Big data driven supply chain innovative capability for sustainable competitive advantage in the food supply chain: Resource-based view perspective. *Business Strategy and the Environment*. https://doi.org/10.1002/bse.3745

Legg, S., & Hutter, M. (2007). Universal intelligence: A definition of machine intelligence. *Minds and Machines*, *17*(4). https://doi.org/10.1007/s11023-007-9079-x

Li, B. h., Hou, B. c., Yu, W. t., Lu, X. b., & Yang, C. w. (2017). Applications of artificial intelligence in intelligent manufacturing: A review. *Frontiers of Information Technology and Electronic Engineering*, *18*(1). https://doi.org/10.1631/FITEE.1601885

Lu, H., Zhao, G., & Liu, S. (2024). Integrating circular economy and Industry 4.0 for sustainable supply chain management: A dynamic capability view. *Production Planning & Control*, *35*(2). https://doi.org/10.1080/09537287.2022.2063198

Modgil, S., Gupta, S., Stekelorum, R., & Laguir, I. (2022). AI technologies and their impact on supply chain resilience during COVID-19. *International Journal of Physical Distribution & Logistics Management*, *52*(2), 130–149.

Modgil, S., Singh, R. K., & Hannibal, C. (2022). Artificial intelligence for supply chain resilience: Learning from Covid-19. *International Journal of Logistics Management*, *33*(4). https://doi.org/10.1108/IJLM-02-2021-0094

Muthaluri, S. (2024). Optimizing supply chain management and marketing strategies: AI and ML integration for competitive advantage. *EATP, 30*(5), 4494. https://doi.org/10.53555/kuey.v30i5.4494

Naz, F., Kumar, A., Majumdar, A., & Agrawal, R. (2022). Is artificial intelligence an enabler of supply chain resiliency post COVID-19? An exploratory state-of-the-art review for future research. *Operations Management Research, 15*(1–2). https://doi.org/10.1007/s12063-021-00208-w

Nikookar, E., & Yanadori, Y. (2022). Preparing supply chain for the next disruption beyond COVID-19: Managerial antecedents of supply chain resilience. *International Journal of Operations & Production Management, 42*(1). https://doi.org/10.1108/IJOPM-04-2021-0272

Nilsson, N. J. (2011). The quest for artificial intelligence: A history of ideas and achievements. In *The quest for artificial intelligence: A history of ideas and achievements*. https://doi.org/10.1017/CBO9780511819346

Nzeako, U. (2024). The role of AI-driven predictive analytics in optimizing IT industry supply chains. *International Journal of Management & Entrepreneurship Research, 6*(5), 1096–1105. https://doi.org/10.51594/ijmer.v6i5.1096

Odimarha, E. (2024). Machine learning's influence on supply chain and logistics optimization in the oil and gas sector: A comprehensive analysis. *Computer Science & IT Research Journal, 5*(3), 976–990. https://doi.org/10.51594/csitrj.v5i3.976

Olan, F., Arakpogun, E. O., Jayawickrama, U., Suklan, J., & Liu, S. (2024). Sustainable supply chain finance and supply networks: The role of artificial intelligence. *IEEE Transactions on Engineering Management*. https://doi.org/10.1109/tem.2021.3133104

Peng, L. (2024). Research on the influence of AI application on business decision making based on machine learning algorithm. *EAI Endorsed Transactions on Industrial Networks and Intelligent Systems, 27*(10), 2341918. https://doi.org/10.4108/eai.27-10-2023.2341918

Piprani, A. Z., Jaafar, N. I., Ali, S. M., Mubarik, M. S., & Shahbaz, M. (2022). Multi-dimensional supply chain flexibility and supply chain resilience: The role of supply chain risks exposure. *Operations Management Research*. https://doi.org/10.1007/s12063-021-00232-w

Polo-Triana, J. (2024). Integration of machine learning in the supply chain for decision making: A systematic literature review. *Journal of Industrial Engineering and Management, 17*(2), 6403. https://doi.org/10.3926/jiem.6403

Pournader, M., Ghaderi, H., Hassanzadegan, A., & Fahimnia, B. (2021). Artificial intelligence applications in supply chain management. *International Journal of Production Economics, 241*. https://doi.org/10.1016/j.ijpe.2021.108250

Queiroz, M. M., Fosso Wamba, S., Raut, R. D., & Pappas, I. O. (2023). Does resilience matter for supply chain performance in disruptive crises with scarce resources? *British Journal of Management*. https://doi.org/10.1111/1467-8551.12748

Rahardjo, B., Wang, F. K., Lo, S. C., & Chu, T. H. (2024). A sustainable innovation framework based on Lean Six Sigma and Industry 5.0. *Arabian Journal for Science and Engineering, 49*(5). https://doi.org/10.1007/s13369-023-08565-3

Rashid, A., Baloch, N., Rasheed, R., & Ngah, A. H. (2024). Big data analytics-artificial intelligence and sustainable performance through green supply chain practices in manufacturing firms of a developing country. *Journal of Science and Technology Policy Management*. (ahead-of-print). https://doi.org/10.1108/JSTPM-04-2023-0050

Rey-Martí, A., Ribeiro-Soriano, D., & Palacios-Marqués, D. (2016). A bibliometric analysis of social entrepreneurship. *Journal of Business Research, 69*(5). https://doi.org/10.1016/j.jbusres.2015.10.033

Ribeiro, J. P., & Barbosa-Povoa, A. (2018). Supply Chain Resilience: Definitions and quantitative modelling approaches – A literature review. *Computers & Industrial Engineering, 115*. https://doi.org/10.1016/j.cie.2017.11.006

Riggs, R., Roldán, J. L., Real, J. C., & Felipe, C. M. (2023). Opening the black box of big data sustainable value creation: The mediating role of supply chain management capabilities and circular economy practices. *International Journal of Physical Distribution & Logistics Management, 53*(7–8). https://doi.org/10.1108/IJPDLM-03-2022-0098

Rogers, E. M. (1995). Diffusion of innovations: Modifications of a model for telecommunications. In *Die diffusion von innovationen in der telekommunikation* (pp. 25–38). https://doi.org/10.1007/978-3-642-79868-9_2

Russel, S., & Norvig, P. (2012). Artificial intelligence—A modern approach. In *The knowledge engineering review* (3rd ed.). https://doi.org/10.1017/S0269888900007724

Sarkıs, J. (2020). Supply chain sustainability: Learning from the COVID-19 pandemic. *International Journal of Operations & Production Management*. https://doi.org/10.1108/ijopm-08-2020-0568

Sharma, R., Shishodia, A., Gunasekaran, A., Min, H., & Munim, Z. H. (2022). The role of artificial intelligence in supply chain management: Mapping the territory. *International Journal of Production Research*, *60*(24). https://doi.org/10.1080/00207543.2022.2029611

Singh, J., Hamid, A. B. A., & Garza-Reyes, J. A. (2023). Supply chain resilience strategies and their impact on sustainability: An investigation from the automobile sector. *Supply Chain Management*, *28*(4), 787–802. https://doi.org/10.1108/SCM-06-2022-0225

Singh, P. K., & Maheswaran, R. (2024). Analysis of social barriers to sustainable innovation and digitisation in supply chain. *Environment, Development and Sustainability*, *26*(2). https://doi.org/10.1007/s10668-023-02931-9

Singh, R. K., Modgil, S., & Shore, A. (2023). Building artificial intelligence enabled resilient supply chain: A multi-method approach. *Journal of Enterprise Information Management*. https://doi.org/10.1108/jeim-09-2022-0326

Vishwakarma, L. P., Singh, R. K., Mishra, R., & Kumari, A. (2023). Application of artificial intelligence for resilient and sustainable healthcare system: Systematic literature review and future research directions. *International Journal of Production Research*. https://doi.org/10.1080/00207543.2023.2188101

Waltman, L., van Eck, N. J., & Noyons, E. C. M. (2010). A unified approach to mapping and clustering of bibliometric networks. *Journal of Informetrics*, *4*(4), 629–635. https://doi.org/10.1016/j.joi.2010.07.002

Wang, X., Xu, Z., & Škare, M. (2020). A bibliometric analysis of Economic Research-Ekonomska Istraživanja (2007–2019). *Economic Research-Ekonomska Istrazivanja*, *33*(1). https://doi.org/10.1080/1331677X.2020.1737558

Wieland, A., & Durach, C. F. (2021). Two perspectives on supply chain resilience. *Journal of Business Logistics*, *42*(3). https://doi.org/10.1111/jbl.12271

Wong, L. W., Tan, G. W. H., Ooi, K. B., Lin, B., & Dwivedi, Y. K. (2024). Artificial intelligence-driven risk management for enhancing supply chain agility: A deep-learning-based dual-stage PLS-SEM-ANN analysis. *International Journal of Production Research*, *62*(15). https://doi.org/10.1080/00207543.2022.2063089

Xu, Z., Wang, X., Wang, X., & Skare, M. (2021). A comprehensive bibliometric analysis of entrepreneurship and crisis literature published from 1984 to 2020. *Journal of Business Research*, *135*. https://doi.org/10.1016/j.jbusres.2021.06.051

Yin, W., & Ran, W. (2021). Theoretical exploration of supply chain viability utilizing blockchain technology. *Sustainability*, *13*(15). https://doi.org/10.3390/su13158231

Zhao, Y. (2023). *The impact of resilient supply chain on enterprise supply chain management—Based on the analysis of e-commerce enterprises under the COVID-19*. https://doi.org/10.2991/978-94-6463-142-5_7

Zhou, J., Hu, L., Yu, Y., Zhang, J. Z., & Zheng, L. J. (2022). Impacts of IT capability and supply chain collaboration on supply chain resilience: Empirical evidence from China in COVID-19 pandemic. *Journal of Enterprise Information Management*. https://doi.org/10.1108/JEIM-03-2022-0091

INDEX

Printed and bound by CPI Group (UK) Ltd, Croydon, CR0 4YY

26/11/2025

14779992-0001